Imbert de Saint-Amand

The Duchess of Berry and the Court of Charles X

Imbert de Saint-Amand

The Duchess of Berry and the Court of Charles X

ISBN/EAN: 9783337417536

Printed in Europe, USA, Canada, Australia, Japan

Cover: Foto ©ninafisch / pixelio.de

More available books at **www.hansebooks.com**

The Duchess of Berry

and the

Court of Charles X

BY

IMBERT DE SAINT-AMAND

WITH PORTRAITS

NEW YORK
CHARLES SCRIBNER'S SONS
1901

COPYRIGHT, 1892, BY
CHARLES SCRIBNER'S SONS.

THE CAXTON PRESS
NEW YORK.

CONTENTS

CHAPTER		PAGE
I.	THE ACCESSION OF CHARLES X.	1
II.	THE ENTRY INTO PARIS	11
III.	THE TOMBS OF SAINT-DENIS	20
IV.	THE FUNERAL OF LOUIS XVIII	29
V.	THE KING	41
VI.	THE DAUPHIN AND DAUPHINESS	48
VII.	MADAME	58
VIII.	THE ORLEANS FAMILY	72
IX.	THE PRINCE OF CONDÉ	81
X.	THE COURT	90
XI.	THE DUKE OF DOUDEAUVILLE	104
XII.	THE HOUSEHOLD OF THE DUCHESS OF BERRY	114
XIII.	THE PREPARATIONS FOR THE CORONATION	123
XIV.	THE CORONATION	139
XV.	CLOSE OF THE SOJOURN AT RHEIMS	152
XVI.	THE RE-ENTRANCE INTO PARIS	160
XVII.	THE JUBILEE OF 1826	166
XVIII.	THE DUCHESS OF GONTAUT	177

CHAPTER		PAGE
XIX.	THE THREE GOVERNORS	187
XX.	THE REVIEW OF THE NATIONAL GUARD	198
XXI.	THE FIRST DISQUIETUDE	208
XXII.	THE MARTIGNAC MINISTRY	217
XXIII.	THE JOURNEY IN THE WEST	224
XXIV.	THE MARY STUART BALL	237
XXV.	THE FINE ARTS	245
XXVI.	THE THEATRE OF MADAME	257
XXVII.	DIEPPE	266
XXVIII.	THE PRINCE DE POLIGNAC	276
XXIX.	GENERAL DE BOURMONT	286
XXX.	THE JOURNEY IN THE SOUTH	292

LIST OF PORTRAITS

MARIÉ CAROLINE . . . . Frontispiece

CHARLES X. . . . . Facing page 42

THE DUKE OF BORDEAUX AND HIS SISTER . . . 182

PRINCE DE POLIGNAC 280

THE DUCHESS OF BERRY AND THE COURT OF CHARLES X

I

THE ACCESSION OF CHARLES X

THURSDAY, the 16th of September, 1824, at the moment when Louis XVIII. was breathing his last in his chamber of the Château des Tuileries, the courtiers were gathered in the Gallery of Diana. It was four o'clock in the morning. The Duke and the Duchess of Angoulême, the Duchess of Berry, the Duke and the Duchess of Orleans, the Bishop of Hermopolis, and the physicians were in the chamber of the dying man. When the King had given up the ghost, the Duke of Angoulême, who became Dauphin, threw himself at the feet of his father, who became King, and kissed his hand with respectful tenderness. The princes and princesses followed this example, and he who bore thenceforward the title of Charles X., sobbing, embraced them all. They knelt about the bed. The *De Profundis* was recited. Then the new King sprinkled holy water on the body of his brother and kissed the icy hand. An instant later M. de Blacas, opening the door of the Gallery of Diana, called out: "Gentlemen, the King!" And Charles X. appeared.

Let us listen to the Duchess of Orleans. "At these words, in the twinkling of an eye, all the crowd of courtiers deserted the Gallery to surround and follow the new King. It was like a torrent. We were borne along by it, and only at the door of the Hall of the Throne, my husband bethought himself that we no longer had aught to do there. We returned home, reflecting much on the feebleness of our poor humanity, and the nothingness of the things of this world."

Marshal Marmont, who was in the Gallery of Diana at the moment of the King's death, was much struck by the two phrases pronounced at an instant's interval by M. de Damas: "Gentlemen, the King is dead! The King, gentlemen!"

He wrote in his Memoirs: "It is difficult to describe the sensation produced by this double announcement in so brief a time. The new sovereign was surrounded by his officers, and everything except the person of the King was in the accustomed order. Beautiful and great thought, this uninterrupted life of the depository of the sovereign power! By this fiction there is no break in this protecting force, so necessary to the preservation of society." The Marshal adds: "The government had been in fact for a year and more in the hands of Monsieur. Thus the same order of things was to continue; nevertheless, there was emotion perceptible on the faces of those present; one might see hopes spring up and existences wither. Every one accompanied the new King to his Pavilion of Marsan. He announced to his ministers that he confirmed them in their functions. Then every one withdrew."

While the Duchess of Berry was present at the death of Louis XVIII., the Duke of Bordeaux and his sister, Mademoiselle, then, the one four, the other five years of age, remained at the Château of Saint Cloud, with the Governess of the Children of France, the Viscountess of Gontaut-Biron. This lady passed the night of the 15th of September in great anxiety. She listened on the balcony, awaiting and dreading the news.

At the moment that the day began to dawn, she heard afar the gallop of a horse that drew near, passed the bridge, ascended the avenue, reached the Château, and in response to the challenge of the guard, she distinguished the words: "An urgent message for Madame the Governess." It was a letter from the new King. Madame de Gontaut trembled as she opened it. Charles X. announced to her, in sad words, that Louis XVIII. was no more, and directed her to made ready for the arrival of the royal family. "Lodge me where you and the governor shall see fit. We shall probably pass three or four days at Saint Cloud. Communicate my letter to the Marshal. I have not strength to write another word."

"The day was beginning to break," we read in the unpublished Memoirs of the Governess of the Children of France. "I went to the bed of Monseigneur. He was awakened. He was not surprised, and said nothing, and allowed himself to be dressed. Not so with Mademoiselle. I told her gently of the misfortune that had come upon her family. I was agitated. She questioned me, asking where was *bon-papa*. I told her that he was still in Paris, but was coming to Saint Cloud; then I added: 'Your *bon-papa*, Mademoiselle, is King, since the King is no more.' She reflected, then, repeating the word: 'King! Oh! that indeed is the worst of the story.' I was astonished, and wished her to explain her idea; she simply repeated it. I thought then she had conceived the notion of a king always rolled about in his chair."

The same day the court arrived. It was no longer the light carriage that used almost daily to bring Monsieur, to the great joy of his grandchildren. It was the royal coach with eight horses, livery, escort, and body-guard. The Duke of Bordeaux and his sister were on the porch with their governess. On perceiving the coach, instead of shouting with pleasure, as was their custom, they remained motionless and abashed. Charles X. was pale and silent. In the vestibule he paused: "What chamber have you prepared for me?" he said sadly to Madame de Gontaut, glancing at the door of his own. The governess replied: "The apartment of Monsieur is ready, and the chamber of the King as well." The sovereign paused, then clasping his hands in silence: "It must be!" he cried. "Let us ascend."

They followed him. He passed through the apartments. On the threshold of the royal chamber Madame de Gontaut brought to Charles X. the Duke of Bordeaux and Mademoiselle and he embraced them. The poor children were disconcerted by so much sadness. "As soon as I can," he said to them, "I promise to come to see you." Then turning to the company: "I would be alone." All withdrew in silence. The Dauphiness was weeping. The Dauphin had disappeared. Everything was gloomy. No one spoke. Thus passed the first day of the reign of Charles X.

The next day the King received the felicitations of the Corps de l'État. Many addresses were delivered. "All contained the expression of the public love," said Marshal Marmont in his Memoirs, "and I believe that they were sincere; but the love of the people is, of all loves, the most fragile, the most apt to evaporate. The King responded in an admirable manner, with appropriateness, intelligence, and warmth. His responses, less correct, perhaps, than those of Louis XVIII., had movement and spirit, and it is so precious to hear from those invested with the sovereign powers things that come from the heart, that Charles X. had a great success. I listened to him with care, and I sincerely admired his facility in varying his language and modifying his expressions according to the eminence of the authority from whom the compliments came."

The reception lasted several hours. When the coaches had rolled away and when quiet was re-established in the Château of Saint Cloud, Charles X., in the mourning costume of the Kings, the violet coat, went to the apartment of the Duke of Bordeaux and his sister. The usher cried: "The King!" The two children, frightened, and holding each other by the hand, remained silent. Charles X. opened his arms and they threw themselves into them. Then the sovereign seated himself in his accustomed chair and held his grandchildren for some moments pressed to his heart. The Duke of Bordeaux covered the hands and the face of his grandfather with kisses. Mademoiselle regarded attentively the altered features of the King and his mourning dress, novel to her. She asked him why he wore such a coat. Charles X. did not reply, and sighed. Then he questioned the governess as to the impression made on the children by the death of Louis XVIII. Madame de Gontaut hesitated to answer, recalling the strange phrase of Mademoiselle: "King! Oh! that indeed is the worst of the story." But the little Princess, clinging to her notion, began to repeat the unlucky phrase. Charles X., willing to give it a favorable interpretation, assured Mademoiselle that he would see her as often as in the past, and that nothing should separate him from her. The two children, with the heedlessness of their age, took on their usual gaiety, and ran to the window to watch the market-men, the coal heavers, and the fishwomen, who had come to Saint Cloud to congratulate the new King.

The griefs of sovereigns in the period of their prosperity do not last so long as those of private persons. Courtiers take too much pains to lighten them. With Charles X. grief at the loss of his brother was quickly followed by the enjoyment of reigning. Chateaubriand, who, when he wished to, had the art of carrying flattery to lyric height, published his pamphlet: *Le roi est mort! Vive le roi!* In it he said: "Frenchmen, he who announced to you Louis le Désiré, who made his voice heard by you in the days of storm, and makes to you to-day of Charles X. in circumstances very different. He is no longer obliged to tell you what the King is who comes to you, what his misfortunes are, his virtues, his rights to the throne and to your love; he is no longer obliged to depict his person, to inform you how many members of his family still exist. You know him, this Bourbon, the first to come, after our disaster, worthy herald of old France, to cast himself, a branch of lilies in his hand, between you and Europe. Your eyes rest with love and pleasure on this Prince, who in the ripeness of years has preserved the charm and elegance of his youth, and who now, adorned with the diadem, still is but *one Frenchman the more in the midst of you.* You repeat with emotion so many happy *mots* dropped by this new monarch, who from the loyalty of his heart draws the grace of happy speech. What one of us would not confide to him his life, his fortune, his honor? The man whom we should all wish as a friend, we have as King. Ah! Let us try to make him forget the sacrifices of his life! May the crown weigh lightly on the white head of this Christian Knight! Pious as Saint Louis, affable, compassionate, and just as Louis XII., courtly as Francis I., frank as Henry IV., may he be happy with all the happiness he has missed in his long past! May the throne where so many monarchs have encountered tempests, be for him a place of repose! Devoted subjects, let us crowd to the feet of our well-loved sovereign, let us recognize in him the model of honor, the living principle of our laws, the soul of our monarchical society; let us bless a guardian heredity, and may legitimacy without pangs give birth to a new King! Let our soldiers cover with their flags the father of the Duke of Angoulême. May watchful Europe, may the factions, if such there be still, see in the accord of all Frenchmen, in the union of the people and the army, the pledge of our strength and of the peace of the world!" The author of the *Génie du Christianisme* thus closed his prose dithyramb: "May God grant to Louis XVIII. the crown immortal of Saint Louis! May God bless the mortal crown of Saint Louis on the head of Charles X.!"

In this chant in honor of the King and of royalty, M. de Chateaubriand did not forget the Duke and Duchess of Angoulême, nor the Duchess of Berry and the Duke of Bordeaux. "Let us salute," he said, "the Dauphin and Dauphiness, names that bind the past to the future, calling up touching and noble memories, indicating the own son and the successor of the monarch, names under which we find the liberator of Spain and the daughter of Louis XVI. The *child of Europe*, the new Henry, thus makes one step toward the throne of his ancestor, and his young mother guides him to the throne that she might have ascended."

Happy in the ease with which the change in the reign had taken place, and seeing the unanimous manifestations of devotion and enthusiasm by which the throne was surrounded, the Duchess of Berry regarded the future with entire confidence. Inclined by nature to optimism, the young and amiable Princess believed herself specially protected by Providence, and would have considered as a sort of impiety anything else than absolute faith in the duration of the monarchy and in respect for the rights of her son. Had any one of the court expressed the slightest doubt as to the future destiny of the *Child of Miracle*, he would have been looked upon as an alarmist or a coward. The royalists were simple enough to believe that, thanks to this child, the era of revolutions was forever closed. They said to themselves that French royalty, like British royalty, would have its Whigs and its Tories, but that it was forever rid of Republicans and Imperialists. At the accession of Charles X. the word Republican, become a synonym of Jacobin, awoke only memories of the guillotine and the "Terror." A moderate republic seemed but a chimera; only that of Robespierre and Marat was thought of. The eagle was no longer mentioned; and as to the eaglet, he was a prisoner at Vienna. What chance of reigning had the Duke of Reichstadt, that child of thirteen, condemned by all the Powers of Europe? By what means could he mount the throne? Who would be regent in his name? A Bonaparte? The forgetful Marie Louise? Such hypotheses were relegated to the domain of pure fantasy. Apart from a few fanatical old soldiers who persisted in saying that Napoleon was not dead, no one, in 1824, believed in the resurrection of the Empire. As for Orleanism, it was as yet a myth. The Duke of Orleans himself was not an Orleanist. Of all the courtiers of Charles X., he was the most eager, the most zealous, the most enthusiastic. In whatever direction she turned her glance, the Duchess of Berry saw about her only reasons for satisfaction and security.

II

THE ENTRY INTO PARIS

THE Duchess of Berry took part in the solemn entry into Paris made by Charles X., Monday, 27th September, 1824. She was in the same carriage as the Dauphiness and the Duchess and Mademoiselle of Orleans. The King left the Château of Saint Cloud at half-past eleven in the morning, passed through the Bois de Boulogne, and mounted his horse at the Barrière de l'Étoile. There he was saluted by a salvo of one hundred and one guns, and the Count de Chambral, Prefect of the Seine, surrounded by the members of the Municipal Council, presented to him the keys of the city. Charles X. replied to the address of the Prefect: "I deposit these keys with you, because I cannot place them in more faithful hands. Guard them, gentlemen. It is with a profound feeling of pain and joy that I enter within these walls, in the midst of my good people, — of joy because I well know that I shall employ and consecrate all my days to the very last, to assure and consolidate their happiness." Accompanied by the princes and princesses of his family and by a magnificent staff, the sovereign descended the Champs-

Élysées to the Avenue of Marigny, followed that avenue, and entered the Rue du Faubourg Saint-Honoré, before the Palace of the Élysée. At this moment, the weather, which had been cold and sombre, brightened, and the rain, which had been falling for a long time, ceased. The King heard two child-voices crying joyously, "*Bon-papa.*" It was the little Duke of Bordeaux and his sister at a window of an entresol of the Élysée which looked out upon the street. On perceiving his two grandchildren, Charles X. could not resist the impulse to approach them. He left the ranks of the cortège, to the despair of the grand-master of ceremonies. The horse reared. A sergeant-de-ville seized him by the bit. Listen to Madame de Gontaut: "I was frightened, and cried out. The King scolded me for it afterward. I confessed my weakness; to fall at the first step in Paris would have seemed an ill omen. The King subdued his fretful horse, said a few tender words to the children, raised his hat gracefully to the ladies surrounding us. A thousand voices shouted: Vive le Roi! The grand-master was reassured, the horse was quieted, and the King resumed his place. The carriage of the princes and princesses passing at that moment, the little princes saw them — it was an added joy."

The cortège followed this route: the Rue du Faubourg Saint-Honoré, the boulevards to the Rue Saint-Denis, the Rue Saint-Denis, the Place du Châtelet, the Pont au Change, the Rue de la Barillerie, the

Marché-Neuf, the Rue Neuve-Notre-Dame, the Parvis. At every moment the King reined in his superb Arab horse to regard more at ease the delighted crowd. He smiled and saluted with an air of kindness and a grace that produced the best impression. Charles X. was an excellent horseman; he presented the figure and air of a young man. The contrast naturally fixed in all minds, between his vigorous attitude and that of his predecessor, an infirm and feeble old man, added to the general satisfaction. The houses were decorated with white flags spangled with fleurs-de-lis. Triumphal arches were erected along the route of the sovereign. The streets and boulevards were strewn with flowers. At the sight of the monarch the happy people redoubled their acclamations. Benjamin Constant shouted: "Vive le roi!"—"Ah, I have captured you at last," smilingly remarked Charles X.

Reaching the Parvis de Notre-Dame, the sovereign, before entering the Cathedral, paused before the threshold of the Hôtel-Dieu. Fifty nuns presented themselves before him, "Sire," said the Prioress, "you pause before the house so justly termed the Hôtel-Dieu, which has always been honored with the protection of our kings. We shall never forget, Sire, that the sick have seen at their bedside the Prince who is to-day their King. They know that at this moment your march is arrested by charity. We shall tell them that the King is concerned for their ills, and it will be a solace to them. Sire, we offer you our homage, our vows, and the assurance that we shall always fulfil with zeal our duties to the sick." Charles X. replied: "I know with what zeal you and these gentlemen serve the poor. Continue, Mesdames, and you can count on my benevolence and on my constant protection."

The King was received at the Metropolitan Church by the Archbishop of Paris at the head of his clergy. The *Domine salvum, fac regem*, was intoned and repeated by the deputations of all the authorities and by the crowd filling the nave, the side-aisles, and the tribunes of the vast basilica. Then a numerous body of singers sang the *Te Deum*. On leaving the church, the King remounted his horse and returned to the Tuileries, along the quais, to the sound of salvos of artillery and the acclamations of the crowd. The Duchess of Berry, who had followed the King through all the ceremonies, entered the Château with him, and immediately addressed to the Governess of the Children of France this note: "From Saint Cloud to Notre-Dame, from Notre-Dame to the Tuileries, the King has been accompanied by acclamations, signs of approval and of love."

Charles X., on Thursday, the 30th September, had to attend a review on the Champ-de-Mars. The morning of this day, the readers of all the journals found in them a decree abolishing the censorship and restoring liberty of the press. The enthusiasm was immense. The *Journal de Paris* wrote: "To-day all is joy, confidence, hope. The enthusiasm excited by the new reign would be far too ill at ease under a censorship. None can be exercised over the public gratitude. It must be allowed full expansion. Happy is the Council of His Majesty to greet the new King with an act so worthy of him. It is the banquet of this joyous accession; for to give liberty to the press is to give free course to the benedictions merited by Charles X."

The review was superb. After having heard Mass in the chapel of the Château of the Tuileries, the King mounted his horse at half-past eleven, and, accompanied by the Dauphin, the Duke of Orleans, and the Duke of Bourbon, proceeded to the Champ-de-Mars. Two calèches followed; the one was occupied by the Dauphiness, the Duchess of Berry, and the Duke of Bordeaux in the uniform of a colonel of cuirassiers,— a four-year old colonel, — the other by the Duchess of Orleans and Mademoiselle of Orleans, her sister-in-law. The weather was mild and clear. The twelve legions of the National Guard on foot, the mounted National Guard, the military household of the King, and all the regiments of the royal guard, which the sovereign was about to review, made a magnificent appearance. An immense multitude covered the slopes about the Champ-de-Mars. Charles X. harvested the effect of the liberal measure that he had first adopted. A thunder of plaudits and cheers greeted his arrival on the ground. At one moment, when he found himself, so to speak, tangled in the midst of the crowd, several lancers of his guard sought to break the circle formed about him by pushing back the curious with the handles of their lances. "My friends, no halberds!" the King called to them. This happy phrase, repeated from group to group, carried the general satisfaction to a climax. A witness of this military ceremony, the Count of Puymaigre, at that time Prefect of the Oise, says in his curious *Souvenirs:* —

"Charles X. appeared to have dissipated all the dangers that for ten years had menaced his august predecessor.

"On all sides there rose only acclamations of delight in favor of the new King, who showed himself so popular, and whose gracious countenance could express only benevolent intentions. I was present, mingling with the crowd, at the first review by Charles X. on the Champ-de-Mars, and the remarks were so frankly royalist, that any one would have been roughly treated by the crowd had he shown other sentiments."

The Duchess of Berry was full of joy. She quivered with pleasure. Very popular in the army and among the people, as at court and in the city, she was proud to show her fine child, who already wore the uniform, to the officers and soldiers. She appeared to all eyes the symbol of maternal love, and the mothers gazed upon her boy as if he had been their own. As soon as the little Prince was seen, there was on every face an expression of kindliness and sympathy. He was the Child of Paris, the Child of France. Who could have foretold then that this child, so loved, admired, applauded, would, innocent victim, less than six years later, be condemned to perpetual exile, and by whom?

Charles X. had won a triumph. Napoleon, at the time of his greatest glories, at the apogee of his prodigious fortunes, had never had a warmer greeting from the Parisian people. In the course of the review the King spoke to all the colonels. On his return to the Tuileries he went at a slow pace, paused often to receive petitions, handed them to one of his suite, and responded in the most gracious manner to the homage of which he was the object. An historian not to be accused of partiality for the Restoration has written: "On entering the Tuileries, Charles X. might well believe that the favor that greeted his reign effaced the popularity of all the sovereigns who had gone before. Happy in being King at last, moved by the acclamations that he met at every step, the new monarch let his intoxicating joy expand in all his words. His affability was remarked in his walks through Paris, and the grace with which he received all petitioners who could approach him." Everywhere that he appeared, at the Hôtel-Dieu, at Sainte-Geneviève, at the Madeleine, the crowd pressed around him and manifested the sincerest enthusiasm. M. Villemain, in the opening discourse of his lectures on eloquence at the Faculty of Letters, was wildly applauded when he pronounced the following eulogium on the new sovereign: "A monarch kindly and revered, he has the loyalty of the antique ways and modern enlightenment. Religion is the seal of his word. He inherits from Henry IV. those graces of the heart that are irresistible. He has received from Louis XIV. an intelligent love of the arts, a nobility of language, and that dignity that imposes respect while it seduces." All the journals chanted his praises. Seeing that the *Constitutionnel* itself, freed from censorship, rendered distinguished homage to legitimacy, he came to believe that principle invincible. He was called Charles the Loyal. At the Théâtre-Français, the line of *Tartufe* —

"Nous vivons sous un prince ennemi de la fraude" —

was greeted with a salvo of applause. The former adversaries of the King reproached themselves with having misunderstood him. They sincerely reproached themselves for their past criticisms, and adored that which they had burned. M. de Vaulabelle himself wrote: —

"Few sovereigns have taken possession of the throne in circumstances more favorable than those surrounding the accession of Charles X."

It seemed as if the great problem of the conciliation of order and liberty had been definitely solved. The white flag, rejuvenated by the Spanish war, had taken on all its former splendor. The best officers, the best soldiers of the imperial guard, served the King in the royal guard with a devotion proof against everything. Secret societies had ceased their subterranean manœuvres. No more disturbances, no more plots. In the Chambers, the Opposition, reduced to an insignificant minority, was discouraged or converted. The ambitious spirits of whom it was composed turned their thoughts toward the rising sun. Peace had happily fecundated the prodigious resources of the country. Finances, commerce, agriculture, industry, the fine arts, everything was prospering. The public revenues steadily increased. The ease with which riches came inclined all minds toward optimism. The salons had resumed the most exquisite traditions of courtesy and elegance. It was the boast that every good side of the *ancien régime* had been preserved and every bad one rejected. France was not only respected, she was *à la mode*. All Europe regarded her with sympathetic admiration. No one in 1824 could have predicted 1830. The writers least favorable to the Restoration had borne witness to the general calm, the prevalence of good will, the perfect accord between the country and the crown. The early days of the reign of Charles X. were, so to speak, the honeymoon of the union of the King and France.

III

THE TOMBS OF SAINT-DENIS

THE funeral solemnities of Louis XVIII. seemed to the people a mortuary triumph of Royalty over the Revolution and the Empire. The profanations of 1793 were expiated. Napoleon was left with the willow of Saint Helena; the descendant of Saint Louis and of Louis XIV. had the basilica of his ancestors as a place of sepulture, and the links of time's chain were again joined. The obsequies of Louis XVIII. suggested a multitude of reflections. It was the first time since the death of Louis XV. in 1774, that such a ceremony had taken place. As was said by the *Moniteur:* —

"This solemnity, absolutely novel for the greater number of the present generation, offered an aspect at once mournful and imposing. A monarch so justly regretted, a king so truly Christian, coming to take his place among the glorious remains of the martyrs of his race and the bones of his ancestors, — profaned, scattered by the revolutionary tempest, but which he had been able again to gather, — was a grave subject of reflection, a spectacle touching in its purpose and majestic in the pomp with which it was surrounded."

Through what vicissitudes had passed these royal tombs, to which the coffin of Louis XVIII. was borne! Read in the work of M. Georges d'Heylli, *Les Tombes royales de Saint-Denis,* the story of these profanations and restorations.

The *Moniteur* of the 6th of February, 1793, published in its literary miscellany, a so-called patriotic ode, by the poet Lebrun, containing the following strophe: —

> " Purgeons le sol des patriotes,
> Par des rois encore infectes.
> La terre de la liberté
> Rejette les os des despotes.
> De ces monstres divinisés
> Que tous les cercueils soient brisés!
> Que leur mémoire soit flétrie!
> Et qu'avec leurs mânes errants
> Sortent du sein de la patrie
> Les cadavres de ses tyrants!"[1]

These verses were the prelude to the discussion, some months later, in the National Convention, of the proposition to destroy the monuments of the Kings at Saint-Denis, to burn their remains, and to send to the bullet foundry the bronze and lead off their tombs and coffins. In the session of July 31, 1793, Barrère, the "Anacreon of the guillotine,"

---

[1] Let us purge the patriot soil — By kings still infected. — The land of liberty — Rejects the bones of despots. — Of these monsters deified — Let all the coffins be destroyed! — Let their memory perish! — And with their wandering manes — Let issue from the bosom of the fatherland — The bodies of its tyrants!

read to the convention in the name of the Committee of Public Safety, a report, which said: —

"To celebrate the day of August 10, which overthrew the throne, the pompous mausoleums must be destroyed upon its anniversary. Under the Monarchy, the very tombs were taught to flatter kings. Royal pride and luxury could not be moderated even on this theatre of death, and the bearers of the sceptre who had brought such ills on France and on humanity seemed even in the grave to vaunt a vanished splendor. The strong hand of the Republic should pitilessly efface these haughty epitaphs, and demolish these mausoleums which might recall the frightful memory of kings."

The project was voted by acclamation. The tombs were demolished between the 6th and 8th of August, 1793, and the announcement was made for the anniversary of the 10th of August, 1792, of "that grand, just, and retributive destruction, required in order that the coffins should be opened, and the remains of the tyrants be thrown into a ditch filled with quicklime, where they may be forever destroyed. This operation will shortly take place."

This was done in the following October. For some days there was carried on a profanation even more sacrilegious than the demolition of the tombs. The coffins containing the remains of kings and queens, princes and princesses, were violated. On Wednesday, the 16th of October, 1793, at the very hour that Marie Antoinette mounted the scaffold, — she who had so wept for her son, the first Dauphin, who died the 4th of June, 1789, at the beginning of the Revolution, — the disinterrers of kings violated the grave of this child and threw his bones on the refuse heap. Iconoclasts, jealous of death, disputed its prey, and they profaned among others the sepulchres of Madame Henrietta of England, of the Princess Palatine, of the Regent, and of Louis XV.

In the midst of these devastations, some men, less insensate than the others, sought at least to rescue from the hands of the destroyers what might be preserved in the interest of art. Of this number was an artist, Alexandre Lenoir, who had supervised the demolition of the tombs of Saint-Denis. He could not keep from the foundry, by the terms of the decree, the tombs of lead, copper, and bronze; but he saved the others from complete destruction — those that may be seen to-day in the church of Saint-Denis. He had them placed first in the cemetery of the Valois, near the ditches filled with quicklime, where had been cast the remains of the great ones of the earth, robbed of their sepulchres. Later, a decree of the Minister of the Interior, Benezech, dated 19 Germinal, An IV., authorizing the citizen Lenoir to have the tombs thus saved from destruction taken to the Museum of French Monuments, of which he was the conservator, and which had been installed at Paris, Rue des Petits Augustins. From thence they were destined to be returned to the Church of Saint-Denis, under the reign of Louis XVIII.

At the height of his power, Napoleon dreamed of providing for himself the same sepulture as that of the kings, his predecessors. He had decided that he would be interred in the Church of Saint-Denis, and had arranged for himself a cortège of emperors about the site that he had chosen for the vault of his dynasty. He directed the construction of a grand monument dedicated to Charlemagne, which was to rise in the "imperialized" church. The great Carlovingian emperor was to have been represented, erect, upon a column of marble, at the back of which statues in stone of the emperors who succeeded him were to have been placed. But at the time of Napoleon's fall, the monument had not been finished. There had been completed only the statues, which have taken their rank in the crypt. They represent Charlemagne, Louis le Débonnaire, Charles le Chauve, Louis le Bègue, Charles le Gros, and even Louis d'Outremer, who, nevertheless, was only a king.

Like the Pharaohs of whom Bossuet speaks, Napoleon was not to enjoy his sepulture. To be interred with pomp at Saint-Denis, while Napoleon, at Saint Helena, rested under a simple stone on which not even his name was inscribed, was the last triumph for Louis XVIII., — a triumph in death. The re-entrance of Louis XVIII. had been not only the restoration of the throne, but that of the tombs. The 21st of January, 1815, twenty-two years, to the very day, after the death of Louis XVI., the remains of the unhappy King and those of his Queen, Marie

Antoinette, were transferred to the Church of Saint-Denis, where their solemn obsequies were celebrated. Chateaubriand cried:—

"What hand has reconstructed the roof of these vaults and prepared these empty tombs? The hand of him who was seated on the throne of the Bourbons. O Providence! He believed that he was preparing the sepulchres of his race, and he was but building the tomb of Louis XVI. Injustice reigns but for a moment; it is virtue only that can count its ancestors and leave a posterity. See, at the same moment, the master of the earth falls, Louis XVIII. regains the sceptre, Louis XVI. finds again the sepulture of his fathers."

At the beginning of the Second Restoration, the King determined, by a decree of the 4th of April, 1816, that search should be made in the cemetery of the Valois, about the Church of Saint-Denis, in order to recover the remains of his ancestors that might have escaped the action of the bed of quicklime, in which they had been buried under the Terror. The same decree declared that the remains recovered should be solemnly replaced in the Church of Saint-Denis.

Excavations were made in January, 1817, in the cemetery of the Valois, and the bones thus discovered were transferred to the necropolis of the kings.

"It was night," says Alexandre Lenoir, in his *Histoire des Arts en France par les Monuments*. "The moon shone on the towers; the torches borne by the attendants were reflected from the walls of the edifice. What a spectacle! The remains of kings and queens, princes and princesses, of the most ancient of monarchies, sought with pious care, with sacred respect, in the ditches dug by impious arms in the evil days. The bones of the Valois and the Bourbons found *pêle-mêle* outside the walls of the church, and brought again, after a long exile, to their ancient burial place."

In a little vault on the left were deposited the coffins containing the bones of earlier date than the Bourbons, and a marble tablet was placed upon it, with the inscription: "Here rest the mortal remains of eighteen kings, from Dagobert to Henry III.; ten queens, from Nantilde, wife of Dagobert, to Marguerite de Valois, first wife of Henry IV.; twenty-four dauphins, princes, and princesses, children and grandchildren of France; eleven divers personages (Hugues-le-grand, four abbés of Saint-Denis, three chamberlains, two constables, and Sédille de Sainte-Croix, wife of the Counsellor Jean Pastourelle). Torn from their violated sepulchres the 17, 18, 19, 20, 21, 22, 23, 24 October, 1793, and 18 January, 1794; restored to their tombs the 19 January, 1817."

On the right were placed the coffins enclosing the remains of the princes and princesses of the house of Bourbon, the list of which is given by a second marble plaque: "Here rest the mortal remains of seven kings, from Charles V. to Louis XV.; seven queens, from Jeanne de Bourbon, wife of Charles V., to Marie Leczinska, wife of Louis XV.; dauphins and dauphinesses, princes and princesses, children and grandchildren of France, to the number of forty-seven, from the second son of Henry IV. to the Dauphin, eldest son of Louis XVI. Torn from their violated sepulchres the 12, 14, 15, and 16 October, 1793; restored to their tombs the 19 January, 1817."

Besides these vaults, there is one that bears the title of the "Royal Vault of the Bourbons," though but a small number of princes and princesses of this family are there deposited. There is where Louis XVIII. was to rest. In 1815, there had been placed in this vault the coffins of Louis XVI. and of Marie Antoinette, recovered on the site of the former cemetery of the Madeleine. On the coffin of the King was carved: "Here is the body of the very high, very puissant, and very excellent Prince, Louis, 16th of the name, by the grace of God King of France and Navarre." A like inscription on the coffin of the Queen recited her titles.

In 1817, there had been put by the side of these two coffins those of Madame Adélaïde and of Madame Victorine, daughter of Louis XV., who died at Trieste, one in 1799, the other in 1800, and whose remains had just been brought from that city to Saint-Denis. There had also been placed in the same vault a coffin containing the body of Louis VII. — a king coming now for the first time, as Alexandre Lenoir remarks, to take a place in the vault of these vanished princes, whose ranks are no longer crowded, and which crime has been more prompt to scatter than has Death been to fill them; also the coffin of Louise de Vaudemont, wife of Henry III., the queen who was buried in the Church of the Capucins, Place Vendôme, and whose remains escaped profanation in 1793. In this same vault were also two little coffins, those of a daughter and a son of the Duke and Duchess of Berry, who died, one in 1817, the other in 1818, immediately after birth, and the coffin of their father, assassinated the 13th of February, 1820, on leaving the Opera. Such were the companions in burial of Louis XVIII.

IV

THE FUNERAL OF LOUIS XVIII

LOUIS XVIII. died the 16th of September, 1824, at the Château of the Tuileries. His body remained there until the 23d of September, when, to the sound of a salvo of one hundred and one guns, it was borne to the Church of Saint-Denis. The coffin remained exposed in this basilica within a *chapelle ardente*, to the 24th of October, the eve of the day fixed for the obsequies, and during all this time the church was filled with a crowd of the faithful, belonging to all classes of society, who gathered from Paris and all the surrounding communes, to render a last homage to the old King. Sunday, 24th of October, at two o'clock in the afternoon, the body was transferred from the *chapelle ardente* to the catafalque prepared to receive it. Then the vespers and the vigils of the dead were sung, and the Grand Almoner, clad in his pontifical robes, officiated. The next day, Monday, the 25th of October, the services of burial took place.

The Dauphin and Dauphiness left the Tuileries at 10.30 A.M., to be present at the funeral ceremony. In conformity with etiquette, Charles X. was not present. He remained at the Tuileries with the Duchess of Berry, with whom he heard a requiem Mass in the chapel of the Château at eleven o'clock. The Duchess was thus spared a painful spectacle. With what emotion would she not have seen opened the crypt in which she believed she would herself be laid, and which was the burial place of her assassinated husband and of her two children, dead so soon after their birth.

The ceremony commences in the antique necropolis. The interior of the church is hung all with black to the spring of the arches, where fleurs-de-lis in gold are relieved against the funeral hangings. The light of day, wholly shut out, is replaced by an immense quantity of lamps, tapers, and candles, suspended from a multitude of candelabra and chandeliers. At the back of the choir shines a great luminous cross. The Dauphiness, the Duchess of Orleans, the princes and princesses, her children, her sister-in-law, are led to the gallery of the Dauphiness. The church is filled with the crowd of constituted authorities. At the entrance to the nave is seen a deputation of men and women from the markets, and others who, according to the *Moniteur*, have won the favor of admission to this sad ceremony by the grief they manifested at the time of the King's death. The Dauphin advances, his mantle borne from the threshold of the church to the choir by the Duke of Blacas, the Duke of Damas, and the Count Melchior de Polignac. The Duke of

Orleans comes next. Three of his officers bear his mantle.

A salvo of artillery, responded to by a discharge of musketry, announces the commencement of the ceremony. The Grand Almoner of France says Mass. After the Gospel Mgr. de Frayssinous, Bishop of Hermopolis, ascends the pulpit and pronounces the funeral oration of the King. At the close of the discourse another salvo of artillery and another discharge of musketry are heard. The musicians of the Chapel of the King, under the direction of M. Plantade, render the Mass of Cherubini. At the *Sanctus*, twelve pages of the King, guided by their governor, come from the sacristy, whence they have taken their torches, salute the altar, then the catafalque, place themselves kneeling on the first steps of the sanctuary, and remain there until after the Communion. The *De Profundis* and the *Libera* are sung. After the absolutions, twelve body-guards advance to the catafalque, which recalls by its form the mausoleums raised to Francis I. and to Henry II. by the architects of the sixteenth century. It occupies the centre of the nave. The cords of the pall are borne by the Chancellor Dambray in the name of the Chamber of Peers, by M. Ravez in the name of the Chamber of Deputies, by the Count de Sèze in the name of the magistracy, by Marshal Moncey, Duke of Conegliano, in the name of the army. The twelve body-guards raise the coffin from the catafalque, and bear it into the royal tomb. Then the

King-at-Arms goes alone into the vault, lays aside his rod, his cap, and his coat-of-arms, which he also casts in, retires a step, and cries: "Heralds-at-Arms, perform your duties."

The Heralds-at-Arms, marching in succession, cast their rods, caps, coats-of-arms, into the tomb, then withdraw, except two, of whom one descends into the vault to place the regalia on the coffin, and the other is stationed on the first steps to receive the regalia and pass them to the one who stands on the steps.

The King-at-Arms begins announcing the regalia. He says: "Marshal, Duke of Ragusa, major-general of the Royal Guard, bring the flag of the Royal Guard." The marshal rises from his place, takes the flag from the hands of the officer bearing it, advances, salutes first the Dauphin, then the Duke of Orleans, approaches the vault, makes a profound bow, and places the flag in the hands of the Herald-at-Arms, standing on the steps. He passes it to the second, who places it on the coffin. The marshal salutes the altar and the princes and resumes his place.

The King-at-Arms continues the calls. "Monsieur the Duke of Mortemart, captain-colonel of the regular foot-guards of the King, bring the ensign of the company which you have in keeping." He summons in the same manner the Duke of Luxembourg, the Duke of Mouchy, the Duke of Gramont, the Duke d'Havré, who bring each the standard of the company of the body-guards of which they are the four captains. The call of the other regalia goes on in the following order: —

"Monsieur the Count of Peyrelongue, Equerry in Ordinary of His Majesty, bring the spurs of the King.

"Monsieur the Marquis of Fresne, Equerry in Ordinary of His Majesty, bring the gauntlets of the King.

"Monsieur the Chevalier de Rivière, Master of the Horse of His Majesty, bring the coat-of-arms of the King.

"Monsieur the Marquis of Vernon, charged with the functions of First Equerry, bring the helmet of the King.

"Monsieur the Duke of Polignac, charged with the functions of Grand Equerry of France, bring the royal sword. (The royal sword is presented before the vault only by the point, and is not carried down.)

"Monsieur the Prince de Talleyrand, Grand Chamberlain of France, bring the banner."

There is seen approaching, the banner in his hand, an old man, slight, lame, clad in satin and covered with embroidery, in gold and jewelled decorations. It is the unfrocked priest who said the Mass of the Champ-de-Mars, for the *Fête de la Fédération;* it is the diplomat who directed the Ministry of Foreign Affairs at the time of the murder of the Duke d'Enghien; it is the courtier, who, before he was Grand

Chamberlain of Louis XVIII. and Charles X., was that of Napoleon. The banner is presented before the vault only by one end. It is inclined over the opening of the crypt, but is not cast in, salutes, for the last time, the dead King, then rises as if to proclaim that the noble banner of France dies not, and that the royalty sheltered beneath its folds descends not into the tomb.

The King-at-Arms again cries:—

"Monsieur the Duke d'Uzès, charged with the functions of Grand Master of France, come and perform your duty." Then the maîtres de l'hôtel, the chambellans de l'hôtel, and the first maître de l'hôtel approach the vault, break their bâtons, cast them in, and return to their places.

The King-at-Arms summons the persons bearing the insignia of royalty.

"Monsieur the Duke of Bressac, bring *la main de justice*.

"Monsieur the Duke of Chevreuse, bring the sceptre.

"Monsieur the Duke of la Trémoïlle, bring the crown."

These three insignia are taken down into the vault, as were the flag and the four standards.

Then the Duke d'Uzès, putting the end of the bâton of Grand Master of France within the vault, cries out: "The King is dead!"

The King-at-Arms withdraws three paces, and repeats in a low voice: "The King is dead! the

King is dead! the King is dead!" Then turning to the assembly he says: "Pray for the repose of his soul!"

At this moment the clergy and all the assistants throw themselves upon their knees, pray, and rise again. The Duke d'Uzès withdraws his bâton from the vault, and brandishing it, calls out: "Long live the King!"

The King-at-Arms repeats: "Long live the King! long live the King! long live the King! Charles, tenth of the name, by the grace of God, King of France and Navarre, very Christian, very august, very puissant, our very honored lord and good master, to whom God grant long and happy life! Cry ye all: Long live the King!" Then the trumpets, drums, fifes, and instruments of the military bands break into a loud fanfare, and their sound is mingled with the prolonged acclamations of the assembly, whose cries "Long live the King! long live Charles X.!" contrast with the silence of the tombs.

"To this outburst of the public hopes," says the *Moniteur*, "succeeded the return of pious and mournful duties; the tomb is closed over the mortal remains of the monarch whose subjects, restored to happiness, greeted him on his return from the land of exile with the name of Louis le Désiré, and who twice reconciled his people with Europe. This imposing ceremony being ended, the princes were again escorted into the Abbey to their apartments, by the Grand Master, the Master of Ceremonies and his aides, preceded by the Master-at-Arms, and the Heralds-at-Arms, who had resumed their caps, coats-of-arms, and rods. Then the crowd slowly dispersed. We shall not try to express the sentiments to which this imposing and mournful ceremony must give rise. With the regrets and sorrow caused by the death of a prince so justly wept, mingle the hopes inspired by a King already the master of all hearts. This funeral ceremony when, immediately after the burial of a monarch whom God had called to Himself, were heard cries of ' Long live Charles X.,' — the new King greeted at the tomb of his august predecessor, — this inauguration, amid the pomps of death, must have left impressions not to be rendered, and beyond the power of imagination to represent."

Reader, if this recital has interested you, go visit the Church of Saint-Denis. There is not, perhaps, in all the world, a spectacle more impressive than the sight of the ancient necropolis of kings. Enter the basilica, admirably restored under the Second Empire. By the mystic light of the windows, faithful reproductions of those of former centuries, — the funerals of so many kings, the profanations of 1793, the restoration of the tombs, — all this invades your thought and inspires you with a dim religious impression of devotion. These stones have their language. *Lapides clamabunt.* They speak amid the sepulchral silence. Listen to the echo of a far-away voice. There, under these arches, centuries old, the 21st of August, 1670, Bossuet pronounced the funeral oration of Madame Henriette of England. He said: —

"With whatever haughty distinction men may flatter themselves, they all have the same origin, and this origin insignificant. Their years follow each other like waves; they flow unceasingly, and though the sound of some is slightly greater and their course a trifle longer than those of others, they are together confounded in an abyss where are known neither princes nor kings nor the proud distinctions of men, as the most boasted rivers mingle in the ocean, nameless and inglorious with the least known streams."

Is not the Church of Saint-Denis itself a funeral discourse in stone more grandiose and eloquent than that of the reverend orator? Regard on either side of the nave these superb mausoleums, these pompous tombs that are but an empty show, and since their dead dwell not in them, contemplate these columns that seem to wish to bear to heaven the splendid testimony of our nothingness! There, at the right of the main altar, descend the steps that lead to the crypt. There muse on all the kings, the queens, the princes, and princesses, whose bones have been replaced at hazard within these vaults, after their bodies had been, in 1793, cast into a common ditch in the cemetery of the Valois to be consumed by quicklime. The great ones of the earth, dispossessed of their sepulchres, could they not say, in the region of shades, in the mournful words of the *Sermonnaire*: —

"Death does not leave us body enough to require room, and it is only the tombs that claim the sight; our body takes another name; even that of corpse, since it implies something of the human form, remains to it but a little time; it becomes a something nameless in any tongue, so truly does everything die in it, even the funeral terms by which its unhappy remains are designated. Thus the Power divine, justly angered by our pride, reduces it to nothingness, and, to level all conditions forever, makes common ashes of us all."

The remains of so many sovereigns and princes are no longer even corpses. The corpses have perished as ruins perish. You may no longer see the coffins of the predecessors of Louis XVI. But those of the Martyr-King, of the Queen Marie Antoinette, of the Duke of Berry, of Louis XVIII., are there before you in the crypt. Pause. Here is the royal vault of the Bourbons. Your glance can enter only a narrow grated window, through which a little twilight filters. If a lamp were not lighted at the back, the eye would distinguish nothing. By the doubtful gleam of this sepulchral lamp, you succeed in making out in the gloom the coffins placed on trestles of iron; to the left that of the Duke of Berry, then the two little coffins of his children, dead at birth; then in two rows those of Mesdames Adélaïde and Victoire, daughters of Louis XV., those of Louis XVI. and Marie Antoinette, those of the two last Princes of Condé, died in 1818 and in 1830, and on the right, at the very extremity of the vault, that of the only sovereign who, for the period of a century, died upon the throne, Louis XVIII.

The royal vault of the Bourbons was diminished more than half to make room for the imperial vault constructed under Napoleon III. The former entrance, on the steps of which stand the Heralds-at-Arms at the obsequies of the kings, has been suppressed. The coffin of Louis XVIII. was not placed on the iron trestles, where it rests to-day, at the time of his funeral. It was put at the threshold of the vault, where it was to have been replaced by that of Charles X.; for by the ancient tradition, when a king of France dies, as his successor takes his place on the throne, so he, in death, displaces his predecessor. But Louis XVIII. waited in vain for Charles X. in the royal vault of the Bourbons; the last brother of Louis XVI. reposes in the chapel of the Franciscans at Goritz.

Charles X. is not alone in being deprived of his rights in his tomb; the Duke and Duchess of Angoulême and the Count of Chambord were so, and also Napoleon III. The second Emperor and Prince Imperial, his son, sleep their sleep in England; for the Bonapartes, like the Bourbons, have been exiled from Saint-Denis. By a decree of the 18th of November, 1858, the man who had re-established the Empire decided that the imperial dynasty should have its sepulture in the ancient necropolis of the kings. Napoleon III. no more realized his dream than

Napoleon I. He had completed under his reign the magnificent vault destined for himself and his race. But once more was accomplished the *Sic vos non vobis*, and no imperial corpse has ever taken its place in the still empty Napoleonic vault. The opening situated in the church, near the centre of the nave, is at present closed by enormous flagstones framed in copper bands; and as there is no inscription on these, many people whose feet tread them in visiting the church do not suspect that they have beneath them the stairway of six steps leading down to the vault that was to be the burial place of emperors. "Oh, vanity! Oh, nothingness! Oh, mortals ignorant of their destinies!" It is not enough that contending dynasties dispute each other's crowns; their covetousness and rivalry must extend to their tombs. Not enough that sovereigns have been exiled from their country; they must be exiled from their graves. Disappointments in life and in death. This is the last word of divine anger, the last of the lessons of Providence.

V

THE KING

BORN at Versailles, the 9th of October, 1757, Charles X., King of France and Navarre, was entering his sixty-eighth year at the time of his accession to the throne. According to the portrait traced by Lamartine, "he had kept beneath the first frosts of age the freshness, the stature, the suppleness, and beauty of youth." His health was excellent, and but for the color of his hair — almost white — he would hardly have been given more than fifty years. As alert as his predecessor was immobile, an untiring hunter, a bold rider, sitting his horse with the grace of a young man, a kindly talker, an affable sovereign, this survivor of the court of Versailles, this familiar of the Petit-Trianon, this friend of Marie Antoinette, of the Princess of Lamballe, of the Duchess of Polignac, of the Duke of Lauzun, of the Prince de Ligne, preserved, despite his devotedness, a great social prestige. He perpetuated the traditions of the elegance of the old régime. Having lived much in the society of women, his politeness toward them was exquisite. This former voluptuary preserved only the good side of gallantry.

The Count d'Haussonville writes in his book entitled *Ma Jeunesse:* —

"I have often seen Charles X. on horseback reviewing troops or following the chase; I have heard him, seated on his throne, and surrounded with all the pomp of an official cortège, pronounce the opening discourse of the session; I have many times been near him at the little select fêtes that the Duchess of Berry used to give, of a morning, in the Pavillon de Marsan, to amuse the Children of France, as they were then called, and to extend their acquaintance with the young people of their own age. One day when I was visiting with my parents some exposition of objects of art or flowers in one of the lower halls of the Louvre, I saw him approach my mother — whom he had known in England — with a familiarity at once respectful and charming. He plainly wished to please those whom he addressed, and he had the gift of doing so. In that kind of success he was rarely wanting, especially with women. His physiognomy as well as his manner helped. It was open and benevolent, always animated by an easy, perhaps a slightly commonplace smile, that of a man conscious that he was irresistible, and that he could, with a few amiable words, overcome all obstacles."

The fiercest adversaries of Charles X. never denied the attraction emanating from his whole personality, the chief secret of which was kindliness. In his constant desire to charm every one that approached

CHARLES X.

him, he had a certain something like feminine coquetry. The Count of Puymaigre, who, being the Prefect of the Oise, saw him often at the Château of Compiègne, says: —

"If the imposing tone of Louis XVIII. intimidated, it was not so with Charles X.; there was rather danger of forgetting, pacing the room with him, that one was talking with a king."

Yet, whatever may be asserted, the new monarch never dreamed of restoring the old régime. We do not believe that for a single instant he had the insensate idea of putting things back to where they were before 1789. His favorite minister, M. de Villèle, was not one of the great nobles, and the men who were to take the chief parts in the consecration were of plebeian origin. The impartial historian of the Restoration, M. de Viel-Castel, remarked it: —

"Charles X. by this fact alone, that for three years he had actively shared in affairs and saw the difficulty of them better, by the fact that he was no longer exasperated by the heat of the struggle and by impatience at the political nullity to which events had so long condemned him, had laid aside a part of his former exaggeration. In the lively satisfaction he felt in entering at last, at the age of sixty-seven, upon the enjoyment of the supreme power by the perspective of which his imagination had been so long haunted, he was disposed to neglect nothing to capture public favor, and thus gain the chance to realize the dreams of his life. His kindliness and natural courtesy would have inspired these tactics, even if policy had not suggested them."

The dignity of the private life of the King added to the respect inspired by his personality. His morals were absolutely irreproachable. His wife, Marie Thérèse of Savoy, died the 2d of June, 1805; he never remarried, and his conduct had been wholly edifying. The sacrifice he made to God, in renouncing the love of women, after he lost his well-beloved Countess of Polastron by death in 1803, was the more meritorious, because, apart from the prestige of his birth and rank, he remained attractive longer than men of his age. No such scandals as had dishonored the court of nearly all his predecessors occurred in his, and the most malevolent could not charge him with having a favorite. In his home he was a man as respectable as he was attractive, a tender father, a grandfather even more tender, an affectionate uncle, a gentle, indulgent master for his servants. None of the divisions that existed in the family of Louis XVIII. appeared in that of his successor; perfect harmony reigned in the court of the Tuileries.

Of a mind more superficial than profound, Charles X. did not lack either in tact or in intelligence. He sincerely desired to do right, and his errors were made in good faith, in obedience to the mandates of his conscience. Lamartine, who had occasion to see him near at hand, thus sums up his character: —

"A man of heart, and impulsive, all his qualities were gifts of nature; hardly any were the fruit acquired by labor and meditation. He had the spirit of the French race, superficial, rapid, spontaneous, and happy in the hazard of repartee, the smile kindly and communicative, the glance open, the hand outstretched, the attitude cordial, an ardent thirst for popularity, great confidence in his relations with others, a constancy in friendship rare upon the throne, true modesty, a restless seeking for good advice, a conscience severe for himself and indulgent for others, a piety without pettiness, a noble repentance for the sole weaknesses of his life, his youthful amours, a rational and sincere love for his people, an honest and religious desire to make France happy and to render his reign fruitful in the moral improvement and the national grandeur of the country confided to him by Providence. All these loyal dispositions were written on his physiognomy. A lively frankness, majesty, kindness, honesty, candor, all revealed therein a man born to love and to be loved. Depth and solidity alone were wanting in this visage; looking at it, you were drawn to the man, you felt doubts of the King."

This remark, just enough at the end of Charles X.'s reign, was hardly so at the outset. In 1824 people had no doubts of the man or of the King. The French were content with Charles X., and Charles X. was content with himself.

The new King said to himself that his policy was the right one, because, from the moment of his accession, all hatreds were appeased. With the absolute calm enjoyed by France he compared the agitations, plots, violence, the troubles and the fury of which it had been the theatre under the Decazes ministry. From the day the Right had assumed power, and Louis XVIII. had allowed his brother to engage in public affairs, the victory of royalty had been complete and manifest. Charles X. thought then that the results had sustained him; that foresight, virtue, political sense, were on his side. Needless to say, every one about him supported him in that idea, that he believed in all conscience that he was in the right, obeying the voice of honor and acting like a king and a Christian. Any other policy than his own would have seemed to him foolish and cowardly. To hear his courtiers, one would have said that the age of gold had returned in France; the felicitations offered him took an idyllic tone. The Count of Chabrol, Prefect of the Seine, said to him, January 1, 1825, at the grand reception at the Tuileries: —

"At your accession, Sire, a prestige of grace and power calmed, in the depths of all hearts, the last murmur of the storm, and the peace that we enjoy to-day is embellished by a charm that is yours alone."

The same day the *Drapeau Blanc* said: —

"Why is there an unusual crowd passing about the palace of the cherished monarch and princes? It is watching with affection for a glance or smile from Charles! These are the new-year gifts for the people moved by love for the noble race of its kings. This glance, expressing only goodness, this smile so full of grace, they long for everywhere and always before their eyes. His classic and cherished features are reproduced in every form; every public place has its bust, every hut its image; they are the domestic gods of a worship that is pure and without superstition, brought to our families by peace and happiness."

The aurora of Charles X.'s reign was like that of his brother Louis XVI. The two brothers resembled travellers who, deceived by the early morning sun and the limpid purity of the sky, set forth full of joy and confidence, and are suddenly surprised by a frightful tempest. The new James II. imagined that his royalty had brought his trials to an end. It was, on the contrary, only a halt in the journey of misfortune and exile. He believed the Revolution finished, and it had but begun.

VI

THE DAUPHIN AND DAUPHINESS

AT the accession of Charles X., the royal family, properly speaking, consisted of six persons only, — the King, the Duke and Duchess of Angoulême, the Duchess of Berry and her two children (the Duke of Bordeaux and Mademoiselle). By the traditions of the monarchy, the Duke of Angoulême, as son and heir of the King, took the title of Dauphin, and his wife that of Dauphiness. The Duchess of Berry, who, under the reign of Louis XVIII. was called Madame the Duchess of Berry, was by right, henceforward, called simply *Madame*, a privilege that belonged to the Duchess of Angoulême before she was Dauphiness. That is why the Gymnase, the theatre under the special protection of the Duchess of Berry, was called, after the new reign began, the *Théâtre de Madame.*

Born at Versailles the 5th of August, 1775, the Duke of Angoulême had just entered on his fiftieth year. A tender and respectful son, an irreproachable husband, a brave soldier, he was lacking in both brilliant and solid qualities. His awkward air, his bashfulness, his myopia, his manners rather *bourgeois* than princely, were against him. He had nothing of the charm and grace of his father. But when one knew him, it was easy to see that he had unquestioned virtues and real worth. To Charles X. he was a most faithful subject and the best of sons. In contrast with so many heirs apparent, who openly or secretly combat the political ideas of their fathers, he was always the humble and docile supporter of the throne. The Spanish expedition brought him credit. In it he showed courage and zeal. The army esteemed him, and he gave serious attention to military matters. A man of good sense and good faith, he held himself aloof from all exaggerations. At the time of the reaction of the White Terror, he had repudiated the fury of the ultras, and distinguished himself by a praiseworthy moderation. He had great piety, without hypocrisy, bigotry, or fanaticism. The Count of Puymaigre, in his curious *Souvenirs*, says:—

"The Duke of Angoulême appeared to me to be always subordinated to the will of the King, and he said to me one day very emphatically that his position forbade any manifestation of personal sentiment, because it was unbecoming in the heir apparent to sustain the opposition. Though very religious, he did not share the exaggerated ideas of what was then called the 'congregation,' and I recall that one day he asked me brusquely: 'Are you a partisan of the missions?' As I hesitated to reply, he insisted. 'No, my lord, in nowise; I think that one good curé suffices for a commune, and that missionaries, by treating the public mind with an unusual fervor, often bring trouble with them and at the same time often lessen the consideration due to the resident priest.'"

Married, on the 10th of June, 1799, to the daughter of Louis XVI. and Marie Antoinette, the Duke of Angoulême had no children; but though the sterility of his wife was an affliction, he never complained of it. He was not known to have either favorites or mistresses. The life of this descendant of Louis XIV. and of Louis XV. was purity itself. There were neither scandals nor intrigues about him. By nature irascible and obstinate, he had modified this tendency of his character by reason and still more by religion. Assiduous in his duties, without arrogance or vanity, regarding his rôle as Prince as a mission given him by Providence, which he wished to fulfil conscientiously, he had not the slightest mental reservation in favor of restoring the old régime, and showed, perhaps, more favor to the lieutenants of Napoleon than to the officers of the army of Condé, his companions in arms. To sum up, he was not an attractive prince, but he merited respect. The Count of Puymaigre thus concludes the portrait traced by him: —

"The manner, bearing, and gestures of the Duke of Angoulême cannot be called gracious, especially in contrast with his father's manners; doubtless it is not fair to ask that a prince, any more than another, should be favored by nature, but it is much to be desired that he shall have an air of superiority. The ruling taste of the Dauphin was for the chase. He also read much and gave much time to the *personnel* of the army. Retiring early, he arose every morning at five o'clock, and lighted his own fire. Far from having anything to complain of in him, I could only congratulate myself on his kindness."

The Dauphiness, Marie-Theresa-Charlotte of France, Duchess of Angoulême, born at Versailles the 19th of December, 1778, was forty-five years old when her uncle and father-in-law, Charles X., ascended the throne. She was surrounded by universal veneration. She was regarded, and with reason, as a veritable saint, and by all parties was declared to be *sans peur et sans reproche.*

The Duchess of Angoulême, shunning the notoriety sought by other princesses, preferred her oratory to the salons. Yet her devotion had nothing mean or narrow in it. Despite the legendary catastrophes that weighed upon her, she always appeared at fêtes where her presence was demanded. She laughed with good heart at the theatre, and there was nothing morose or ascetic in her conversation. She never spoke of her misfortunes. One day she was pitying a young girl who suffered from chilblains. "I know what it is," she said; "I have had them." Then she added, without other comment: "True, the winters were very severe at that time." She did not wish to say that she had had these chilblains while a prisoner in the Temple, when fuel was refused to her.

But if the Princess never spoke of herself, she never ceased to think of the martyrs for whom she wept. At the Tuileries, she occupied the Pavillon de l'Horloge and the Pavillon de Flore, the first floor apartments that had been her mother's. She used for her own a little salon hung with white velvet sown with marguerite lilies. This tapestry was the work of the unhappy Queen and of Madame Elisabeth. In the same room was a stool on which Louis XVII. had languished and suffered. It served as *prie-dieu* to the Orphan of the Temple. There was in this stool a drawer where she had put away the remaining relics of her parents: the black silk vest and white cravat worn by Louis XVI. the day of his death; a lace bonnet of Marie Antoinette, the last work done by the Queen in her prison of the Conciergerie, which Robespierre had had taken from her on the pretext that the widow of the Christian King might kill herself with her needle or with a lace-string; finally some fragments of the fichu which the wind raised from the shoulders of Madame Elisabeth when the angelic Princess was already on the scaffold. The Dauphiness, who usually dined with the King, dined alone on the 21st of January and the 16th of October. She shut herself in the chamber where she had collected these relics and passed the whole day and evening there in prayer.

The charity of the pious Princess was inexhaustible. Almost all her revenue was expended in alms. She would not have receipts signed by those to whom she distributed relief. "The duty of givers," she said, "is to forget their gifts and the names of those who receive them; it is for those who receive to remember." Nor did she ever ask the political opinions of those she relieved. To be unfortunate, sufficed to excite her interest. One day Sister Rosalie, charged by the Princess with paying a pension to a man whose ill conduct she had discovered, thought it her duty to notify the benefactress, and suspend the succor. "My sister," replied the Dauphiness, "continue to pay this man his pension. We must be charitable to the good that they may persevere, and to the bad that they may become better." Sunday, when the Princess did no work, she passed the evening in detaching the wax seals from letters and envelopes. This wax, converted into sticks, produced one thousand francs a year, which she sent to a poor family. She gave much, but only to Frenchmen and Frenchwomen. She replied to every demand for aid for foreigners that she was sorry not to comply with the request, but she should feel that she was doing an injustice to give to others while there was a single Frenchman in need. On each anniversary of mourning she doubled her alms.

The existence of the Dauphiness at the Tuileries passed with extreme regularity. A very early riser, like her husband, she made her toilet herself, having learned to help herself in her captivity in the Temple. She used to breakfast at six o'clock, and at seven daily attended the first Mass in the chapel of the Château. There was a second at nine o'clock for the Dauphin, and a third at eleven for the King. From eight to eleven she held audiences. She retired at ten o'clock, and only prolonged the evening to eleven when she visited the Duchess of Berry, for whom she had a great affection, and whose children she saw two or three times a day. A devoted companion of Charles X., she always went with him to the various royal châteaux. The Count of Puymaigre says in his *Souvenirs:* —

"The Dauphiness having by her kindness accustomed me to speaking freely, I used this privilege without embarrassment, but always observing that measure which keeps a man of good society within just limits, equally careful not to put himself ridiculously at ease and not to be so abashed by exaggerated respect as to become insipid. I have always thought that a princess no more than any other woman likes to be bored. I talked much with her in the carriage, seeking to amuse the Princess with a few anecdotes, and I did not fear to discuss serious things with her, on which she expressed herself with real sagacity. When she was accused of want of tact in the numerous receptions of which one had to undergo the monotony, it was often the fault of her immediate companions, who neglected to give her suitable information as to the various persons received. How many times I have hinted to her to speak to some devoted man, who regarded a word from the Princess as a signal favor, to yield to requests, perhaps untimely, to visit some establishment, to receive the humble petitions of a mayor, a curé, or a municipal council. I will not deny that she had a sort of brusqueness, partly due to an exceedingly high voice, and moments of ill humor, transient no doubt, but which nevertheless left a painful impression on those who were subjected to them. Madame the Dauphiness made no mistake as to the state of France; she was not the dupe of the obsequiousness of certain men of the court, and merit was certain to obtain her support whether it had been manifested under the old or the new régime; but she had not the influence she was supposed to have, and I doubt if she tried to acquire it."

One day the Princess was talking to the Prefect of the Oise about the great noblemen who had possessions in the Department.

"Have they any influence over the people?" she asked him.

"No, Madame, and it is their own fault. M. de La Rochefoucauld is the only one who is popular, but his influence is against you. As to the others, greedy of the benefits of the court, they come to their estates only to save money, to regulate their accounts with their managers, and the people, receiving no mark of their interest, acknowledge no obligation to them."

"You are perfectly right," replied the Dauphiness, "that is not the way with the English aristocracy."

"She saw with pain," adds M. de Puymaigre, "the marriages for money made by certain men of the court, but not when they allied themselves with an honorable plebeian family; her indignation was justly shown toward those who took their wives in families whose coveted riches came from an impure source."

The extraordinary catastrophes that had fallen on the daughter of Louis XVI. and Marie Antoinette had been a great experience for her, and she was not surprised at the recantations of the courtiers. The Hundred Days had, perhaps, suggested even more reflections to her than her captivity in the Temple or her early exile. She could not forget how, in 1815, she had been abandoned by officers who, but the day before, had offered her such protestations and such vows. In the midst of present prosperity she had a sort of instinct of future adversity. Something told her that she was not done with sorrow, and that the cup of bitterness was not drained to the dregs. While every one about her contemplated the future with serene confidence, she reflected on the extreme mobility of the French character, and still distrusted inconstant fortune. The morrow of the birth of the Duke of Bordeaux one of her household said to her: —

"Your Highness was very happy yesterday."

"Yes, very happy yesterday," responded the daughter of Louis XVI., "but to-day I am reflecting on the destiny of this child."

To any one inclined to be deceived by the illusions of the prestige surrounding the accession of Charles X., it ought to have sufficed to cast a glance on the austere countenance of the Orphan of the Temple, to be recalled to the tragic reality of things. The King had for his niece and daughter-in-law an affection blended with compassion and respect. The pious and revered Princess gave to the court a character of gravity and sanctity.

VII

MADAME

THE Duchess of Angoulême and the Duchess of Berry lived on the best of terms, showing toward each other a lively sympathy. Yet there was little analogy between their characters, and the two Princesses might even be said to form a complete contrast, one representing the grave side, the other the smiling side of the court.

Born November 7, 1798, and a widow since February 14, 1820, Madame (as the Duchess of Berry was called after the Duchess of Angoulême became Dauphiness) was but twenty-five when her father-in-law, Charles X., ascended the throne. She was certainly not pretty, but there was in her something seductive and captivating. The vivacity of her manner, her spontaneous conversation, her ardor, her animation, her youth, gave her charm. Educated at the court of her grandfather, Ferdinand, King of Naples, who carried *bonhomie* and familiarity to exaggeration, and lived in the company of peasants and lazzaroni, she had a horror of pretension and conceit. Her child-like physiognomy had a certain playful and rebellious expression; slightly indecorous speech did not displease her. This idol of the aristocracy was simple and jovial, mingling in her conversation Gallic salt and Neapolitan gaiety. In contrast with so many princesses who weary their companions and are wearied by them, she amused herself and others. Entering a family celebrated by its legendary catastrophes, she had lost nothing of the playfulness which was the essence of her nature. The Tuileries, the scene of such terrible dramas, did not inspire her as it did the Duchess of Angoulême, with sad reflections. When she heard Mass in the Chapel of the Château, she did not say to herself that here had resounded the furies of the Convention. The grand apartments, the court of the Carrousel, the garden, could not recall to her the terrible scenes of the 20th of June and the 10th of August. When she entered the Pavillon de Flore, she did not reflect that there had sat the Committee of Public Safety. The Tuileries were, to her eyes, only the abode of power and pleasure, an agreeable and beautiful dwelling that had brought her only happiness, since there she had given birth to the Child of Europe, the "Child of Miracle."

The Duchess of Berry thought that a palace should be neither a barracks nor a convent nor a prison, and that even for a princess there is no happiness without liberty. She loved to go out without an escort, to take walks, to visit the shops, to go to the little theatres, to make country parties. She was like a bird in a gilded cage, which often escapes and returns with pleasure only because it has escaped. She was neither worn out nor *blasée;* everything interested her, everything made her gay; she saw only the good side of things. In her all was young — mind, character, imagination, heart. Thus she knew none of those vague disquietudes, that causeless melancholy, that unreasoned sadness, from which suffer so many queens and so many princesses on the steps of a throne.

Gracious and simple in her manners, modest in her bearing, more inclined to laughter and smiles than to sobs and tears, satisfied with her lot despite her widowhood, she felt happy in being a princess, in being a mother, in being in France. Flattered by the homage addressed to her on all sides, but without haughty pride in it, she protected art and letters without pedantry, rejuvenated the court, embellished the city, spread animation wherever she was seen, and appeared to the people like a seductive enchantress. Those who were at her receptions found themselves not in the presence of a coldly and solemnly majestic princess, but of an accomplished mistress of the house bent on making her salon agreeable to her guests. There was in her nothing to abash, and by her gracious aspect, her extreme affability, she knew how to put those with whom she talked at their ease, while wholly preserving her own rank. She was not only polite, she was engaging, always seeking to say something flattering or kindly to those who had the honor to approach her. If she visited a studio, she congratulated the artist; in a shop she made many purchases and talked with the merchants with a grace more charming to them, perhaps, than even her extreme liberality. If she went to a theatre, she enjoyed herself like a child. The select little fêtes given by her always had a character of special originality and gaiety.

The Dauphiness had a higher rank at court than Madame, because she was married to the heir of the throne. But as she took much less interest in social matters, she did not shine with so much *éclat*. The Duchess of Berry was the queen of elegance. In all questions of adornment, toilet, furniture, she set the fashion. A commission as "tradesman of Madame" was the dream of all the merchants. Sometimes, on New Year's Day, her purchases at the chief shops were announced in the *Moniteur*. There were hardly any *chroniques* in the journals under the Restoration. A simple "item" sufficed for an account of the most dazzling fêtes. If the customs of the newspapers had been under the reign of Charles X. what they are now, the Duchess of Berry would have filled all the "society notes," and the objective point of every "reporter," to use an American expression, would have been the Pavillon de Marsan, the "Little Château," as it was then called. There indeed shone in all their splendor the stars of French and foreign nobility, the women who possessed all sorts of aristocracy — of birth, of fortune, of wit, and of beauty. This little circle of luxury and elegance excited less jealousy and less criticism than did the intimate society of Marie Antoinette in the last part of the old régime, because in the Queen's time, to frequent the Petit Trianon was the road to honors, while under Charles X. the intimates of the Pavillon de Marsan did not make their social pleasures the stepping-stone to fortune.

The Duchess of Berry never meddled in politics. Doubtless her sympathies, like those of the Dauphiness, were with the Right, but she exercised no influence on the appointment of ministers and functionaries. Charles X. never consulted her about public affairs; the idea would never have occurred to the old King to ask counsel of so young and inexperienced a woman.

It is but justice to the Princess to say that while wholly inclined toward the Right, she had none of the exaggeration of the extremists in either her ideas or her attitude, and that, repudiating the arrogance and prejudices of the past, she never, in any way, dreamed of the resurrection of the old régime. She was liked by the army, being known as a good rider and a courageous Princess. When she talked with officers she had the habit of saying things that went straight to their hearts. There was no difference in her politeness to the men of the old nobility or to the parvenus of victory. The former servitors of Napoleon were grateful for her friendliness to them, and perhaps they would always have respected the white flag — the flag of Henry IV., had it been borne by the gracious hand of his worthy descendant. To sum up, she was what would be called to-day a very "modern" Princess; her rôle might well have been to share the ideas and aspirations of the new France.

The Duchess of Berry led a very active life. When she came to France she was in the habit of rising late. But her husband, who believed the days to be shorter for princes than for other men, showed that he disliked this, and after that the Princess would not remain in bed after six o'clock, winter or summer. As soon as she was ready she summoned her children, and for half an hour gave them her instructions. On leaving them, she went to hear Mass, and then breakfasted. Next came the walks, almost always with a useful object in view. Sometimes it was a hospital to which Madame carried relief, sometimes an artist's studio, a shop, an industrial establishment that she encouraged by her purchases and her presence. On her return she busied herself with the tenderest and most conscientious care in the education of the two daughters whom her husband had left to her, and who have since become, one the Baroness of Chorette, the other the Princess of Lucinge. Audiences took up the remainder of the morning, sometimes lasting to dinner time. When some one said to her one day that she must be very tired of them, she replied: "During all that time I am told the truth, and I find as much pleasure in hearing it as people of society do in reading romances."

Madame was very charitable. She devoted to the poor an ordinary and an extraordinary budget. The tenth of her revenue was always applied to the relief of the unfortunate, and was deposited by twelfths, each month, with her First Almoner. This tithe was distributed with as much method as sagacity. A valet de chambre, each evening, brought to the Princess the day's petitions for relief. Madame classified them with her own hand in alphabetical order, and registered and numbered them. Whatever the hour, she never adjourned this task to the morrow. The private secretary then went over these petitions and presented an analysis of them to the Princess, who indicated on the margin what she wished to give. This was the ordinary budget of the poor, the tenth of Madame's revenue. But she had, besides, an extraordinary budget of charity for the unfortunate who were the more to be respected because they concealed themselves in obscurity and awaited instead of seeking help. It often happened that the Princess borrowed in order to give more. The total of her revenues amounted to 1,730,000 francs, — 1,500,000 francs from the Treasury, 100,000 francs in Naples funds, coming from her dower, and 130,000 francs from her domain of Rosny. Madame expended all in alms or in purchases intended to encourage the arts and commerce.

The Duchess of Angoulême and the Duchess of Berry each had in the environs of Paris a pleasure house, which was their Petit Trianon, where they could lead a simpler life, less subject to the laws of etiquette than in the royal Châteaux. That of the Dauphiness was Villeneuve-l'Étang; and that of Madame, Rosny. The first had been bought of Marshal Soult by the Duchess of Angoulême in 1821. When she rode from Paris, this was always her destination. When she lived at Saint Cloud, she often set out on foot in the early morning alone, and followed across the park a little path known as the "road of the Dauphiness," to a little gate of the Château of Villeneuve-l'Étang, of which she carried the key.

Rosny is a château situated in the Department of Seine-et-Oise, seven kilometres from Mantes, where Sully, the famous minister of Henry IV., was born, and which had been bought in 1818 by the Duke of Berry. It was the favorite resort of Madame. She went there often and passed a great part of the summer. There she lived the life of a simple private person, receiving herself those who came to offer homage or request aid. The village of Rosny profited by the liberality of the Château. *La Quotidienne* said in an article reproduced by the *Moniteur:* —

"Since Her Royal Highness the Duchess of Berry has owned the estate of Rosny, her sole occupation has been to secure the happiness of this country. Every journey she makes is marked by some act of goodness. Besides the Hospital of Saint-Charles, a monument of her beneficence and piety, which is open to all the sick of the country, she sends out relief to the homes of the needy every day. The houses that rise in the village replace wretched huts, and give a more agreeable and cheerful aspect to the place. The children of either sex, the object of her most tender solicitude, are taught at her expense. At every journey Madame honors them with a visit and encourages them with prizes which she condescends to distribute herself."

In his *Souvenirs Intimes* the Count de Mesnard, First Equerry of the Duchess of Berry, writes:—

"The King, Charles X., did not recognize in his daughter-in-law nearly the solidity that she had. He believed her to be light-minded, and only looked upon her as a great child, though he loved her much and her gaiety pleased him beyond measure, being himself of a gay nature. You may have heard that one day Madame rode in an omnibus. That is not correct. But it is true that one day Her Royal Highness said to the King:—

"'Father, if you will wager ten thousand francs, I will ride in an omnibus to-morrow.'

"'It's the last thing I should do, my dear,' replied His Majesty. 'You are quite crazy enough to do it.'"

M. de Mesnard adds this reflection: "What the King regarded as folly was only the appearance of it. There was in Madame a rich fund of reason, justice, and humanity. Independently of all the acts of beneficence daily done here, Madame employs still more considerable sums in the support of young girls in the convents of Luçon and Mantes, and in several other establishments. There are in the colleges a large number of young people of families of modest fortune, whose expenses she pays. The Hospital of Rosny alone costs Madame from twenty thousand to twenty-five thousand francs a year. The exhaustless bounty of this august Princess extends to all. There is no sort of aid that Her Royal Highness does not take pleasure in according: subscriptions without interest for her, for concerts that she will not hear, for benefit performances that she will not see, everything gets a subscription from her, and it all costs more than is convenient with the Princess's revenue. Sometimes it happens that her funds are exhausted, and as her benevolence never is, embarrassment follows."

Apropos of this the Count de Mesnard relates a touching anecdote. One winter exceedingly cold, the Duchess of Berry was about to give a fête in the Pavillon de Marsan. During the day she had supervised the preparations. Things were arranged perfectly, when all at once her face saddened. She was asked respectfully what had displeased her. "What icy weather!" she cried. "Poor people may be dying of cold and hunger to-night while we are taking our delights. That spoils my pleasure." Then she added emphatically: "Go call the Marquis de Sassenay" (her Treasurer).

The Marquis came promptly.

"Monsieur," said the good Princess, "you must write instantly to the twelve mayors of Paris, and in each letter put one thousand francs to be expended in wood, and distributed this very night to the poor families of each arrondissement. It is very little, but it may save some unfortunates."

The Treasurer responded: "Madame, I should be eager to obey the orders of Her Royal Highness, but she has nothing, or almost nothing, in her treasury."

A feeling of discontent was strongly depicted on the face of Madame, who was about to give expression to it, when M. de Mesnard hastened to say that the funds of the First Equerry were in better state than those of the Treasurer, and remitted to the latter the twelve thousand francs, which were distributed to the poor that evening according to the Princess's wishes.

The Duchess of Berry had the double gift of pleasing and making herself loved. All the persons of her household, all her servitors, from the great nobles and great ladies to the domestics and the chambermaids, were deeply devoted to her. Poor or rich, she had attentions for all. Listen to the Count de Mesnard: —

"Madame is incessantly making presents to all who approach her. At New Year's her apartments are a veritable bazaar furnished from all the shops of Paris; her provision, made from every quarter, is universal, from bon-bons to the most precious articles — everything is there. Madame has thought of each specially; the people of her own service are not forgotten any more than the ladies and officers of her household; father, mother, children, every one, is included in the distribution. The royal family naturally comes first; next, the numerous relatives of the Palais Royal, of whom she is very fond; then her family at Naples, which is also numerous; and finally all of us, masters and servants, we all have our turn."

No one, we think, has made a more exact portrait of the Duchess of Berry than the Count Armand de Pontmartin, who is so familiar with the Restoration. In his truthful and lively *Souvenirs d'un vieux critique*, how well he presents "this flower of Ischia or of Castellamare, transplanted to the banks of the Seine, under the gray sky of Paris, to this Château des Tuileries, which the revolutions peopled with phantoms before making it a spectre."

How really she was "this good Duchess, so French and so Neapolitan at once, half Vesuvius, half school-girl, whom nothing must prevent us from honoring and loving." The chivalric and sentimental rhetoric of the time, the elegies of the poets, the noble prose of Chateaubriand, the tearful articles of the royalist journals, have condemned her to appear forever solemn and sublime. It was sought to confine her youth between a tomb and a cradle. But as M. de Pontmartin so finely remarks: "At the end of two or three years her true nature appears beneath this artificial drapery. Amusements recommence, distractions abound. The Princess is no longer a heroine; she is a sprite. The beach of Dieppe sings her praises better, a thousand times better, than the chorus of courtiers. She loves pleasure, but she wishes every pleasure to be a grace or a benefit. She creates a mine of gold under the sand of the Norman coast; she pacifies political rancor and soothes the wounds of the grumblers of the Grand Army. She makes popular the name of Bourbon, which had suffered from so much ingratitude. The Petit-Château, as her delightful household was called, renews the elegant manners, the exquisite gallantries of the court of Anne of Austria, and offers to the romancers the models of which Balzac, later, made so much too free use. There I see our amiable Duchess in her true element, not on the kind of Sinai on which the writers of the white flag have perched her, prodigal in their imitations of Bossuet, — between Jeanne d'Arc and Jeanne Hachette, between Valentine de Milan and the Widow of Malabar."

To sum up, the Duchess of Berry was to the court of Charles X. what the Duchess of Burgundy was to that of Louis XIV. Her lovely youth brightened everything. Let us do her this justice: despite a character in appearance frivolous, she carried to a kind of fanaticism the love of France and passion for French glory. There was one thing that the gracious widow took very seriously, — the rights of her son. She would have risked a thousand deaths to defend that child, who represented in her heart the cause of the fatherland. Where he was concerned there was in the attitude of this frail young woman something firm and decided. To a sagacious observer, the amazon was already manifest under the lady of society. She was like those officers who shine equally at the ball and on the field of battle. Recognizing in her more than one imperfection, she cannot be denied either courage, or intelligence, or heart. By her qualities as by her defects she was of the race of Henry IV. But she was more frank and more grateful than the Béarnais. Doubtless she did not have the genius, the prodigious ability, the fine and profound political sense, of that great man; but her nature was better, her generosity greater, her character more sympathetic.

VIII

THE ORLEANS FAMILY

AT the accession of Charles X., Louis Philippe, Duke of Orleans, chief of the younger branch of the Bourbons, born at Paris, October 6th, 1773, was not yet fifty-seven years old. He married November 25th, 1809, Marie-Amélie, Princess of the Two Sicilies, whose father, Ferdinand I., reigned at Naples, and whose mother, the Queen Marie-Caroline, sister of Marie Antoinette, died at Venice, September 7th, 1814. Marie-Amélie, born April 26th, 1782, was forty-two years old when Charles X. ascended the throne. Of her marriage with the Duke of Orleans there were born five sons and four daughters:—

1. Ferdinand-Philippe-Louis-Charles-Henri-Roulin, Duke of Chartres, born at Palermo, September 3d, 1810. (When his father became King, he took the title of Duke of Orleans, and died from a fall from his carriage going from the Tuileries to Neuilly on the Chemin de la Révolte, July 13th, 1842.)

2. Louise-Marie-Thérèse-Caroline-Elisabeth, Mademoiselle d'Orléans, born at Palermo the 3d of April, 1812. (She married the King of the Bel-

gians, Leopold I., August 9th, 1832, and died October 11th, 1850.)

3. Marie-Christine-Caroline-Adélaïde-Françoise-Léopoldine, Mademoiselle de Valois, born at Palermo, April 12th, 1813. (She was designated by the name of the Princess Marie, distinguished herself in the arts, made the famous statue of Jeanne d'Arc, married October 17th, 1837, the Duke Frederic William of Würtemberg, and died January 2d, 1839.)

4. Louis-Charles-Philippe-Raphaël, Duke of Nemours, born at Paris, October 25th, 1814.

5. Marie-Clémentine-Caroline-Léopoldine, Mademoiselle de Beaujolais, born at Neuilly June 3d, 1817. (She was designated by the name of the Princess Clémentine, and married, April 20th, 1843, the Prince August, of Saxe-Coburg-Gotha.)

6. François-Ferdinand-Philippe-Louis-Marie, Prince de Joinville, born at Neuilly, August 14th, 1818.

7. Charles-Ferdinand-Louis-Philippe-Emmanuel, Duke of Penthièvre, born at Paris, January 1st, 1820. (He died July 25th, 1828.)

8. Henri-Eugène-Philippe-Louis, Duke d'Aumale, born at Paris, January 16th, 1822.

9. Antoine-Marie-Philippe-Louis, Duke of Montpensier, born at Neuilly, July 5th, 1824.

The Duke of Orleans had a sister who lived with him at the Palais Royal, and was reputed to be his Egeria. She was Louise-Marie-Adélaïde-Eugénie, Mademoiselle d'Orléans, as she was called under the

Restoration. Born August 23d, 1777, she had been educated by Madame de Genlis, with her brother, and was said to be attached to the ideas of the Liberal party. (It was she who in 1830 decided Louis-Philippe to accept the crown, took the name of Madame Adélaïde, and died, unmarried, some days before the revolution of the 24th of February, 1848.)

Marie-Amélie, Duchess of Orleans, was the sister of the Prince Royal of the Two Sicilies, Ferdinand, father of the Duchess of Berry, and the niece was very fond of her aunt. The two Princesses were united by other bonds than those of blood. During all her infancy the Duchess of Berry had lived with her aunt at Palermo and Naples. Both were descended in direct line from the great Empress, Maria Theresa. Both had greatly loved the Queen Marie-Caroline, of whom one was the granddaughter, the other the daughter. Both professed great admiration for the Martyr-Queen, Marie Antoinette, of whom one was the grand-niece, the other the niece. The devotion and family feeling of the Duchess of Orleans won every one's sympathy for her, and the Duchess of Berry had a respectful attachment for her. Their relations were as constant as they were friendly. There existed between the Palais Royal and the Pavillon de Marsan, dwellings so near each other, a friendship and neighborliness that left nothing to be desired.

The Duke of Bordeaux and his sister, Mademoiselle, were very fond of their little Orleans cousins.

There was a certain pleasure in thinking that the Duke of Chartres might one day become the husband of Mademoiselle. This young Prince, already very amiable and sympathetic, was the favorite of the Duchess of Berry. She said to herself that he would be the son-in-law of her dreams. Every time that she went to the Palais Royal, where her visits were incessant, she was received with transports of affection. Nowhere did she enjoy herself more. Louis-Philippe treated her with deference and courtesy. She believed sincerely in his friendship, and any one who had shown in her presence the least doubt of the loyalty of her aunt's husband would not have ventured to complete the phrase expressing it. The Duchess of Berry was to preserve this confidence until the Revolution of 1830.

Charles X. had a kindly feeling, founded on very real sympathy, for the Duke of Orleans and all his family. During the Emigration, as under the reign of Louis XVIII., he had always maintained very cordial relations with the Duke, and had tried to efface the bad memories of Philippe Égalité. Charles X. was as confiding as Louis XVIII. was distrustful. Optimist, like all good natures, the new King would not believe evil. He attributed to others his own good qualities. Louis XVIII. always had suspicions as to the Duke of Orleans. "Since his return," he said, in 1821, "the Duke of Orleans is the chief of a party without seeming to be. His name is a threatening flag, his palace a rallying-place. He makes no stir, but I can see that he makes progress. This activity without movement is disquieting. How can you undertake to check the march of a man who makes no step?" Every time the Duke attempted to bring up the question of exchanging his title of Most Serene Highness for that of Royal Highness, the King stubbornly resisted. "The Duke of Orleans is quite near enough to the throne already," he replied to all solicitations. "I shall be careful to bring him no nearer."

This refusal was very depressing to the Duke. One circumstance rendered it still more annoying. As a king's daughter, his wife was a Royal Highness. By this title she enjoyed honors denied to her husband. When she was present at court with him she was first announced, both doors of the salon being opened: "Her Royal Highness, Madame the Duchess of Orleans." Then one door having been closed, the usher announced: "His Most Serene Highness, Monseigneur the Duke of Orleans." This distinction was very disagreeable to the Duke. Charles X. hastened to abolish it. September 21st, 1824, he accorded the title of Royal Highness to the Duke of Orleans, and three days later he conferred this title, so much desired, on the children of the sister of the Duke. The latter showed his great pleasure. Though he might favor liberalism and give pledges to democracy, he remained a Prince to the marrow of his bones. He loved not only money, but honors, and attached extreme importance to questions of etiquette. The memories of his childhood and his early youth bound him to the old régime and despite appearances to the contrary, this Prince, so dear to the *bourgeois* and to the National Guard, was always by his tastes and aspirations a man of Versailles.

Charles X. would gladly have said to the Duke of Orleans, as Augustus to Cinna, speaking of his benefits: —

"Je t'en avais comblé, je t'en veux accabler."

He was not content with according him a title of honor; he gave him something much more solid, by causing to be returned to him, with the consent of the Chambers, the former domain and privileges of the House of Orleans. This was not easy. It required not only the good-will of the Château, but the vote of the Chambers, and the majority was hardly favorable to the Duke of Orleans, of whom it cherished the same suspicions as Louis XVIII. The Duchess of Berry pleaded warmly the cause of her aunt's husband, and conspired with Charles X. against the Right, the members of which in this case believed it a service to royalty to disobey the King. The opposition to the project seemed likely to be so strong, that the government was obliged to commit a sort of moral violence upon the Chamber of Deputies. The King directed his ministers to join in some way the question of the apanages of the House of Orleans with the disposition of his own civil list. The King thought that the sentiments of the Chamber for himself and his family would make them adopt the whole *en bloc*. It was a device of his kindliness, a sort of smuggling in the King's coach, as was said by M. de Labourdonnaye. A large number of deputies demanded a division of the question. The ministers had to make great efforts and mount the tribune many times to defend the measure, which passed only by a very feeble majority. The Duke of Orleans, now at the very height of his desires, thanked Charles X. with effusion.

Nor was this all; from the millions of indemnity to the *émigrés*, the Duke of Orleans drew 14,000,000 francs. The opposition chiefs of the Left imitated the Prince and profited largely by the law that they had opposed and condemned. The Duke of Choiseul obtained 1,100,000 francs, the Duke of La Rochefoucauld-Liancourt 1,400,000 francs, M. Gaétan de La Rochefoucauld 1,429,000 francs, General Lafayette himself 1,450,000 francs.

The Orleanist party was already beginning to take form, perhaps without the knowledge of its chief. In his pamphlets of 1824, Paul-Louis Courier devoted himself to separating the older from the younger branch of the House, declaring that he should like to be a resident of a commune of Paris if the Duke of Orleans were its mayor, for from a Prince the Duke had become a man during the Emigration, and had never begged bread of a foreign hand. Louis-Philippe continued prudently the rôle he had played at the end of the first Restoration and during the Hundred Days. While professing an obsequious and enthusiastic respect for Charles X., he secretly flattered the Bonapartists and the Liberals. He sent his eldest son to the public school, as if to insinuate that he remained faithful to the ideas of equality from which his father had gained his surname. He made very welcome the coryphées of the Opposition, such as General Foy and M. Laffitte, to the Palais Royal, and received them in halls where the brush of Horace Vernet had represented the great battles of the tricolor flag. When General Foy died, in November, 1825, the Duke of Orleans put his name for ten thousand francs to the subscription opened to provide a fund for the children of the General. Some friendly representations were made from the Château to the Palais Royal on this matter. It was answered that the Duke of Orleans had subscribed not as Prince, but as a friend, and in private called attention to the modesty of the gift compared with others, with that of M. Casimir Périer, for example, which amounted to fifty thousand francs. This excuse was satisfactory at the Tuileries.

Is this saying that Louis-Philippe was already at this time thinking of dethroning his benefactor, his relative, and his King? We think not. He profited by the errors of Charles X.; but if Charles X. had not committed them, the idea of usurpation would not have occurred to the mind of the chief of the younger branch. Men are not so profoundly good or so profoundly wicked. They let themselves be carried further than they wish, and if the acts they are to commit some day were foretold them, the prophecies would most often seem to them as impossible as insulting.

Madame de Gontaut, Governess of the Children of France, recounts an incident that took place at the Louvre, December 22d, 1824, at the opening of the session of the Chambers: "The crowd was prodigious. The Dauphiness and the Duchess of Berry and Mademoiselle d'Orléans were present in one of the bays. The Children of France were there. The Duchess of Berry took the Duke of Bordeaux by her side. The Duchess of Orleans called Mademoiselle, whom she loved tenderly, to her. The canon announced the approach of the King. At the moment of his appearance the hall resounded with acclamations. The platform for the royal family was the one prepared for the late King; there had been left a slight elevation in it, that the King did not see, and he stumbled on it. With the movement his hat, held on his arm, fell; the Duke of Orleans caught it. The Duchess of Orleans said to me:—

"'The King was about to fall; my husband sustained him.'

"I answered: 'No, Madame; Monseigneur has caught His Majesty's hat.'

"The Dauphiness turned and looked at me. We did not speak of it until six months after. Neither of us had forgotten it."

A few years more and Charles X. was to drop, not his hat, but his crown.

IX

THE PRINCE OF CONDÉ

AT the time of the accession of Charles X., the family of Condé was represented only by an old man of sixty-eight, Louis-Henri-Joseph de Bourbon-Condé, born April 13th, 1756. At the death of his father in 1818, he had taken the title of Prince of Condé, while retaining that of Duke of Bourbon, by which he had previously been designated. On the 10th of January, 1822, he lost his wife, Princess Louise-Marie-Thérèse-Bathilde, sister of the Duke of Orleans, mother of the unfortunate Duke d'Enghien, and he lost, on March 10th, 1824, his sister, Mademoiselle de Condé, the nun whose convent of the Perpetual Adoration was situated in the Temple near the site of the former tower where Louis XVI. and his family had been confined.

The Duke of Bourbon, in his youth, had had a famous duel with the Count of Artois, the future Charles X. No resentment subsisted between the two princes, who afterwards maintained the most cordial relations. During the Emigration, the Duke of Bourbon served with valor in the army of his father, the Prince of Condé. While the white flag floated at the head of a regiment he was found fighting for the royal cause; then, the struggle ended, he retired to England, where he had lived near Louis XVIII., and always at his disposition. Returning to France at the Restoration, he had since resided almost always at Chantilly or at Saint-Leu, without his wife, from whom he had long been separated. He was ranked as a reactionary, but busied himself little with politics, and exerted no influence.

The Count of Puymaigre, who, in his office as Prefect of the Oise, at the commencement of the reign of Charles X., often went to Chantilly, speaks of him in his *Souvenirs:*—

"The name of my father, much beloved by the late Prince of Condé, more than my title of Prefect, caused me to be received with welcome, and I took advantage of it the more gladly, because I have never seen a house where one was more at one's ease, and where there was more of that comfortable life known before the Revolution as the château life. There was little of the prince in him; he was more like an elderly bachelor who liked to have about him joy, movement, pleasure, a wholly Epicurean life. The society of Chantilly ordinarily consisted of the household of the Prince; that is to say, old servitors of his father, some ladies whose husbands held at this little court the places of equerries or gentlemen of the chamber, some persons who were invited, or like myself, had the right to come when they wished, and among this number I frequently saw the Prince of

Rohan, relative of the Duke of Bourbon, disappointed since of the portion of the inheritance he hoped for; finally, some Englishmen and their wives. The tone was quite free, since the Prince set the example. And I recall that one day he recommended me to be gallant with one of the English ladies, who, he said, would like nothing better than to receive such attentions. That seemed very likely to me, but she was not young enough to tempt me to carry the adventure very far."

The real châtelaine of this little court of Chantilly was a beautiful Englishwoman, Sophie Dawes, married to a French officer, the Baron of Feuchères. Born about 1795, in the Isle of Wight, Sophie Dawes was the daughter of a fisherman. It is said that she was brought up by charity, and played for some time at Covent Garden Theatre, London. But her early life is unknown, and what is told of it is not trustworthy. In 1817, she was taken into the intimacy of the Duke of Bourbon, and afterwards acquired an irresistible ascendancy over him. When she became his inseparable companion, she explained her presence with him by the story that she was his natural daughter, and the Duke avoided confirming or denying this assertion. In 1818, he arranged a marriage between his favorite and a very honorable officer, the Baron of Feuchères, who believed, in good faith, that Sophie Dawes was really the daughter of the Duke of Bourbon, and not his mistress. The marriage was celebrated in England, but the pair returned to Chantilly. The Baron of Feuchères figures in the royal Almanacs of 1821, 1822, 1823, as lieutenant-colonel, gentleman in ordinary to the Duke of Bourbon, Prince of Condé, but not in the Almanac of 1824.

In a very interesting work, the *Vie de Charles X.* by the Abbé de Védrenne, the reader will find: —

"By the marriage of Sophie Dawes, did the Duke of Bourbon wish to break away from a guilty bond? It is generally believed. As to M. de Feuchères, convinced that his wife was the daughter of the Prince, he had no suspicion. It was Sophie Dawes herself who enlightened him, to drive him away. The effect of the revelation was terrible. M. de Feuchères, indignant, quitted his wife. There no longer remained about the Prince any but the creatures of Madame de Feuchères. Every one did her bidding at Chantilly, and the Prince most of all."

The favorite sought to palliate her false situation in the eyes of society by doing good with the Prince's money. The Count of Puymaigre relates that she many times took him to the Hospital of Chantilly, endowed by the munificence of the great Condé, the revenues of which she wished to increase. He adds: "I urged her to this good work as much as I could; for good, by whatever hand done, endures."

One day the Duchess of Angoulême asked him if he went often to Chantilly.

"I go there," replied the Prefect, "to pay my court to the Duke of Bourbon, whom I have the honor of having in my department."

"That is very well," responded the Dauphiness, "but I hope that Madame de Puymaigre does not go."

The grand passion of the Duke of Bourbon was hunting. The Prefect of the Oise says:—

"It was particularly during the hunts of Saint-Hubert that Chantilly was a charming abode. The start was made at seven o'clock in the morning, and usually I was in the carriage of the Prince with the everlasting Madame de Feuchères. The hunting-lodge was delightful and in a most picturesque situation. There twenty or thirty persons met to the sound of horns, in the midst of dogs, horses, and huntsmen. The coursing train of the Prince was finer and more complete than that of the King. A splendid breakfast was served at the place of rendezvous, built and furnished in the Gothic style of the thirteenth century, and there the chase began. Although I told the Prince that I was no hunter, he often made me mount my horse and accompany him; but often having enjoyed the really attractive spectacle of the stag, driven by a crowd of dogs, which launched themselves after him across the waters of a little lake, I hastened back to the Gothic pavilion where the ladies and a few men remained."

The Prince said one day to the Prefect:—

"Decidedly, you do not love hunting."

"But I might love it, my lord, if I had such an outfit."

"That's because you don't know anything about

it, my dear Puymaigre; when I was in England, hunting all alone in the marshes with my dog Belle, I enjoyed it much more than here."

The Prefect thus concludes his description of life at Chantilly: —

"Dinner was at six o'clock in the magnificent gallery where the souvenirs of the great Condé were displayed in all their pomp, and the eyes fell on fine pictures of the battles of Rocroy, Senef, Fribourg, and Nordlingen, inspiring some regret for the life led by the heir of so much glory. After dinner society comedy was played on a very pretty stage, where the luxury of costumes was very great and the *mise-en-scène* carefully attended to; and this did not make the actors any better, although the little plays were tolerable. But Madame de Feuchères wishing to play **Alzire** and to take the principal part, which she doled out with sad monotony, without change of intonation from the first line to the last, and with a strongly pronounced English accent, it was utterly ridiculous, and Voltaire would have flown into a fine passion had he seen one of his *chefs-d'œuvres* mangled in that way. Who could have told that this poor Prince, who, if he had neither the virtues nor the dignity proper to his rank, was nevertheless a very good fellow, would perish in 1830, in such a tragic manner?"

Charles X. had a long standing affection for the Duke of Bourbon. On September 21st, 1824, he conferred on him at the same time as on the Duke of Orleans, the title of Royal Highness. The last of the Condés was, besides, Grand Master of France. This court function was honorary rather than real, and the Prince appeared at the Tuileries only on rare occasions. Charles X. loved him as a friend of his childhood, a companion of youth and exile, but he had a lively regret to see him entangled in such relations with the Baroness of Feuchères. The advice he gave him many times to induce him to break this liaison was without result. Finally the King said: "Let us leave him alone; we only give him pain." He never went to Chantilly, in order not to sanction by his royal presence the kind of existence led there by his old relation; and the Prince knowing the sentiments of his sovereign, gave him but few invitations, which were always evaded under one pretext or another.

People wondered at the time who would be the heirs of the immense fortune of the Condés, whose race was on the point of extinction. The Prince's mother was Charlotte-Élisabeth de Rohan-Soubise, and the Rohans thought themselves the natural heirs. But such a combination would not have met the views of Madame de Feuchères, who, not content with having got from the Prince very considerable donations, counted on figuring largely in his will.

Nevertheless she was not without lively anxiety in that regard. The Rohans had refused all compromise with her. If they were disinherited, what would they say? Would they not attack the will on the ground of undue influence? Such was the eventuality against which the prudent Baroness intended to guard herself. In consequence she conceived the bold project of sheltering her own wealth under the patronage of some member of the royal family, in having him receive the fortune of the old Prince under a will which at the same time should consecrate the part to be received by her, and put it beyond all contest. She would have wished the old Prince to choose his heir in the elder branch of the House of Bourbon. But the Duchess of Berry, who was disinterestedness itself, declined any arrangement of that nature. To the insinuations made to her in favor of her son, she responded: —

"Henri will be King. The King of France needs nothing."

She did more. It is said that to the persons who bore these advances to her, she suggested the idea of having the heritage of the Condés pass to the family of the Duke of Orleans. But the thing was not easy. It is true that the children of the Duke were, by their mother, Bathilde d'Orléans, nephews of the wife of the Duke of Bourbon. But this Prince had led a bad life with his wife, from whom he had separated immediately after the birth of the Duke d'Enghien, and the souvenirs of the Revolution separated him widely from a family whose political ideas were not his. Yet the Duke and Duchess of Orleans were not discouraged. They entered on negotiations a long time in advance with the Baroness of Feuchères, who was in reality the arbiter of the situation. M.

Nettement relates that the first time that Marie-Amélie pronounced the name of the Baroness in the presence of the Duchess of Angoulême, the daughter of Louis XVI. said to her: "What! you have seen that woman!" The Duchess of Orleans responded: "What would you have? I am a mother. I have a numerous family; I must think before all of the interests of my children."

What is certain is that the Prince was induced to be the godfather of the Duke d'Aumale, born the 6th of January, 1822, and that was a sort of prelude to the will of 1830.

X

THE COURT

NOW let us throw a general glance over the court of the King, Charles X., in 1825, the year of the consecration.

The civil household of the King comprised six distinct services: those of Grand Almoner of France, of the Grand Master of France, of the Grand Chamberlain of France, of the Grand Equerry of France, of the Grand Huntsman of France, and of the Grand Master of Ceremonies of France.

The Grand Almoner was the Cardinal, Prince of Croy, Archbishop of Rowen; the First Almoner, Mgr. Frayssinous, Bishop of Hermopolis; the confessor of the King, the Abbé Jocard. Charles X., this monarch, surrounded by great lords, knelt before a plebeian priest and demanded absolution for his sins. There were, besides, in the service of the Grand Almoner of France, eight almoners, eight chaplains, and eight pupils of the chapel, serving in turns of four.

The function of the Grand Master of France had as titulary the Duke of Bourbon, Prince of Condé. But this Prince performed his duties only in very rare and solemn circumstances. In fact, the service of the Grand Master of France was directed by the First Steward, the Count of Cossé-Brissac. There were besides four chamberlains of the House, the Count de Rothe, the Marquis of Mondragon, the Count Mesnard de Chousy, the Viscount Hocquart, and several stewards.

The Grand Chamberlain of France was the Prince de Talleyrand. He discharged his functions only on solemn occasions, such as the funeral of Louis XVIII. and the consecration of Charles X. and the arrival of the Duchess of Berry. In fact, the service of the Grand Chamberlain of France was directed by one of the first gentlemen of the chamber. They were four in number, — the Duke d'Aumont, the Duke of Duras, the Duke of Blacas, the Duke Charles de Damas, — and performed their functions in turn a year each. Every four years the King designated those who were to serve during each of the following four years. Thus, the Royal Almanac of 1825 has this notice: —

First gentlemen of the chamber: 1825, the Duke d'Aumont; 1826, the Duke of Duras; 1827, the Duke of Blacas; 1828, Count de Damas (afterwards Duke).

The first chamberlains, masters of the wardrobe, were five in number: the Marquis de Boisgelin, the Count de Pradel, the Count Curial, the Marquis d'Avaray, the Duke d'Avaray. There were besides thirty-two gentlemen of the chamber, without counting those that were honorary. To this same service belonged the readers, the first valets-de-chambre, the ushers of the chamber, the musicians of the chamber, those of the chapel and the service of the faculty. The *entrées*, a matter so important in the ceremonies of courts, were also attached to this service.

By virtue of royal regulations of November 1st, December 31st, 1820, and January 23d, 1821, the *entrées* at the Château of the Tuileries were established as follows: They were divided in six classes: the grand *entrées*, the first *entrées* of the Cabinet, the *entrées* of the Cabinet, those of the Hall of the Throne, those of the first salon preceding the Hall of the Throne, and last, those of the second salon.

The grand *entrées* gave the privilege of entering at any time the sleeping-room of the King. They belonged to the Grand Chamberlain, to the first chamberlains — masters of the wardrobe. Next came the first *entrées* of the Cabinet (this was the name of the hall which, during the reign of Napoleon III., was designated as the Salon de Louis XIV., because it contained a Gobelins tapestry representing the Ambassadors of Spain received by the King). Persons who have the first *entrées* of the Cabinet have the right to enter there at any time in order to have themselves announced to the King, and there to await permission to enter the main apartment. These first *entrées* of the Cabinet belong to those who have to take the orders of the sovereign — to the grand officers of his civil and military households, or, in their absence, to the first officer of each service, to the major-general of the royal guard on service, to the Grand Chancellor, to the minister-secretaries of State, to the Grand Chancellor of the Legion of Honor, to the captains of the King's bodyguard, to the Grand Quartermaster.

Next come the *entrées* of the Cabinet (which must not be confused with the first *entrées* of the Cabinet). These give to persons enjoying them the right to enter that room usually a little before the hour fixed by the King to hear Mass, and to remain there at will during the day, up to the hour of the evening when the sovereign gives out the watchword. They belong to the grand officers and to the first officers of the civil and military households of the King, to the major-generals of the royal guard and the lieutenant-general in service, to the cardinals, to the Chancellor of France, to the minister-secretaries of State, to the Grand Chancellor of the Legion of Honor, to the marshals of France, to the Grand Referendary of the Chamber of Peers, to the President of the Chamber of Deputies, and to all the officers of the King's household on service.

The persons and functionaries civil or military with a lower rank in the hierarchy of the court have their *entrées*, some to the Hall of the Throne, others to the first salon preceding the Hall of the Throne (the Salon d'Apollon under Napoleon III.), and still others to the second salon (communicating with the

Hall of the Marshals, and called, under Napoleon III., the Salon of the First Consul).

The collective audience given to all having their *entrées* was called the public audience of the King. It took place when the King went to hear Mass in his chapel, only on his return to re-enter his inner apartment. Followed by all his grand officers and his first officers in service, Charles X. passed to and paused in each of the rooms in his outer apartment, in order to allow those having the right to be there to pay their court to him. When he attended Mass in his inner apartment, he gave a public audience only after that ceremony. He paused in his Grand Cabinet, then in the Hall of the Throne, and successively in the other rooms.

When the King was ready to receive, the First Gentleman of the Chamber gave notice to the grand officers and the first officers that they might present themselves. Moreover, he placed before the King the list of persons having *entrées* to his apartments or to whom he had accorded them. On this list Charles X. indicated those he wished invited.

There was no titular Grand Equerry of France. The First Equerry, charged with the saddle-horses of the King, was the Duke of Polignac, major-general. The two equerries-commandant were the Marquis of Vernon and Count O'Hégerthy, major-general. There were, besides, four equerries, masters of the horse, three each quarter, namely: for the January quarter the Chevalier de Rivière, major-general; the Count Defrance, lieutenant-general; the Baron Dujon, major-general;—for the April quarter, the Colonel Viscount de Bongars; the Baron Vincent, major-general; the Viscount Domon, lieutenant-general;—for the July quarter, the Colonel Marquis de Martel, the Viscount Vansay, the Count Frederic de Bongars;—for the October quarter, the Count de Fezensac, major-general; the Colonel Marquis Oudinot, the Colonel Marquis de Chabannes. The chief Equerries of the stable were the Viscount d'Abzac and the Chevalier d'Abzac, both colonels. There were, besides, the equerries in ordinary and the pupil-equerries. The pages belonged to the service of the Grand Equerry of France.

The Grand Huntsman was the Marshal Marquis of Lauriston, and the First Huntsman, the Lieutenant-General Count de Girardin. There were also huntsmen for the hunting-courses and huntsmen for the gunning-hunts of the King.

The Grand Master of Ceremonies was the Marquis of Dreux-Brézé, and the Master of Ceremonies the Marquis of Rochemore, major-general. There were, besides, the aides, a king-at-arms and heralds-at-arms.

All the civil household of the King worked with the greatest regularity. Etiquette, carefully observed, though stripped of the ancient minutiæ, recalled the old usages of the French monarchy. All that had been suppressed was what was puerile and weariness for the courtiers and for the King himself.

The military household of the King was a group of chosen troops. The horse body-guards comprised five companies, each bearing the name of its chief. The Duke d'Havré et de Croy, the Duke of Gramont, the Prince of Poix, Duke de Mouchy, the Duke of Luxembourg, the Marquis de Rivière. The chiefs of these companies, all five lieutenants-general, were entitled captains of the guard. There was, besides, a company of foot-guards in ordinary to the King, whose chief, the Duke of Mortemart, major-general, had the title of captain-colonel, and whose officers were some French, some Swiss. There was a Chief Quartermaster, the Lieutenant-General Marquis de La Suze.

The royal guard, composed of two divisions of infantry, two divisions of cavalry, and a regiment of artillery, was under the command of four marshals of France, Victor, Duke de Bellune; Macdonald, Duke de Tarente; Oudinot, Duke de Reggio; Marmont, Duke de Raguse, all four of whom had the title of major-general.

The body-guards, the Swiss, the royal guard, were the admiration of all connoisseurs. The Emperor Napoleon never had had troops better disciplined, of better bearing, clad in finer uniforms, animated by a better spirit.

To the household of the King must be added those of the Dauphin, the Dauphiness, and the Duchess of Berry. The Dauphin had as first gentlemen, the Duke of Damas and the Duke of Guiche, both lieutenants-general; for gentlemen, the Count d'Escars and the Baron of Damas, lieutenants-general; the Count Melchior de Polignac, major-general; the Viscount de Saint Priest, and the Count de Bordesoulle, lieutenants-general; the Count d'Osmond, lieutenant-colonel. For aides-de-camp, the Baron de Beurnonville and the Count de Laroche-Fontenille, major-generals; the Viscount of Champagny, the Count of Montcalm, and the Baron Lecouteulx de Canteleu, colonels; the Viscount de Lahitte, and the Duke de Ventadour, lieutenant-colonels; the Count de La Rochefoucauld, chief of battalion.

The household of the Dauphiness was composed as follows: a First Almoner, the Cardinal de La Fare, Archbishop of Sens, with two almoners serving semiannually, and a chaplain; a lady-of-honor, the Duchess of Damas-Cruz; a lady of the bed chamber, the Viscountess d'Agoult; seven lady companions, the Countess of Béarn, the Marchioness of Biron, the Marchioness of Sainte-Maure, the Viscountess of Vaudreuil, the Countess of Goyon, the Marchioness de Rougé, the Countess of Villefranche; two gentlemen-in-waiting, the Marquis of Vibraye and the Duke Mathieu de Montmorency, major-general; a First Equerry, the Viscount d'Agoult, lieutenant-general, and two equerries, the Chevalier de Beaune and M. O'Hégerthy.

We shall devote a special chapter to the household of the Duchess of Berry.

The Count Alexandre de Puymaigre has left in

his *Souvenirs* an account of the manner in which the court employed the two weeks passed at Compiègne in the month of October of each year. At 8 A.M., the King heard Mass, where attendance was very exact except when the King omitted to come, when no one came. At nine o'clock they set out for the hunt, almost always with guns. One hundred to one hundred and fifty hussars or chasseurs of the guard in garrison at Compiègne beat the field, marching in line of battle, with the King in the middle: he had at his right the Dauphin, at his left a captain of the guards, or such person of the court as he was pleased to designate. These were the three who alone had the right to fire.

Behind the sovereign, apart from some persons connected with the service of the hunt, came a master of the horse, the first huntsman, and some persons admitted to the hunt. The King, who used a flint-lock gun, was a very good marksman. About five or six in the evening he returned to the Château. The people of the court were gathered on the steps, awaiting him. He usually addressed some affable words to them, and then went to dress in order to be in the salon at seven o'clock.

The captain of the guards, the first gentleman, the first huntsman, the ladies and gentlemen in waiting of the princesses, the masters of the horse, the colonel of the guard, dined with the King. The dinner was choice, without being too sumptuous, but the wines were not of the first order. The company remained at the table an hour, and each talked freely with his or her neighbor, except those by the side of the Dauphin or a Princess. There was music during the repast, and the public was admitted to circulate about the table. The royal family liked the attendance of spectators to be considerable. Thus care was taken to give out a number of cards, in order that the promenade about the table during the second service should be continuous. Often the princesses spoke to the women of their acquaintance and gave candy to the children passing behind them.

After the coffee, which was taken at table, Charles X. and his guests traversed the Gallery of Mirrors, leading to the salon between two lines of spectators eager to see the royal family. The King next played billiards while a game of écarté was started. The agents for the preservation of the forests and the pages of the hunt remained by the door, inside, without being permitted to advance into the salon, which was occupied only by persons who had dined with the King.

After having had his game of billiards and left his place for other players, Charles X. took a hand at whist, while the écarté went on steadily until, toward ten o'clock, the King retired. He was followed to his sleeping-room, where he gave the watchword to the captain of the body-guards, and indicated the hour of the meet for the next day.

"Sometimes we then returned to the salon," adds the Count of Puymaigre, who, in virtue of his office as Prefect of the Oise, dined with the King, as well as the Bishop of Beauvais and the general commanding the sub-division. "M. de Cossé-Brisac, the first steward, had punch served, and we continued the écarté till midnight or one o'clock, when we could play more liberally, the Dauphiness having limited the stakes to five francs. The Duchess of Berry was less scrupulous. After the withdrawal of the princes we were glad to be more at ease; the talk became gay and even licentious, and I will say here that all the men of the court whom I have seen near the King, far from being what could be called devout or hypocritical, as was believed in the provinces, were anything but that; that they no more concealed their indifference in religious matters than they did their diversity of political opinions, royalist doubtless, but of divers grades; that no one was more tolerant than the King; finally, that if an occult power, the existence of which I do not deny, but the force of which has been exaggerated, acted on the mind of the King, it had not its seat in what was called the court."

Charles X. was deeply religious, a fervent believer, sincerely Christian, and this Prince who but for his great piety might perhaps have given excuse for scandal, led a life without reproach. But as indulgent for others as he was severe to himself, he forced no one to imitate his virtues, and his palaces were in no way like convents. As was said by the Duke Ambroise de Doudeauville, for three years the minister of the King's household, "his religion, despite all the stupid things said of it, was very frank, very real, and very well understood."

Rarely has a sovereign given such a good example to those about him. No mistresses, no favorites, no scandal, no ruinous expenditures, no excess of luxury; a gentle piety, extreme affability, perfect courtesy, a constant desire to render France happy and glorious. The appearance of Charles X. was that of a fine old man, gracious, healthy, amiable, and respected. Persons of plebeian origin at his court were treated by him with as much politeness and attention as the chiefs of the ancient houses of France. His manners were essentially aristocratic, but without arrogance or pretension. Full of goodness toward his courtiers and his servitors, he won the love of all who approached him. His tastes were simple, and personally he required no luxury. Habituated during the Emigration to go without many things, he never thought of lavish expenditure, of building palaces or furnishing his residences richly. "Never did a king so love his people," says the Duke Ambroise de Doudeauville, "never did a king carry self-abnegation so far. I urged him one day to allow his sleeping-room to be furnished. He refused. I insisted, telling him that it was in a shocking condition of neglect.

"'If it is for me,' he replied with vivacity, 'no; if it is for the sake of the manufactures, yes.'

"It was the same in everything. He had no

whims and never listened to a proposition by which he alone was to profit. He joined to these essential qualities, manners that were wholly French, and *mots* that often recalled Henry IV. We were always saying to each other, my colleagues and I, 'If a king were made to order for France, he would not be different.' What a misfortune for France, which he loved so much, that he was not known better and more appreciated. This portrait, I protest, is in nowise flattering; if this poor Prince were still reigning, I would not say so much of him, above all in his presence; but he is persecuted and is an exile; I owe my country the truth, nothing but the truth."

Let us add to the honor of Charles X. that he made of his personal fortune and his civil list the noblest and most liberal use.

"On the throne," says the Viscount Sosthènes de La Rochefoucauld, "he was generous to excess. In his noble improvidence of the future, he considered his civil list as a sort of loan, made by the nation for the sake of its grandeur, to be returned in luxury, magnificence, and benefits. A faithful depositary, he made it a duty to use it all, so that, stripped of his property, he carried into exile hardly enough for the support of his family and some old servitors."

To sum up, all who figured at the court of Charles X. agree in recognizing that he was not a superior man, but a prince, chivalrous and sympathetic, honest and of good intentions, who committed grave errors, but did not deserve his misfortunes. In his appearance, in his physiognomy, in thought and language, there was a mingling of grace and dignity of which even his adversaries felt the charm. If posterity is severe for the sovereign, it will be indulgent for the man.

XI

THE DUKE OF DOUDEAUVILLE

AT the time of the consecration of Charles X., the minister of the King's household was the Duke Ambroise de Doudeauville, father of the Viscount Sosthènes de La Rochefoucauld. A philanthropic nobleman, devoted to the throne, the altar, the Charter, and to liberty, respectful for the past but thoughtful for the future, joining intelligent toleration to sincere piety, faithful servitor but no courtier to the King, the Duke of Doudeauville enjoyed the esteem of all and had at court a high standing, due even more to his character than to his birth. The volume of Memoirs that he has left does honor to his heart as well as to his mind. There is grace and gaiety, depth and charm, wisdom and courage, in this short but substantial book, where appears in full light one of the most distinct types of the ancient French society. "My years of grandeur and splendor," this author wrote, "have passed like a dream, and I have beheld the awakening with pleasure. I know not what my destiny shall be. As to my conduct, I believe that I can affirm that it will be always that of an honest man, a good Frenchman, a servant of God, desiring a Christian close to an honorable life, the crown of every human edifice."

The details given by the Duke of Doudeauville as to his early years are very characteristic. He was born in 1765. He was entrusted to the care of a nurse living two leagues from Paris in a little village, the wife of a post-rider. His parents, when they came to see him, found "their eighteen-months-old progeny astride of one of the horses of his foster-father." Like Henry IV., he was raised roughly, leading the life of a real peasant, running the day long, in sabots, through the snow and ice and mud. "My nurse, who was retained as maid," he says, "was a good peasant, and thoroughly proletarian. Afterwards, transferred to the capital, she there preserved with her simple cap her frank and rustic manners, to the admiration of all who knew her, and esteemed her loyal character and her plain ways. It is to her, and to her alone, that I am indebted for receiving any religious instruction either in infancy or youth. Everything about me was wholly foreign to those ideas; my religion was none the less fervent for that. From my earliest years, being born brave, I felt the vocation of the martyr the most desirable means of being joined to our Father which is in Heaven, and I have always thought that to end one's days for one's God, one's wife and family, was a touching and enviable death."

The Duke of Doudeauville was still a child, and a little child — in point of age he was fourteen and a day, in size he was four feet seven inches — when he was married. He espoused Mademoiselle de Montmirail, of the family of Louvois, who brought him, with a beauty he did not then prize, a considerable fortune, the rank of grandee of Spain, and, worth more than all, rare and precious qualities. Nevertheless, the little husband was very sad. When his approaching marriage was announced to him, he cried out, "Then I can play no longer!" When, after the first interview, he was asked how he liked his *fiancée*, whose fresh face, oval and full, was charming, he responded: "She is really very beautiful; she looks like me when I am eating plums." Listen to his story of the nuptials. "Imagine my extreme embarrassment," he says, "my stupid disappointment, with my excessive bashfulness amid the numerous concourse of visitors and spectators attracted by our wedding. The grandfather of Mademoiselle de Montmirail, being captain of the Hundred-Swiss, a great part of this corps was there, and, as if to play me a trick, all these Hundred-Swiss were six feet tall, sometimes more. One would have said, seeing me by the side of them, the giants and the dwarf of the fair. Every one gazed at the bride, who, although she was only fifteen, was as tall as she was beautiful, and every one was looking for the bridegroom, without suspecting that it was this child, this schoolboy, who was to play the part."

Is it not amusing, this picture of a marriage under the old régime? The little groom was so disturbed when he went to the chapel and during the ceremony, that, though his memory was excellent, he never could recall what passed at that time. "I only remember," he says, "the sound of the drums that were beating during our passage, and cheered me a little; it was the one moment of the day that was to my taste. How long that day seemed! You may imagine it was not from the motives common in like cases, but because I drew all glances upon me, and all vied in laughing at and joking me, pointing their fingers at me."

The day ended with a grand repast that lasted two or three hours. A crowd of strangers strolled around the table all the while. Although the precaution had been taken to put an enormous cushion on the chair of the husband, his chin hardly came above the table. Seated by the side of his young wife, he did not dare look at her. For days beforehand he had been wondering if he should always be afraid of her.

"After this solemn banquet," he adds, "came the soirée, which did not seem any more amusing; after the soirée the return to my parents' home was no more diverting; nevertheless, it was made in the company of my dear spouse, who henceforth was to dwell at my father's house. They bundled me into a wretched cabriolet with my preceptor, and sent me to finish my education at Versailles, and to learn to ride at the riding-school of the pages."

We must note that the marriage thus begun was afterwards a very happy union, and that there was never a pair more virtuous and more attached to each other than the Duke and Duchess of Doudeauville.

In 1789, the Duke was major of the Second Regiment of Chasseurs. He emigrated, though the Emigration was not at all to his liking. "This measure," he said, "appeared to me in every way unreasonable, and yet, to my great chagrin, I was forced to submit to it. The person of the King was menaced, right-thinking people compromised, the tranquillity and prosperity of France lost; they were arming abroad, it was said, to provide a remedy for these evils. The nobles hastened hither. Distaffs were sent to all who refused to rally on the banks of the Rhine. How, at twenty-five, could one resist this tide of opinion?" When he perceived, in the foreign powers, the design of profiting by the discords in France instead of putting an end to them, he laid aside his arms, and never resumed them during the eight years of the Emigration. "This resolve," he said, "was consistent with my principles. Always a good Frenchman, I desired only the good of my country, the happiness of my fellow-countrymen; my whole life, I hope, has been a proof of this view. All my actions have tended to this end."

During his eight years of emigration, the Duke of Doudeauville was constantly a prey to anxiety, grief, poverty, trials of every kind. Thirteen of his relatives were put to death under the Terror. His wife was imprisoned, and escaped the scaffold only through the 9th Thermidor. He himself, having visited

France clandestinely several times, ran the greatest risks. In the midst of such sufferings his sole support was the assistance of a devoted servant. "At the moment that I write these lines," he says in his Memoirs, "I am about to lose my domestic Raphaël, the excellent man who, for fifty years, has given me such proofs of fidelity, disinterestedness, and delicacy; I have treated him as a friend; I shall grieve for him as for a brother."

Misfortune had fortified the character of the Duke of Doudeauville. Unlike other *émigrés*, he had learned much and forgotten nothing. His attitude under the Consulate and the Empire was that of a true patriot. Without joining the Opposition, he wished no favor. The sole function he accepted was that of councillor-general of the Department of the Marne, where he could be useful to his fellow-citizens without giving any one the right to accuse him of ambitious motives. Nothing would have been easier for him than to be named to one of the high posts in the court of Napoleon, whose defects he disapproved, but whose great qualities he admired. "Bonaparte," he said in his Memoirs, "had monarchical ideas and made much of the nobility, especially that which he called historic. I must confess, whatever may be said, that the latter under his reign was more esteemed, respected, fêted, than it has been since under Louis XVIII. or Charles X. The princes feared to excite toward it and toward themselves the envy of the *bourgeois* classes, who would have no supremacy but their own. Napoleon, on the contrary, having frankly faced the difficulty, created a nobility of his own. Those who belonged to it, or hoped to, found it quite reasonable that they should be given as peers the descendants of the first houses of France." The Duchess of Doudeauville was a sister of the Countess of Montesquiou, who was governess of the King of Rome, and whose husband had replaced the Prince de Talleyrand as Grand Chamberlain of the Emperor. Very intimate with the Count and Countess, the Duke of Doudeauville had some trouble in avoiding the favors of Napoleon, who held him in high esteem. He found a way to decline them without wounding the susceptibilities of the powerful sovereign.

Under the Restoration, the Duke of Doudeauville distinguished himself by an honest liberalism, loyal and intelligent, with nothing revolutionary in it, and by an enlightened philanthropy that won him the respect of all parties. When he was named as director of the post-office in 1822, many people of his circle blamed him for taking a place beneath him. "Congratulate me," he said, laughing, "that I have not been offered that of postman; I should have taken it just the same if I had thought I could be useful." And he added: "It was thought that it would be a sinecure for me. Far from that, I gave myself up wholly to my new employment, and I worked so hard at it, than in less than a year my eyes, previously excellent, were almost ruined. I always occupied fifteen or twenty places, each more gratuitous than the others. To make the religion that I practise beloved and to serve my neighbor, has always seemed to me the best way to serve God. So I believe that I can say without fear of contradiction that I have never done any one harm, and that I have always tried to do all the good possible."

In the month of August, 1824, the Duke of Doudeauville was named minister of the King's household. In this post he showed administrative qualities of a high order. In April, 1827, not wishing to share in a measure that he regarded as both inappropriate and unpopular, the disbanding of the Parisian National Guard, he gave in his resignation. "I did not wish," he said, "to join the Opposition. The popularity given me by my resignation would have assured me a prominent place, but this rôle agreed neither with my character nor with my antecedents. I resolved on absolute silence and complete obscurity; I even avoided showing myself in Paris, where I knew that manifestations of satisfaction and gratitude would be given to me." King Louis Philippe said one day to Marshal Gérard: "Had they listened to the Duke of Doudeauville, and not broken up the National Guard of Paris, the revolution would not have taken place."

The great lord, good citizen, and good Christian, who, at periods most disturbed by changes of régime, had always been as firm in the application of his principles as he was moderate in his actions and gentle in his method, made himself as much respected under Louis Philippe as under the Restoration. During the cholera, he set the example of absolute devotion and was constantly in the hospitals. He continued to sit in the Chamber of Peers until the close of the trial of the Ministers, in the hope of saving the servitors of Charles X. But when Louis Philippe quitted the Palais Royal to install himself at the Tuileries, he resigned as Peer of France. He no longer wished to reappear at the Château where he had seen Louis XVIII. and Charles X., and in a letter to the Queen Marie-Amélie, who had a real veneration for him, he wrote: "My presence at the Tuileries would be out of place, and even the new hosts of that palace would be astonished at it." The Duke of Doudeauville, who died at a great age, in 1841, devoted his last years to good works, to charity, to the benevolent establishments of which he was the president. One day at the Hôtel de Ville, he drew applause from an assembly far from religious, by the words we are about to cite, because they discovered in them his whole mind and heart: "A husband would like a wife reserved, economical, a good housekeeper, an excellent mother for his family, charming, eager to please him — him only, adorning herself with virtue, the one ornament that is never ruinous, having great gentleness for him, great strength as against all others; he would wish, in fine, a perfect wife. I should like to believe that there are many such, especially among my listeners, but I should think it a miracle if one of them united all these qualities without having the principles of religion. A woman, pretty, witty, agreeable, would like her husband to think she was so, that he should be as amiable for her, or almost, as for those he saw for the first time; that he should not keep his ill humor and his brusqueness for his home and lavish his care and attention on society; that he should forget sometimes that he is a master, — in some ways a despotic master, — despite the liberalism of the century and the progress of philosophy; that he should be willing to be a friend, even if he ceased to be a lover; finally, that he should not seek from others what he will more surely find at home. Let this tender wife invoke religion, let her cause her husband to love it, let her win him to it; she will get what she hopes for and thank me for the recipe."

Our lady readers will thank us, we hope, for having spoken of a man who gives them such good advice; and it is with pleasure that we have taken the occasion to render homage to the memory of a great lord, who doubly deserved the title, by the elevation of his ideas and the nobility of his sentiments. Such men — alas! they are rare — would have saved the Restoration if the Restoration could have been saved.

XII

THE HOUSEHOLD OF THE DUCHESS OF BERRY

WE shall now, commencing with the ladies, throw a rapid glance over the persons who, at the time of the consecration, formed the household of the Duchess of Berry. The Princess had one lady of honor, one lady of the bedchamber, and eleven lady companions, of whom three were honorary. All were distinguished as much by their manners and sentiments as by birth and education.

The lady of honor was the Maréchale Oudinot, Duchess of Reggio, a lady of the highest rank, who joined a large heart to a firm mind. Attached, through her family, to the religious and monarchical principles of the old régime, by her marriage to the glories of the imperial epic, she represented at the court the ideas of pacification and fusion that inspired the policy of Louis XVIII. Born in 1791, of Antoine de Coucy, captain in the regiment of Artois, and of Gabrielle de Mersuay, she was but two years old when her father and mother were thrown into the dungeons of the Terror. Carried in the arms of a faithful serving-woman, she visited the two prisoners, who escaped death. She married one of Napoleon's most illustrious companions in arms, the "modern Bayard," as he was called, the Marshal Oudinot, Duke of Reggio, who had received thirty-two wounds on the field of battle, and who, by securing the passage of Beresina, deserved to be called the "saviour of the army." He was wounded at the close of the Russian campaign. Then his young wife crossed all Europe to go and care for him and saved him. She was but twenty. She was only twenty-four when Louis XVIII. named her lady of honor to the Duchess of Berry. Despite her extreme youth, she filled her delicate functions with exquisite tact and precocious wisdom, and from the first exercised a happy influence over the mind of the Princess, who gladly listened to her counsels. Very active in work, the lady of honor busied herself with untiring zeal with the details of her charge. She was the directress, the secretary, the factotum, of the Duchess of Berry. The Abbé Tripied, who pronounced her funeral eulogy at Bar-le-Duc, May 21st, 1868, traced a very lifelike portrait of her. Let us hear the ecclesiastic witness of the high virtues of this truly superior woman.

"She bore," he said, "with equal force and sagacity her titles of lady of honor and Duchess of Reggio. Proud of her *blason*, where were crossed the arms of the old and of the new nobility, and where she saw, as did the King, a sign, as it were, of reconciliation and peace, she bore it high and firm, and defended it in its new glories, against insulting attacks. An ornament to the court, by her graces and her high distinction, she displayed there, for the cause of the good, all the resources of her mind and the riches of her heart. But none of the seductions and agitations she met there disturbed the limpidity of her pure soul. Malignity, itself at bay, was forced to recognize and avow that in the Duchess of Reggio no other stain could be found than the ink-stains she sometimes allowed her pen to make upon her finger. In her greatness, this noble woman saw, before all, the side of duty."

In 1832, when the Duchess of Berry was imprisoned in the citadel of Blaye, her former lady of honor asked, without being able to obtain that favor, the privilege of sharing her captivity. The Duchess of Reggio to the last set an example of devotion and of all the virtues. She was so gracious and affable that one day some one remarked: "When the Duchess gives you advice, it seems as if she were asking a service of you." When the noble lady died, April 18th, 1868, at Bar-le-Duc, where her good works and her intelligent charity had made her beloved, they wished to give her name to one of the streets of the city, and as they already had the Rue Oudinot and the Place Reggio, one of the streets was called the Rue de La Maréchale.

The lady of the bedchamber of the Duchess of Berry and her lady companions all belonged to the old aristocracy. The Countess of Noailles, lady of the bedchamber, a woman full of intelligence, and very beautiful, a mother worthy of all praise, was the daughter of the Duke de Talleyrand, the niece of the Prince de Talleyrand, the wife of Count Just de Noailles, second son of the Prince of Poix.

The Duchess of Berry had eight lady companions: the Countess of Bouillé, the Countess d'Hautefort, the Marchioness of Béthisy, the Marchioness of Gourgues, the Countess of Castéja, the Countess of Rosanbo, the Marchioness of Podenas; and three whose title was honorary, the Marchioness of Lauriston, the Countess Charles de Gontaut, and the Countess de La Rochejaquelein.

The Countess of Bouillé, who at the time of the coronation of Charles X. was about forty years old, was a creole, very agreeable and much respected.

The Countess d'Hautefort, *née* Maillé-Latour-Landry, forty-one years old, married to a colonel who belonged to the fourth company of the body-guards, was a woman of much intelligence, charmingly natural, and an excellent musician. She shared in 1832 the captivity of the Duchess of Berry.

Very distinguished in manner and sentiment as in birth, the Marchioness Charles de Béthisy, married to a lieutenant-general and peer of France; the Countess of Gourgues, *née* Montboissier, married to a master of requests, a deputy; the Countess of Mefflay, a young and charming woman, daughter of the Countess of Latour, whom the Duchess of Berry had as governess in the Two Sicilies, and wife of the Count Meffray, receiver-general of Gers; the Viscountess of Castéja, daughter of the Marquis of Bombelles, major-general, ambassador of Louis XVI. at Lisbon and Vienna, then priest, Canon of Breslau, Bishop of Amiens, First Almoner of the Duchess of Berry (he died in 1822, and one of his sons, Charles de Bombelles, married morganatically the Empress Marie-Louise, in 1833); the Countess of Rosanbo, daughter of the Count of Mesnard; the Marchioness of Podenas, wife of a lieutenant-colonel; the Marchioness of Lauriston, wife of the marshal, formerly lady of the palace to the Empress Josephine and the Empress Marie-Louise; the Countess Charles de Gontaut, whose husband was chamberlain of the Emperor, a very young and very pretty woman, remarkable for the vivacity of her mind; the Countess de La Rochejaquelein, *née* Duras, a very pious and very charitable woman, whose husband was a major-general. In fact, the circle around the Duchess of Berry was perfection. The greatest ladies of France were by her side, and the society of the *Petit Château,* as the Pavillon de Marsan was called, was certainly fitted to give the tone to the principal salons of Paris.

The Duchess of Berry had as chevalier d'honneur a great lord, very learned, known for his unchangeable devotion to royalty, the Duke de Sévis (born in 1755, died in 1830). The Duke, who emigrated and was wounded at Quiberon, held himself apart during the Empire, and published highly esteemed writings on finance, some Memoirs, and a *Recueil de Souvenirs et Portraits.* He was a peer of France and member of the French Academy. For adjunct to the chevalier d'honneur, the Duchess had the Count Emmanuel de Brissac, one of the finest characters of the court, married to a Montmorency.

Her first equerry was the Count Charles de Mesnard, a Vendéan gentleman of proven devotion. The Count Charles de Mesnard was born at Luçon, in 1769, the same year as Napoleon, whose fellow-pupil he was at Brienne. Belonging to one of those old houses of simple gentlemen who have the antiquity of the greatest races, he was son of a major-general who distinguished himself in the Seven Years War, and who at the close of the old régime was gentleman of the chamber of the Count of Provence (Louis XVIII.), and captain of the Guards of the Gate of this Prince. He emigrated, and served in the ranks of the army of Condé, with his older brother, the Count Édouard de Mesnard, married to Mademoiselle de Caumont-Laforce, daughter of the former governess of the children of the Count d'Artois (Charles X.), and sister of the Countess of Balbi. The Count Édouard de Mesnard, having entered Paris secretly, was shot there as *émigré,* October 27th, 1797, despite all the efforts of the wife of General Bonaparte to save him. When he was going to his death, his eyes met, on the boulevard, those of one of his friends, the Marquis of Galard, who had returned with him secretly. The condemned man had the presence of mind to seem not to recognize the passerby, and the latter was saved, as he himself related with emotion sixty years afterward.

At the commencement of the Empire, the Count Charles de Mesnard was living at London, where he was reduced to gaining his living by copying music, when the Emperor offered to restore his confiscated property if he would come to France and unite with the new régime. The Count of Mesnard preferred to remain in England near the Duke of Berry, who showed great affection for him. The Restoration compensated the faithful companion of exile. He was a peer of France and Charles X. treated him as a friend. He had married, during the Emigration, an English lady, Mrs. Sarah Mason, widow of General Blondell, by whom he had a daughter, Aglaé, who was named a lady companion to the Duchess of Berry, at the time of her marriage, in 1825, with the Count Ludovic de Rosanbo, and a son, Ferdinand, married in 1829, to Mademoiselle de Bellissen.

The Princess had for equerry-de-main, the Viscount d'Hanache; for honorary equerry, the Baron of Fontanes; for equerry porte-manteau, M. Gory. Her secretary of orders was the Marquis de Sassenay, who bore, besides, the title of Administrator of the Finances and Treasurer of Madame. He had under his orders a controller-general, M. Michals, who was of such integrity and devotion that when, after the Revolution of July, he presented himself at Holyrood to give in his accounts to the Duchess of Berry, she made him a present of her portrait.

There was not a private household in France where more order reigned than in that of Madame. The chief of each service, — the Duchess of Reggio, the Viscount Just de Noailles, the Count Emmanuel de Brissac, and the Count of Mesnard, presented his or her budget and arranged the expenditures in advance with the Princess. This budget being paid by twelfths before the 15th of the following month, she required to have submitted to her the receipts of the month past. This did not prevent Madame from being exceedingly generous. One day she learned that a poor woman had just brought three children into the world and knew not how to pay for three nurses, three layettes, three cradles. Instantly she wished to relieve her. But it was the end of the month; the money of all the services had been spent.

"Lend me something," she said to the controller-general of her household; "you will trust me; no one will trust this unfortunate woman."

As M. Nettement remarked: "The Duchess of Berry held it as a principle that princes should be like the sun which draws water from the streams only to return it in dew and rain. She considered her civil list as the property of all, administered by her. She was to be seen at all expositions and in all the shops, buying whatever was offered that was most remarkable. Sometimes she kept these purchases, sometimes she sent them to her family at Naples, Vienna, Madrid, and her letters used warmly to recommend in foreign cities whatever was useful or beautiful in France. She was thus in every way the Providence of the arts, of industry, and commerce."

To sum up, the household of the Duchess of Berry worked to perfection, and Madame, always affable and good, inspired a profound devotion in all about her.

XIII

THE PREPARATIONS FOR THE CORONATION

THE coronation of Louis XVI. took place the 11th of June, 1775, and since that time there had been none. For Louis XVII. there was none but that of sorrow. Louis XVIII. had desired it eagerly, but he was not sufficiently strong or alert to bear the fatigue of a ceremony so long and complicated, and his infirmities would have been too evident beneath the vault of the ancient Cathedral of Rheims. An interval of fifty years — from 1775 to 1825 — separated the coronation of Louis XVI. from that of his brother Charles X. How many things had passed in that half-century, one of the most fruitful in vicissitudes and catastrophes, one of the strangest and most troubled of which history has preserved the memory!

Chateaubriand, who, later, in his *Mémoires d'outre-tombe*, so full of sadness and bitterness, was to speak of the coronation in a tone of scepticism verging on raillery, celebrated at the accession of Charles, in almost epic language, the merits of this traditional solemnity without which a "Very Christian King" was not yet completely King. In his pamphlet, *Le roi est mort! Vive le roi!* he conjured the new monarch to give to his crown this religious consecration. "Let us humbly supplicate Charles X. to imitate his ancestors," said the author of the *Génie du Christianisme*. "Thirty-two sovereigns of the third race have received the royal unction, that is to say, all the sovereigns of that race except Jean 1er, who died four days after his birth, Louis XVII., and Louis XVIII., on whom royalty fell, on one in the Tower of the Temple, on the other in a foreign land. The words of Adalbéron, Archbishop of Rheims, on the subject of the coronation of Hugh Capet, are still true to-day. 'The coronation of the King of the French,' he says, 'is a public interest and not a private affair, *Publica sunt hæc negotia, non privata.*' May Charles X. deign to weigh these words, applied to the author of his race; in weeping for a brother, may he remember that he is King! The Chambers or the Deputies of the Chambers whom he may summon to Rheims in his suite, the magistrates who shall swell his cortège, the soldiers who shall surround his person, will feel the faith of religion and royalty strengthened in them by this imposing solemnity. Charles VII. created knights at his coronation; the first Christian King of the French, at his received baptism with four thousand of his companions in arms. In the same way Charles X. will at his coronation create more than one knight of the cause of legitimacy, and more than one Frenchman will there receive the baptism of fidelity."

Charles X. had no hesitation. This crowned representative of the union of the throne and the altar did not comprehend royalty without coronation. Not to receive the holy unction would have been for him a case of conscience, a sort of sacrilege. In opening the session of the Chambers in the Hall of the Guards at the Louvre, December 22d, 1824, he announced, amid general approval, the grand solemnity that was to take place at Rheims in the course of the following year. "I wish," he said, "the ceremony of my coronation to close the first session of my reign. You will attend, gentlemen, this august ceremony. There, prostrate at the foot of the same altar where Clovis received the holy unction, and in the presence of Him who judges peoples and kings, I shall renew the oath to maintain and to cause to be respected the institutions established by my brother; I shall thank Divine Providence for having deigned to use me to repair the last misfortunes of my people, and I shall pray Him to continue to protect this beautiful France that I am proud to govern."

If Napoleon, amid sceptical soldiers, former *conventionnels*, and former regicides, had easily secured the adoption of the idea of his coronation at Notre-Dame, by so much the more easy was it for Charles X. to obtain the adoption, by royalist France, of the project of his coronation at Rheims. "The King saw in this act," said Lamartine, "a real sacrament for the crown, the people a ceremony that carried its imagination back to the pomps of the past, politicians a concession to the court of Rome, claiming the investiture of kings, and a denial in fact of the principle, not formulated but latent since 1789, of the sovereignty of the people. But as a rule, there was no vehement discussion of an act generally considered as belonging to the etiquette of royalty, without importance for or against the institutions of the country. It was the fête of the accession to the throne — a luxury of the crown. The oaths to exterminate heretics, formerly taken by the kings of France at their coronation, were modified in concert with the court of Rome and the bishops. For these was substituted the oath to govern according to the Charter. Thus it was in reality a new consecration of liberty as well as of the crown." The French love pomp, ceremonies, spectacles. The idea of a consecration was not displeasing to them, and with rare exceptions, the Voltaireans themselves refrained from criticising the ceremony that was in the course of preparation. It soon became the subject of conversation on every side.

Six millions voted by the two Chambers for the expenses of the coronation, at the time that the civil list was regulated at the beginning of the reign, permitted the repairs required by the Cathedral of Rheims to be begun in January, 1825. The arches that had sunken, or threatened to do so, were strengthened; the ancient sculptured decorations were restored; the windows were completed; the fallen statues were raised. It was claimed that even the holy ampulla had been found, that miraculous oil, believed, according to the royal superstitions of former ages, to have been brought from heaven by a dove for the anointing of crowned heads. The Revolution thought that it had destroyed this relic forever. The 6th of October, 1793, a commissioner of the Convention, the representative of the people, Ruhl, had, in fact, publicly broken it on the pedestal of the statue of Louis XV. But it was related that faithful hands had succeeded in gathering some fragments of the phial as well as some particles of the balm contained in it. The 25th of January, 1819, the Abbé Seraine, who in 1793 was curé of Saint-Remi of Rheims, made the following declaration: —

"The 17th of October, 1793, M. Hourelle, then municipal officer and first warden of the parish of Saint-Remi, came to me and notified me, from the representative of the people, Ruhl, of the order to remit the reliquary containing the holy ampulla, to be broken. We resolved, M. Hourelle and I, since we could do no better, to take from the holy ampulla the greater part of the balm contained in it. We went to the Church of Saint-Remi; I withdrew the reliquary from the tomb of the saint, and bore it to the sacristy, where I opened it with the aid of small iron pincers. I found placed in the stomach of a dove of gold and gilded silver, covered with white enamel, having the beak and claws in red, the wings spread, a little phial of glass of reddish color about an inch and a half high corked with a piece of crimson damask. I examined this phial attentively in the light, and I perceived a great number of marks of a needle on the sides; then I took from a crimson velvet bag, embroidered with fleurs-de-lis in gold, the needle used at the time of the consecration of our kings, to extract the particles of balm, dried and clinging to the glass. I detached as many as possible, of which I took the larger part, and remitted the smaller to M. Hourelle."

The particles thus preserved were given into the hands of the Archbishop of Rheims, who gathered them in a new reliquary.

Sunday, the 22d of May, 1825, the day of the feast of the Pentecost, the Archbishop of Rheims assembled in a chapel of that city the metropolitan clergy, the principal authorities, and the persons who had contributed to the preservation of the particles of the precious relic, in order to proceed, in their presence, to the transfusion of those particles into the holy chrism, to be enclosed in a new phial. A circumstantial report of this ceremony was prepared in duplicate.

"Thus," said the *Moniteur*, May 26, "there remains no doubt that the holy oil that will flow on the forehead of Charles X. in the solemnity of his consecration, is the same as that which, since Clovis, has consecrated the French monarchs."

The day of the consecration approached. The Mayor of Rheims, M. Ruinard de Brimont, had not a moment's rest. At the consecration of Louis XV., about four hundred lodgings had been marked with chalk. For that of Charles X. there were sixteen hundred, and those who placed them at the service of the administration asked no compensation. The 19th of May was begun the placing of the exterior decorations on the wooden porch erected in front of the door of the basilica. It harmonized so completely with the plan of the edifice that "at thirty *toises*," it seemed a part of the edifice. The centrings and the interior portières of this porch presented to the view a canopy sown with fleurs-de-lis in the midst of which stood out the royal cipher and the crown of France, modelled in antique fashion. These decorations were continued from the portal along the beautiful gallery that led to the palace. The palace itself, whose apartments had been adorned and furnished with royal magnificence, was entered by a very elegant porch. The grand feasting-hall, with its Gothic architecture, its colored glass, its high chimney-piece covered with escutcheons and surmounted by a statue of Saint-Remi, its portraits of all the kings of France, was resplendent. Three tables were to be set in the royal feasting-hall, — that of the King, that of the Dauphiness, and that of the Duchess of Berry. A gallery enclosed in glass, where there was a table of one hundred and thirty covers, had been built as by enchantment. On leaving the feasting-hall, one entered the covered gallery, which, by a gentle incline, led to the Cathedral. This gallery was formed of twenty-four arcades of fifteen feet each, and joined at right angles the porch erected before the portal. By this arrangement the King could proceed on a level from his apartment to the Cathedral.

In the middle of the nave was erected a magnificent jubé, where the throne of Charles X. was placed. The cornice of the Corinthian order was supported by twenty columns. At the four corners there were gilded angels. The summit was surmounted by a statue of Religion and an angel bearing the royal crown. This jubé, glittering with gold, was placed about one hundred and fifty feet from the portal. There was a passage under it to reach the choir, and the ascent to it was by a staircase of thirty steps. As it was open, the King upon his throne could be seen from all parts of the basilica. At the end of the choir, to the right on entering, was the gallery of the Dauphiness and the Duchess of Berry; to the left, opposite, was that of the princes and princesses of the blood; lower, toward the jubé, and also on the left, that of the ambassadors and strangers of distinction; by the side of the jubé, the gallery of the first gentlemen of the chamber of the King. There were, moreover, two rows of galleries on each side of the nave. The sanctuary was beaming with gold. The pillars, surrounded with wainscoting, were covered with rich Gothic ornaments. Above each of the galleries was a portrait of a king of France seated on his throne; still higher, portraits of bishops and statues of the cities of France in niches. At the back, a platform had been constructed for the musicians of the Chapel of the King. The choir and the sanctuary were to be lighted by thirty-four grand chandeliers, besides the candelabra attached to each pillar.

Some days before the coronation, which excited the curiosity of all Europe, the city of Rheims was filled with a crowd of tourists. The streets and promenades of the city, usually so quiet, presented an extraordinary animation. There had been constructed a bazaar, tents, cafés, places for public games, and at the gates of the city there was a camp of ten thousand men. To visit this camp was a favorite excursion for the people and for strangers. The soldiers assembled each evening before their tents and sang hymns to the sovereign and the glory of the French arms. In the evening of the 22d of May, these military choruses were closed by the *Serment Français*, sung by all voices. At the words "Let us swear to be faithful to Charles!" all heads were uncovered, and the soldiers waving their helmets and shakos in the air, cried over and again, "Long live the King!"

On May 24th, the King left Paris with the Dauphin. Before going to Rheims he stopped at the Château of Compiègne, where he remained until the 27th, amid receptions and fêtes and hunts.

M. de Chateaubriand was already at Rheims. He wrote on May 26: —

"The King arrives day after to-morrow. He will

be crowned Sunday, the 29th. I shall see him place upon his head a crown that no one dreamed of when I raised my voice in 1814. I write this page of my Memoirs in the room where I am forgotten amid the noise. This morning I visited Saint-Remi and the Cathedral decorated in colored paper. The only clear idea that I can have of this last edifice is from the decorations of the *Jeanne d'Arc* of Schiller, played at Berlin. The opera-scene painters showed me on the banks of the Spree, what the opera-scene painters on the banks of the Vesle hide from me. But I amused myself with the old races, from Clovis with his Franks and his legion come down from heaven, to Charles VII. with Jeanne d'Arc."

The writer, who some weeks earlier had expressed himself in terms so dithyrambic as to the consecration, now wrote as follows of this religious and monarchical solemnity: —

"Under what happy auspices did Louis XVI. ascend the throne! How popular he was, succeeding to Louis XV.! And yet what did he become? The present coronation will be the representation of a coronation. It will not be one; we shall see the Marshal Moncey, an actor at that of Napoleon, the Marshal who formerly celebrated the death of the tyrant Louis XVI. in his army, brandish the royal sword at Rheims in his rank as Count of Flanders or Duke of Aquitaine. To whom can this parade really convey any illusion? I should have wished no pomp to-day; the King on horseback, the church bare, adorned only with its ancient arches and tombs; the two Chambers present, the oath of fidelity to the Charter taken aloud on the Bible. This would have been the renewal of the monarchy; they might have begun it over again with liberty and religion. Unfortunately there was little love of liberty, even if they had had at least a taste for glory."

This is not all; the curious royalist, as if disabused as to Bourbon glories, so extolled by him, glorifies, apropos of the coronation of Charles X., the Napoleon whom in 1814 he called disdainfully "Buonaparte," loading him with the most cutting insults:—

"After all, did not the new coronation, when the Pope anointed a man as great as the chief of the second race, by a change of heads alter the effect of the ancient ceremony of our history? The people have been led to think that a pious rite does not dedicate any one to the throne, or else renders indifferent the choice of the brow to be touched by the holy oil. The supernumeraries at Notre-Dame de Paris, playing also in the Cathedral of Rheims, are no longer anything but the obligatory personages of a stage that has become common. The advantage really is with Napoleon, who furnishes his figurants to Charles X. The figure of the Emperor thenceforth dominates all. It appears in the background of events and ideas. The leaflets of the good time to which we have attained shrivel at the glance of his eagles."

Charles X. left Compiègne the 27th of May in the

morning, and slept at Fismes. The next day, the 28th, he had just quitted this town and was descending a steep hill, when several batteries of the royal guard fired a salute at his departure; the horses, frightened, took flight. Thanks to the skill of the postilion, there was no accident to the King; but a carriage of his suite, in which were the Duke of Aumont, the Count de Cossé, the Duke of Damas, and the Count Curial, was overturned and broken, and the last two wounded. At noon Charles X. arrived at a league and a half from Rheims, at the village of Tinqueux, where he was awaited by the Dukes of Orleans and Bourbon, the officers of his civil and military household, the authorities of Rheims, the legion of the mounted National Guard of Paris, etc. He entered the gold carriage, — termed the coronation carriage, — where the Dauphin and the Dukes of Orleans and Bourbon took their places beside him. The cortège then took up its march. From Tinqueux to Rheims, the royal coach, gleaming with gold, passed under a long arcade of triumphal arches adorned with streamers and foliage. From the gates of the city to the Cathedral, flowers strewed the sand that covered the ground. All the houses were hung with carpets and garlands; at all the windows, from all the balconies, from all the roofs, innumerable spectators shouted their acclamations; the cortège advanced to the sound of all the bells of the city, and to the noise of a salvo of artillery of one hundred and one guns. The King was received under a daïs at the door of the metropolitan church, by the Archbishop of Rheims in his pontifical robes, and accompanied by his suffragans, the Bishops of Soissons, Beauvais, Châlons, and Amiens. The Archbishop presented the holy water to the sovereign, who knelt, kissed the Gospels, then was escorted processionally into the sanctuary. His *prie-dieu* was placed at fifteen feet from the altar, on a platform, about which was a magnificent canopy hung from the ceiling of the Cathedral.

The Dauphiness had entered her gallery with the Duchess of Berry and the princesses of the blood. The Archbishop celebrated the vespers, and then the Cardinal de La Fare ascended the pulpit and delivered a sermon in which he said: —

"God of Clovis, if there is here below a spectacle capable of interesting Thy infinite Majesty, would it not be that which in this solemnity fixes universal attention and invites and unites all prayers? These days of saintly privilege, in which the hero of Tolbiac, and thirteen centuries after him, the sixty-fifth of his successors have come to the same temple to receive the same consecration, can they be confounded with the multitude of human events, to be buried and lost in the endless annals? To what, O great God! if not to the persistence of Thy immutable decrees, can we attribute, on this earth, always so changing and mobile, the supernatural gift of this miraculous duration?"

The Cardinal covered with praises not only the

King, but the Dauphin, the Dauphiness, the Duchess of Berry, the Duke of Bordeaux. He cried: —

"Constantly happy as King, may Charles X. be constantly happy as father!

"May his paternal glances always see about him, shining with a brilliancy that nothing can change, this family so precious, the ornament of his court, the charm of his life, the future of France!

"This illustrious Dauphin, the terror of the genius of evil, the swift avenger of the majesty of kings, conquering hero and peace-maker!

"This magnanimous Princess, the living image of celestial charity, the visible Providence of the unfortunate, the model of heroism as of virtue!

"This admirable mother of the Child of Miracle, who restored hope to the dismayed nation, astonished it by her courage and captivates it by her goodness!

"This tender scion of the first branch of the lilies, the object, before his birth, of so many desires, and now of so many hopes."

The Prince of the Church, amid general emotion, thus closed his discourse: —

"May it be, O Lord! thy protecting will, that if the excess of ills has surpassed our presentiments and our fear, the reality of good may, in its turn, surpass our hopes and our desires.

"Condescend that the lasting succor of Thy grace may guide in an unbroken progress of prosperity and lead to happiness without vicissitude or end, our King, Thy adorer, and his people, who, under his laws, shall be more than ever religious and faithful."

After the sermon, the Archbishop celebrated the *Te Deum*, to which Charles X. listened standing. Then after having kissed the altar and a reliquary in which was a piece of the true cross, the sovereign returned to his apartments in the Archbishop's palace.

Thus passed the eve of the consecration. The same day M. de Chateaubriand wrote:—

"Rheims, Saturday, the eve of the consecration. I saw the King enter. I saw pass the gilded coaches of the monarch who, a little while ago, had not a horse to mount; I saw rolling by, carriages full of courtiers who had not known how to defend their master. This herd went to the church to sing the *Te Deum*, and I went to visit a Roman ruin, and to walk alone in an elm grove called the *Bois d'Amour*. I heard from afar the jubilation of the bells; I contemplated the towers of the Cathedral, secular witnesses of this ceremony always the same and yet so different in history, time, ideas, morals, usages, and customs. The monarchy perished, and for a long time the Cathedral was changed to a stable. Does Charles X., when he sees it again to-day, recall that he saw Louis XVI. receive anointment in the same place where he in his turn is to receive it? Will he believe that a consecration shelters him from misfortune? There is no longer a hand with virtue enough to cure the king's evil, no ampulla with holy power sufficient to render kings inviolable."

Such was the disposition of the great writer, always content with himself, discontented with others. The crowd of royalists, far from showing themselves sceptical and morose, as he was, was about to attend the ceremony of the morrow in a wholly different mood. It had long been ready with its enthusiasm, and awaited with impatience mingled with respect the dawn of the day about to rise.

XIV

THE CORONATION

SUNDAY, the 29th of May, 1825, the city of Rheims presented, even before sunrise, an extraordinary animation. From four o'clock in the morning vehicles were circulating in the streets, and an hour after people with tickets were directing their steps toward the Cathedral, the men in uniform or court dress, the women in full dress. The sky was clear and the weather cool.

Let us listen to an eye-witness, the Count d'Haussonville, the future member of the French Academy:—

"Need I say that the competition had been ardent among women of the highest rank to obtain access to the galleries of the Cathedral, which, not having been reserved for the dignitaries, could receive a small number of happy chosen ones? Such was the eagerness of this feminine battalion to mount to the assault of the places whence they could see and be seen, that at six o'clock in the morning when I presented myself at the Gothic porch built of wood before the Cathedral, I found them already there and under arms. They were in court dress, with trains, all wearing, according to etiquette, uniform coiffures of lace passed through the hair (what they called *barbes*), and which fell about their necks and shoulders, conscientiously *décolletés*. For a cool May morning it was rather a light costume; they were shivering with cold. In vain they showed their tickets, and recited, in order to gain entrance, their titles and their rank; the grenadier of the royal guard, charged with maintaining order until the hour of the opening of the doors, marched unmoved before these pretty beggars, among whom I remember to have remarked the Countess of Choiseul, her sister, the Marchioness of Crillon, the Countess of Bourbon-Bosset, etc. He had his orders from his chief to let no one enter, and no one did."

Finally the doors were opened. At a quarter after six all the galleries were filled. The foreign sovereigns were represented by especial ambassadors: the King of Spain by the Duke of Villa-Hermosa, the Emperor of Austria by Prince Esterhazy, the King of England by the Duke of Northumberland, the Emperor of Russia by the Prince Wolkonski, the King of Prussia by General de Zastrow. These various personages were objects of curiosity to the crowd, as was Sidi-Mahmoud, ambassador of the Bey of Tunis. The rich toilets and dazzling jewels of the ladies of the court were admired; all eyes were fixed on the gallery where were the Dauphiness, the Duchess of Berry, and the Duchess and Mademoiselle d'Orléans, all four resplendent with diamonds. The spectacle was magnificent. An array of marvels attracted attention. Behind the altar the sacred vessels in gold, of antique form, the crown in diamonds surmounted by the famous stone, the "Regent," the other attributes of royalty on a cushion of velvet embroidered with fleurs-de-lis; on the front of the altar the royal mantle, open, not less than twenty-four feet in length; on the altar of green-veined marble, superb candelabra in gold; on the centre of the cross of the church, suspended from the ceiling above the choir and the *prie-dieu* of the King, an immense canopy of crimson velvet, sown with golden fleurs-de-lis; at the back of the choir, toward the nave, about one hundred and fifty feet from the portal, the gigantic jubé with its staircase of thirty steps; upon this the throne; all around a swarm of standards, those of the five companies of the King's body-guard, and the flag of his foot-guards, borne by the superior officers; on the two sides of the stairway, ranged *en échelon*, the flags and standards of the regiments of the guard and of the line in camp under the walls of Rheims; a splendor of light, banishing all regret for the sun, from candelabra at the entrance of the choir, from chandeliers in the galleries, from chandeliers full of candles suspended from the ceiling, from tapers on the columns.

The Cardinals de Clermont-Tonnerre and de La Fare, preceded by the metropolitan chapter, came to seek the King in his apartment in the palace. The Grand Preceptor knocked at the door of the royal chamber; the Grand Chamberlain said in a loud voice: —

"What do you seek?" The Cardinal de Clermont-Tonnerre responded: —

"Charles X., whom God has given us for King."

Then the ushers opened the doors of the chamber. The two cardinals entered and saluted the sovereign, who rose from his chair, bowed, and received the holy water. The Cardinal de Clermont-Tonnerre recited a prayer. The cortège was formed, and in the following order traversed the great covered gallery which had been built along the right side of the Cathedral: —

The metropolitan chapter; the King's foot-guards; the band; the heralds-at-arms; the king-at-arms; the aides de cérémonies; the Grand Master of Ceremonies, Marquis de Dreux-Brézé; the four knights of the Order of the Holy Spirit, who were to carry the offerings, viz. the Duke de Vauguyon the wine in a golden vase, the Duke of Rochefoucauld the *pain d'argent*, the Duke of Luxembourg the *pain d'or*, the Duke of Gramont the ewers filled with silver medals; the King's pages on the flanks; the Marshal Moncey, Duke of Conegliano, charged with the functions of constable, holding in his hand his naked sword; the Duke of Mortemart, captain-colonel of the foot-guards in ordinary to the King; the Marshal Victor Duke of Bellune, major-general of the royal guard; the Marshal Marquis de Lauriston, the Count de Cossé, and the Duke de Polignac, named by the

King to bear his train in the church; then, with his two attendant cardinals, de Clermont-Tonnerre and de La Fare, one at his right, the other at his left, the King.

There was a movement of curiosity, attention, and respect. Charles X. had entered the Cathedral. The moment his foot crossed the threshold, Cardinal de La Fare pronounced a prayer: —

"O God, who knowest that the human race cannot subsist by its own virtue, grant Thy succor to Charles, Thy servant, whom Thou hast put at the head of Thy people, that he may himself succor and protect those subject to him."

Here, then, is Charles X. in that basilica where fifty years before, Sunday, June 11, 1775, he assisted at the coronation of his brother Louis XVI. Then he was seventeen. Ah! what would have been his surprise had it been foretold to him by what strange and horrible series of gloomy and bloody dramas he should himself come to be crowned in this Cathedral of Rheims! What a contrast between the religious pomps of June 11, 1775, and the sacrilegious scaffolds of January 21 and October 16, 1793! What a difference between the royal mantle of the sovereign and the humble costume of the captive of the Temple, between the resplendent toilet of the Queen of France and Navarre and the patched gown of the prisoner of the Conciergerie! What a road travelled between the hosannas of the priests and the insults of the Furies of the Guillotine! What reflections might one make who had been present at both the ceremonies! How much must such an one have been moved were he the King himself, the brother of Louis XVI., Charles X.! But the 29th of May, 1825, all hearts inclined to confidence and joy. Peoples forget quickly, and there were but few to call up sinister memories. The sovereign appeared in his first costume, a camisole of white satin, with a cap rich with diamonds, surmounted by black and white plumes. Despite his sixty-seven years, Charles X. had a fine presence, a slender form, a manner almost youthful. State costumes became him perfectly. He wore them with the elegance of the men of the old court.

Let us listen again to Count d'Haussonville:—

"At the moment Charles X. crossed the nave, clad in a gown of white satin, opened over a doublet of the same color and the same material, a general thrill evoked a thousand little cries of ecstasy from my lady neighbors. With that sensitiveness to grace innate with women, and which never fails to delight them, how could they help applauding the royal and supremely elegant fashion in which Charles X., despite his age, wore this strange and slightly theatrical costume? No one was better adapted than he, in default of more solid qualities, to give a becoming air to the outward manifestations of a royalty that was at once amiable and dignified."

It is half-past seven in the morning. The ceremony begins. Escorted by his two attendant cardinals, the King reaches the foot of the altar and kneels. Mgr. de Latil, Archbishop of Rheims, standing and without his mitre, pronounces this prayer: —

"Almighty God, who rulest all above us, and who hast deigned to raise to the throne Thy servant Charles, we implore Thee to preserve him from all adversity, to strengthen him with the gift of the peace of the Church, and to bring him by Thy grace to the joys of a peace eternal!"

The King is now escorted by the two cardinals to the seat prepared for him in the centre of the sanctuary, under the great dais, a little in advance of the first of the steps that divide the sanctuary from the choir. At his right are the Dauphin, the Duke of Orleans, and the Duke of Bourbon, their ducal crowns on their heads.

The *Veni Creator* having been sung, the Archbishop takes the book of the Gospels, on which he places a piece of the true cross, and holds it open before the monarch. Charles X., seated, his head covered, his hand on the Gospels and the true cross, pronounces in a strong voice the oath of coronation: —

"In the presence of God, I promise to my people to maintain and honor our holy religion, as belongs to the very Christian King and eldest son of the Church; to render good justice to all my subjects; finally, to govern according to the laws of the kingdom and the Constitutional Charter, which I swear faithfully to observe, so help me God and His holy Gospels."

The King next takes two other oaths, the first as sovereign chief and grand master of the Order of the Holy Spirit, the others as sovereign chief and grand master of the military and royal Order of Saint Louis and of the royal Order of the Legion of Honor. He swears to maintain these orders and not to allow them to fail of their glorious prerogatives. Then his gown is removed by the First Gentleman of the Chamber, and he gives his cap to the First Chamberlain. He now bears only the robe of red satin with gold lace on the seams. He is seated. The Marquis of Dreux-Brézé, Grand Master of Ceremonies, goes to the altar and takes the shoes of violet velvet sown with golden fleurs-de-lis, and Prince Talleyrand, Grand Chamberlain, puts them on the feet of the King.

Then the Archbishop blesses the sword of Charlemagne, placed on the altar in its scabbard:—

"*Exaudi Domine*," he says, "grant our prayers, and deign to bless with Thy hand this sword with which Thy servant Charles is girt, that he may use it to protect the churches, the widows, and the orphans, and all Thy servants; and may this sword inspire dread and terror to whoever shall dare to lay snares for our King. We ask it through our Lord Jesus Christ."

The Archbishop draws the sword from the sheath, and places it naked in the hands of the King, who, having lowered it, offers it to God and replaces it upon the altar.

To the ceremony of the sword succeeds the preparation of the holy chrism. The Archbishop has the reliquary opened containing the holy ampulla, which is taken from a little chest of gold; he withdraws from it, by means of a golden needle, a particle which he mingles with the holy chrism on the patin. Meanwhile the choir chants: —

"The holy Bishop Remi, having received from Heaven this precious balm, sanctified the illustrious race of the French in the baptismal waters and enriched them with the gift of the Holy Spirit."

Then the two attendant cardinals undo the openings made in the garments of the King for the anointings, and escort His Majesty to the altar. A large carpet of velvet with fleurs-de-lis is stretched in front, and on this are two cushions of velvet, one over the other. The King prostrates himself, his face against the cushions. The Archbishop, holding the golden patin of the chalice of Saint Remi, on which is the sacred unction, takes some upon his thumb, and consecrates the King, who is kneeling.

The Archbishop then proceeds to the seven anointings: on the crown of the head, on the breast, between the shoulders, on the right shoulder, on the left shoulder, in the bend of the right arm, in the bend of the left arm, making the sign of the cross at each, and repeating seven times: *Ungo te in regem de oleo sanctificato, in nomine Patris et Filii et Spiritus Sancti.*

Aided by the attendant cardinals, he then closes the openings in the King's garments.

The Grand Chamberlain advances, and puts upon His Majesty the tunic and dalmatica of violet satin sown with fleurs-de-lis in gold, which the Master of Ceremonies and an aide have taken from the altar. The Grand Chamberlain places over these the royal mantle of violet velvet sown with golden fleurs-de-lis, lined and bordered with ermine. Charles X., clad in the royal robes, kneels. The Archbishop, seated, with the mitre on his head, anoints the palms of his hands, saying: *Ungentur manus istæ de oleo sanctificato.* The King then receives the gloves sprinkled with holy water, the ring, the sceptre, the *main de justice.*

The Dauphin, the Duke of Orleans, and the Duke of Bourbon advance. The Archbishop, mitre on head, takes with both hands from the altar the crown of Charlemagne and holds it above the King's head without touching it. Immediately the three princes put out their hands to support it. The Archbishop, holding it with the left hand only, with the right makes the sign of benediction: *Coronat te Deus corona gloriæ atque justitiæ.* After which he places the crown on the head of the King, saying: *Accipe coronam regni in nomine Patris et Filii et Spiritus Sancti.*

Now that the King is crowned, he ascends the steps of the jubé, and seats himself upon the throne. The religious silence, maintained to that moment, is broken by cries of "Long live the King!" which rise from all parts of the Cathedral. The ladies in the galleries wave their handkerchiefs. The enthusiasm reaches a paroxysm. Flourishes of trumpets resound. The people enter the Cathedral amid acclamations. Three salutes are fired by the infantry of the royal guard. The artillery responds from the city ramparts. The bells ring. The heralds-at-arms distribute the medals struck for the coronation. The people rush to get them. The keepers release the birds, which fly here and there beneath the vaulted roof, dazzled, terrified by the shining chandeliers. The *Te Deum* is sung. High Mass begins. At the offertory the King leaves the throne to go to the altar with the offerings. Reaching the front of the altar, he hands his sceptre to Marshal Soult, Duke of Dalmatia, the *main de justice* to Marshal Mortier, Duke of Treviso. Then, after having presented in succession the offerings, — viz. the wine in a vase of gold, the *pain d'argent*, the *pain d'or*, — he resumes his sceptre and his *main de justice* and returns to the throne.

After the benediction, the Grand Almoner goes and takes the kiss of peace from the Archbishop, and then goes and gives it to the King. The Dauphin, the Duke of Orleans, and the Duke of Bourbon, laying aside their ducal crowns, come and receive the kiss from the King.

After the *Domine salvum fac regem* Charles X. again descends from the throne, and returns to the altar. There he removes his crown and retires behind the altar to his confessional, where he remains three minutes. During this time the holy table is prepared. The cloth is held on one side by the Bishop of Hermopolis, First Almoner of the King, and on the other by the Grand Almoner. Charles X. kneels on a cushion before the holy table, which is supported by the Dauphin and the Duke of Orleans. The King receives the communion in both kinds. The whole assembly kneels. The great crown of Charlemagne is handed to Marshal Jourdan, who bears it in front of the King. The Archbishop then places the diamond crown on the King's head, who resumes his sceptre and his *main de justice*, while the choir chants the *Exaudiat*, and returns with his cortège to the Archbishop's palace, passing through the church and the covered gallery. It is half-past eleven in the morning. The ceremony of consecration is finished. It has lasted four hours.

Reaching his apartments, Charles X. passes the sceptre to Marshal Soult, the *main de justice* to Marshal Mortier. The shirt and the gloves touched by the holy unction must be burned. The great officers of the crown then escort the monarch to the royal banquet in the great hall. There he eats under a daïs with the Dauphin, the Duke of Orleans, and the Duke of Bourbon, with their ducal crowns, and he with the diamond crown upon the head.

The royal insignia have been placed upon the table which is served by the great officers and the officers of the household. The marshals of France stand before the sovereign ready to resume the insignia. Around about are five other tables, where are placed the members of the diplomatic corps, the peers of France, the deputies, the cardinals, archbishops, and bishops. The royal banquet lasts half an hour to the sound of military music. In the evening the city of Rheims is everywhere illuminated.

XV

CLOSE OF THE SOJOURN AT RHEIMS

AFTER his coronation Charles X. remained at Rheims during the 30th and 31st of May. On the 30th the ceremony of the Order of the Holy Spirit was celebrated in the Cathedral. The interior presented the same aspect as the day before. At 1 P.M. the order passed in procession through the covered gallery as follows: the usher, the herald, Marquis d'Aguessau, Grand Master of Ceremonies of the order, having at his right the Count Desèze, Commander Grand Treasurer, at his left Marquis de Villedeuil, Commander Secretary, the Chancellor, two columns of Knights of the Holy Spirit. In the right hand column, the Viscount of Chateaubriand, the Duke of San-Carlos, the Prince of Castelcicala, the Viscount Laîné, the Marquis of Caraman, the Marquis Dessole, Marshal Marquis of Viomesnil, the Duke d'Avaray, the Marshal Duke of Ragusa, the Marshal Duke of Taranto, the Marshal Duke of Conegliano, the Duke of Lévis, the Duke of Duras, the Duke d'Aumont, the Duke of Luxembourg, the Prince of Hohenlohe, the Duke de La Vauguyon. In the left column, the Marquis of Talaru, the Duke of Doudeauville, the Count of Villèle, the Marshal Marquis of Lauriston, the Count Charles de Damas, the Baron Pasquier, the Duke of Blacas d'Aulps, the Marquis of Rivière, the Marshal Duke of Reggio, the Duke of Dalberg, the Prince de Poix, the Duke de Gramont, Prince Talleyrand, the Duke de La Rochefoucauld. Then came the Dauphin, the Duke of Orleans, the Duke of Bourbon, the King.

The vestments of the monarch, of a silver stuff, were covered by a mantle of the order in black velvet, lined with green silk stitched with gold. His head-dress was also in black velvet, surmounted by an aigrette of heron plumes. The knights of the order had their mantles with the Holy Spirit in silver spangles on the shoulder; the grand collar, the facings of their mantles, caught up in front, were of green velvet sown with gold flames. They made their entry into the Cathedral in two columns, which deployed on either side of the altar. The King, who followed them, seated himself on a throne in the choir and they arranged themselves in their stalls to the right and left. The princesses occupied the same gallery as the day before. The clergy chanted the vespers. Then the two columns formed in a double rank and the ceremony commenced. There was a long series of obeisances. The King made twenty himself, eleven before vespers, nine after. The reception began with the ecclesiastical commanders and the laymen came afterwards.

The solemnity was less imposing than that of the

coronation. Count d'Haussonville remarked it: "The military array of so many marshals and generals clad in brilliant uniforms, the pomp of the ceremonies to the slow and majestic sound of the organ filling the vast nave of the church, had succeeded, the preceding day, in redeeming for the spectators, and for me particularly, whatever was a little superannuated in the minute observance of a ritual that had come down from the Middle Ages. I felt myself, on the contrary, rather surprised than edified by the character, partly religious, partly worldly, but far more worldly than religious, that I witnessed on the morrow. Most of these gentlemen were known to me. I had met nearly all of them in my mother's or grandmother's salon. I had not been insensible to the fine air given them by the *cordon bleu* (worn under the frock coat, usually, or on great occasions over a coat covered with gold lace and shining decorations), the traditional object of ambition for those most in favor at court; but they seemed to me to present a constrained figure, as I saw them soberly ranged in the stalls of the canons, clad in a costume of no particular epoch, wrapped in long mantles of motley color, and following, with a distracted air, the phases of a ceremony to which they were so little accustomed that they were constantly rising, sitting down, and kneeling at the wrong time."

The receptions took place as follows: the herald-at-arms of the order called in groups of four the new members from each column, and escorted them to the middle of the sanctuary. There the four knights, abreast, saluted together, first the altar, then the sovereign. Then they advanced in line toward the throne, and after a second obeisance, knelt, placed the right hand on the book of the Gospels spread out on the knees of the monarch, and took the oath. The King decorated each with his own hand. He passed over their coats, from right to left, the *cordon bleu* with the cross of gold suspended from it, placed the collar on the mantle, gave a book of hours and a decastich to each one, who kissed his hand, rose, and returned to his place.

By a curious coincidence, M. de Chateaubriand and M. de Villèle, two inveterate adversaries, were one in the column on the right, the other in that on the left, and the herald-at-arms of the order called both at once to the foot of the throne. Listen to the author of the *Mémoires d'outre-tombe:* —

"I found myself kneeling at the feet of the King at the moment that M. de Villèle was taking the oath. I exchanged a few words of politeness with my companion in knighthood, apropos of a plume detached from my hat. We quitted the knees of the King, and all was finished. The King, having had some trouble in removing his gloves to take my hands in his, had said to me, laughing, 'A gloved cat catches no mice.' It was thought that he had spoken to me for a long time, and the rumor spread of my nascent favor. It is likely that Charles X., thinking that the Archbishop had told me of his favorable sentiments, expected a word of thanks and that he was shocked at my silence."

The ceremony of the reception of the knights once finished, the King quitted his throne in the sanctuary, after having made the required obeisances. The completory was next sung. Then all the members of the order re-escorted the monarch to his apartments in the same order and with the same ceremony that he had been escorted to the Cathedral.

After the ceremony, Charles X. held a chapter of the order, in which he named twenty-one *cordons bleus:* the Dukes d'Uzès, de Chevreuse, de Boissac, de Mortemart, de Fitz-James, de Lorges, de Polignac, de Maillé, de Castries, de Narbonne, the Marshal Count Jordan, the Marshal Duke of Dalmatia, the Marshal Duke of Treviso, the Marquis de la Suze, the Marquis de Brézé, Marquis de Pastoret, Count de La Ferronays, Viscount d'Agoult, Marquis d'Autichamp, Ravez, Count Juste de Noailles. By an ordinance of the same day he named to be Dukes, the Count Charles de Damas, Count d'Escars, and the Marquis de Rivière.

The next day, May 31, the King after having heard Mass in his apartments, left the palace at ten o'clock with a brilliant cortège. Preceded by the hussars of the guard, and by the pages, and followed by a numerous staff, he was in the uniform of a general officer, on a white horse, whose saddle of scarlet velvet was ornamented with embroideries and fringe of gold. He had at his right the Dauphin on a white horse, and the Duke of Bourbon on a bay horse; at his left the Duke of Orleans, who wore the uniform of a colonel-general of hussars, and rode an iron-gray horse. Following the cortège was an open carriage; at the back the Dauphiness with the Duchess of Berry at her left, and in front the Duchess of Orleans and Madame of Orleans, her sister-in-law. The route lay through an immense crowd to the Hospital of Saint Marcoul. When he arrived there, the King dismounted and offered up a prayer in the chapel. Then he ascended to the halls, where were assembled one hundred and twenty-one scrofulous patients. He touched them, making a cross with his finger on the brow, while the first physician held the head and the captain of the guard the hand. The King said to each: "May God heal thee! The King touches thee!" Then he thanked the sisters who had charge of the hospital for all the care they gave to the solacing of suffering humanity. The pious sisters knelt at the feet of the sovereign, and begged his benediction, according to an ancient custom. The King gave it to them, and allowed them to kiss his hand. The holy women wept with joy.

Charles X., followed by his cortège, next proceeded to the abbey of Saint Remi, which dates from the eleventh century, and performed his devotions on the tomb of the saint whose shrine had been discovered. Then he remounted and went to review the troops of the camp of Saint Léonard, under the walls of the city, in a vast plain, along the river Vesle, on the right of the road to Châlons. In the midst of this plain rises a grassy hillock, above which was placed the portrait of the King; below, on a background of soil, was this inscription in bluets and marguerites, —

"A moment in the camp — always in our hearts."

Not far from there an altar had been erected under a tent before the royal tent. All the road from Châlons, opposite the lines, was covered with a shouting and cheering crowd. Charles X. was accompanied by the princes and a brilliant staff. The carriage of the princesses followed him. He distributed to the officers, sub-officers, and soldiers the crosses of the Legion of Honor which he had accorded to them. The review, which was magnificent, lasted from noon to 3 P.M. Before returning to the palace, the sovereign visited the bazaar established along the promenades of the lawn. He dismounted, and the princesses descended from their carriage to traverse the shops.

At five o'clock the cortège, which had set out at 10 A.M., returned to the palace. On each of the four nights that Charles X. passed at Rheims, the streets of the city were illuminated. It was clear weather, and by the light of the illuminations, amid the crowd in the streets, there were everywhere to be seen the generals, the officers of the King's household, and the great personages of the court in grand uniform. Charles X. set out from Rheims the morning of June 1, and the city, after some days of dazzling pomp, resumed its accustomed calm. Things had passed off well, and the monarch was fully satisfied.

The poets had tuned their lyres. Barthélemy, himself, the future author of the *Némésis*, celebrated in enthusiastic verses the monarchical and religious solemnity; Lamartine, future founder of the Second Republic, published *Le Chant du Sacre ou la Veillée des Armes;* Victor Hugo, the future idol of the democracy, sang his dithyrambic songs. Yet, in this concert of enthusiasm there were some discordant notes. Béranger circulated his ironic song *Le Sacre de Charles le Simple.*

As for Chateaubriand, the most illustrious of the royalist writers, he was to close his chapter of the *Mémoires d'outre-tombe* as follows:—

"So I have witnessed the last consecration of the successors of Clovis. I had brought it about by the pages in which in my pamphlet, *Le Roi est mort! Vive le Roi!* I had described it and solicited it. Not that I had the least faith in the ceremony, but as everything was wanting to legitimacy, it had to be sustained by every means, whatever it might be worth."

XVI

THE RE-ENTRANCE INTO PARIS

CHARLES X. made a solemn re-entrance into Paris, June 6, 1825. According to the *Moniteur*, Paris was divided between a lively desire for the day to come and fear that the weather, constantly rainy, should spoil the splendor of the royal pomp. At the barrier of La Villette there had been erected amphitheatres and a triumphal arch. The streets were hung with white flags and the arms of the sovereign, with the inscription: "Long live Charles X.! Long live our well-beloved King!" The Rue Saint Denis, the Rue du Roule, the Rue Saint Honoré, presented a picturesque spectacle. The merchants of these business streets had converted the façades of their houses into an exposition of the rich tissues of their shops, and the cortège was thus to traverse a sort of bazaar. What a pity if the rain was going to spoil so many fine preparations! By a good luck, on which every one congratulated himself, the weather in the morning ceased its gloomy look, and a merchant of the Rue Saint Denis inscribed on his balcony these two celebrated lines, —

"Nocte pluit tota, redeunt spectacula mane,
    Divisum imperium cum Jove Cæsar habet."

At 1 P.M. a salvo of one hundred and one guns announced the arrival of the monarch at the barrier of La Villette. The Prefect of the Seine addressed him an allocution and presented him the keys of the city. The King responded: "I feel a great satisfaction in re-entering these walls. I always recall with lively emotion the reception given me eleven years ago when I preceded the King, my brother. I return here, having received the holy unction that has given me new strength. I consecrate it all, and all that I have of life and all my resources, to the happiness of France. It is my firm resolve, gentlemen, and I give you the assurance of it."

The cortège then took up its march. It was formed of a squadron of gendarmerie, several squadrons of the lancers and cuirassiers of the royal guard, the mounted National Guard of Paris, the staff of the garrison and of the first military division, a numerous group of general and superior officers.

The Count d'Haussonville wrote on the subject:—

"I was in the cortège, and as the staff of the National Guard followed pretty close to the royal carriage, I had occasion to note how far below what had been hoped was the reception at the gate of La Villette, where a triumphal arch had been erected. Some groups, plainly soldiers, after the discourse of the Prefect of Paris and the response of the King, uttered some huzzas that found no echo. When we approached the boulevards, the public warmed up a little. The windows were lined with women, of whom the greater number waved their handkerchiefs in sign of welcome. Around Notre-Dame, whither the cortège proceeded on its way to the Tuileries, the crowd was enormous behind the line of soldiers charged with restraining it. There was nothing offensive in their remarks; neither was there any emotion or sympathy. The magnificence of the equipages and the costumes, the beauty of the military uniforms, particularly of the *corps d'élite*, such as the Hundred Swiss and the body-guard, were the only things spoken of. The spectators sought to guess and name to each other the prominent persons."

During the passage the King received bouquets offered him by the market men and women, as well as by a number of workmen's corporations preceded by their banners. At the entrance of the Cathedral he was congratulated by the Archbishop of Paris at the head of the clergy. A *Te Deum* was sung and the *Marche du Sacre* of Lesueur was played. Then the King returned to his carriage and directed his course to the Tuileries.

As the cortège drew near to the Château, the welcome grew more and more cordial. The balconies of many of the houses were draped. Women of the court, in rich toilet, threw bouquets and flowers to the King. The Count d'Haussonville says: —

"The untiring good grace with which the King returned the salutations of the crowd, and by gestures full of *bonhomie* and affability, responded to the cries of persons whom he recognized as he passed, added every moment to his personal success. In fact, when, June 6, 1825, at evening, he descended from the magnificent coronation coach, to mount the stairs of the palace of his fathers, Charles X. had reason to be content with the day. I doubt whether among the witnesses of the splendid fêtes that had followed without interruption at Rheims and at Paris, there were many who would not have been strongly surprised if there had been announced to them by what a catastrophe, in five years only, an end was to be put to the reign inaugurated under the happiest auspices."

The 8th of June, the city of Paris offered to the King a fête at which there were eight thousand guests. The sovereign made his entry, having the Dauphiness on his right, and on the left the Duchess of Berry, who opened the ball. A cantata was sung with words by Alexandre Soumet, and the music by Lesueur.

The 10th of June, the King went to the Opera with the Dauphin, the Dauphiness, and the Duchess of Berry. The back of the stage opened and showed, in an immense perspective, the most illustrious kings of France; at the farthest line were the statue of Henry IV., Paris, its monuments, the Louvre. The 19th of June, Charles X. again accompanied by the family went to the Théâtre-Italien. *Il viaggio a Reims* was played. *Le Moniteur*, apropos of this work, said:—

"It is an opera of a mould which, under the forms

of the *Opera buffa*, presents some ideas not destitute of comedy, in which homage of love and respect is at times expressed with an art that French taste cannot disavow. The author, M. Bellochi, has conceived the praiseworthy idea of introducing personages of all the nations of Europe, joining with the French in their prayers for the happiness of our country and of the august family that governs us. The composer is M. Rossini. The *morceaux* are worthy of the reputation of this celebrated master. Madame Pasta displayed all the resources of her admirable talent. Bouquets of roses and lilies were distributed to the ladies."

There was an endless series of fêtes, receptions, balls at court, at the houses of the ministers of the foreign ambassador, theatrical representations retracing the incidents of the coronation. The cities of the provinces imitated the example of Paris. All this movement stimulated business, and France appeared happy. But to an acute observer it was plain that the pomps of the coronation and the fêtes that followed it pleased the people of the court more than the *bourgeoisie*. The Count d'Haussonville says, apropos of the nobility at that time:—

"I had the feeling—educated as I was at college, and provided early with a sort of precocious experience, the precious fruit of public education—that the nobility was a world a little apart. I instinctively perceived how much the preoccupations of the persons with whom I was then passing my time were of a nature particular, special to their class, not opposed — that would be saying too much certainly — but a little foreign to the great currents that swayed the opinion of their contemporaries. They had their way of loving the King and their country which was not very comprehensible, nor even, perhaps, very acceptable, to the mass of the people and the *bourgeois* classes, who were rather inclined to remain cold or even sullen in the presence of certain manifestations of an ultra-royalism, the outward signs of which were not always at this time entirely circumspect."

To one regarding the horizon attentively there were already some dark spots on the bright azure of the heavens. The struggles of the rival classes of French society existed in a latent state. The white flag had not made the tricolor forgotten. Charles X., consecrated by an archbishop, did not efface the memory of Napoleon crowned by a pope, and beneath royalist France were pressing upward already Bonapartist France and Revolutionary France.

XVII

THE JUBILEE OF 1826

THE dominant quality of Charles X., his piety, was the one that was to be most used against him. There was in this piety nothing morose, hypocritical, fanatical, and not an idea of intolerance or persecution mingled with it. Conviction and feeling united in the heart of the King to inspire him with profound faith. In 1803, before the death-bed of a beloved woman, he had sworn to renounce earthly for divine love, and from that time he had kept his vow. The woman by whom this conversion was made was the sister-in-law of the Duchess of Polignac, Louise d'Esparbès, Viscountess of Polastron. The Duchess of Gontaut recounts in her unpublished Memoirs the touching and pathetic scene of the supreme adieu of this charming woman and of Charles X., then Count d'Artois. It was in England during the Emigration. The Viscountess of Polastron was dying with consumption, and the approach of the end reawakened in her all the piety of her childhood. A holy priest, the Abbé de Latil, demanded the departure of the Prince. "I implore Monseigneur," he said, "to go into the country; you shall see the poor penitent again; she herself desires it, having one word to say to you, one favor to ask, but it cannot be until at the moment of death."

The Prince, who, even at the time of his greatest errors, had never ceased to love and honor religion, obeyed the command of the priest. He awaited in cruel anguish the hour when he should be permitted to return. It was authorized only when death was very near. The Duchess of Gontaut says: —

"The doors of the salon were opened. Monsieur dared not approach; I was near the dying woman and held her hand; it was trembling. She perceived Monsieur. He was about to rush toward her. 'Come no nearer,' said the Abbé, in a firm voice. Monsieur did not venture to cross the threshold. The agitation redoubled; the agony increased. She raised her hands to heaven, and said: —

"'One favor, Monseigneur, one favor — live for God, all for God.'

"He fell upon his knees, and said: 'I swear it, God!' She said again, 'All for God!' Her head fell on my shoulder; this last word was her last breath: she was no more. Monsieur raised his arms to heaven, uttered a horrible cry: the door was closed."

The Count d'Artois was then but forty-five, but from that day he never gave occasion for the least scandal, and led an exemplary life. As Louis XIV. had held in profound esteem the courageous prelates who adjured him to break with his mistresses,

Charles X. was attached to the truly Christian priest who had converted him by the death-bed of the Viscountess of Polastron. The Abbé de Latil, the obscure ecclesiastic of the Emigration, became, under the Restoration, the Archbishop of Rheims and Cardinal. It was not without profound emotion that the very Christian King saw himself consecrated by the priest who twenty-two years before had caused him to return to virtue. This memory was imposed on the mind and heart of the monarch, and under the vault of the ancient Cathedral, he certainly thought of Madame de Polastron, as of a good angel, who, from the height of heaven, watched over him, and who, by her prayers, had aided him to traverse so many trials, to reach the religious triumph of the coronation.

Charles X. was happy then. Profoundly sincere in his ardent desire to make France happy, he believed himself at one with God and with his people, and rejoiced in that supreme good, so often wanting to sovereigns, — peace of heart. Could he be reproached for having taken the ceremony of his coronation seriously? A king who does not believe in his royalty is no more to be respected than a priest who does not believe in his religion. Charles X. was convinced, as the Archbishop of Rheims had said in his letter of 29th May, 1825, that kings exercise over their subjects the power of God Himself, and that they have that sacred majesty, upon which, in the fine expression of Bossuet, God, for the good of things human, causes to shine a portion of the splendor of divine majesty.

This disposition of mind in Charles X. fortified his piety, so that, at the time of the jubilee of 1826, he seized eagerly the opportunity to affirm his religious faith, and to return thanks to the God of his fathers, who at this epoch of his life was loading him with favors.

The jubilee is a time of penitence and pardon, when the Pope accords plenary indulgence to all Catholics who submit to certain practices and assist at certain pious ceremonies. The grand jubilee was formerly celebrated only once in a hundred years; afterwards it took place every fifty, and then every twenty-five years. 1825 was the time of its first celebration in the nineteenth century, and it drew to Rome that year more than ten thousand pilgrims. The Pope had celebrated the close of it the 24th of December, 1825, but yielding to the prayers of several Catholic powers, he accorded to them, by special bulls, the privilege of celebrating the same solemnity in 1826.

The opening of the French jubilee took place February 15, 1826, at Notre-Dame de Paris. The papal bull, borne on a rich cushion, was remitted to the Archbishop for public reading. The nuncio chanted the *Veni Creator*. Mass was said by the Cardinal, Prince of Croï, Archbishop of Rouen, Grand Almoner of France. The relics of the apostles Saint Peter and Saint Paul were borne around the Place du Parvis, in the midst of a cortège, in which were present the marshals of France, the generals, and the four princesses. The order of the Archbishop of Paris prescribed four general processions. The first took place with great pomp the 17th of March, 1826. The King and the royal family, the princes and princesses of the blood, all the court, the marshals, a multitude of high functionaries, peers of France, deputies, officers, assisted at this ceremony in which appeared the Archbishop of Paris and his grand vicars, the metropolitan chapter, the pupils of all the seminaries in surplice, the priests of all the Paris churches with their sacerdotal armaments. It was a veritable army of ecclesiastics that traversed the capital. In the midst of the cortège, the reliquary containing the relics of Saint Peter and Saint Paul was the object of the devotion of the faithful. Surrounded by the Dauphin, the Duke of Orleans, the young Duke of Chartres, the great officers of the crown, of the Hundred Swiss, and of the body-guard, Charles X., in a costume half religious, half military, walked between a double hedge formed by the royal guard and the troops of the line. The Place du Parvis-Notre-Dame was hung with draperies in fleur-de-lis, and all the streets to be traversed by the procession had been draped and sanded. The first stop of the cortège was under the peristyle of the Hotel-Dieu, where an altar had been erected; the second, at the Church of the Sorbonne; the third, at that of Sainte Geneviève. The two other processions had no less *éclat*, and their pauses being fixed in the churches of the principal parishes, they passed through the busiest and most populous quarters of Paris.

The fourth and last procession, that of the 3d of May, was the most important of all. It was to close by an expiatory ceremony in honor of Louis XVI., by the laying and benediction of the corner-stone of the monument voted by the Chamber of 1815, and which still awaited its foundation. It is at the very place where the unfortunate sovereign had been executed that the monument was to be constructed. The cortège left Notre-Dame and directed its course first to the Church of Saint-Germain-l'Auxerrois. The Chamber of Peers, the Chamber of Deputies, all the functionaries, all the authorities of the Department of the Seine, followed the King and Dauphin, who advanced, accompanied by the ministers, the marshals, the officers of their houses, *cordons bleus*, *cordons rouges*. Never since the end of the old régime had such a multitude of priests been seen defiling through the streets of Paris. The pupils of all the seminaries, the almoners of all the colleges, the priests of all the parishes and all the chapels, stretched out in an endless double line, at the end of which appeared the Nuncio of the Pope, Cardinals de Latil, de Croï, and de La Fare, the Archbishop of Paris, and a crowd of prelates. After the station of Saint-Germain-l'Auxerrois, there was a second at Saint-Roch, then a third and last at the Assumption.

When the special prayers of the close of the jubilee had been said at this last parish, the immense cortège resumed its march to the place where Louis XVI. had brought his head to the sacrilegious scaffold. The day chosen for the expiatory solemnity was the 3d of May, the anniversary of the return of Louis XVIII. to Paris in 1814, and then a political idea was connected with the religious ceremony. A vast pavilion surmounted by a cross hung with draperies in violet velvet, and enclosing an altar, which was reached on four sides by four stairways of ten steps each, occupied the very place where, the 10th of January, 1793, the scaffold of the Martyr-King had been erected, in the middle of the Place called successively the Place Louis XV. and the Place de La Concorde, and which was thenceforth to be called the Place Louis XVI.

The account in the *Moniteur* says: —

"A first salvo of artillery announced the arrival of the procession. It presented as imposing a tableau as could be contemplated. This old French nation — the heir of its sixty kings at the head — marched, preceded by the gifts made by Charlemagne to the Church of Paris, and the religious trophies that Saint Louis brought from the holy places. The priests ascend to the altar. Three times in succession they raise to heaven the cry for pardon and pity. All the spectators fall upon their knees. A profound, absolute silence reigns about the altar and over all the Place; a common sorrow overwhelms the people; the King's eyes are filled with tears."

In this multitude the absence of the Dauphiness, the daughter of Louis XVI., is remarked. The Orphan of the Temple had made it a law for herself never to cross the place where her father had perished. She went to the expiatory chapel of the Rue d'Anjou-Saint-Honoré, to pass in prayer the time of the ceremony.

M. de Vaulabelle makes this curious comparison: —

"Behind Charles X. there knelt his Grand Chamberlain, Prince Talleyrand, covered with gleaming embroideries, orders, and cordons. It was the ecclesiastical dignitary whom Paris had beheld celebrating the Mass of the Federation on the Champ-de-Mars, the wedded prelate who, as Minister of the Directory, had for some years observed as a national festival the anniversary of this same execution, now the subject of so many tears."

Religious people rejoiced at the ceremony that was celebrated; but the Voltairians and the enemies of royalty complained bitterly at the sight of the quays, the streets, the squares of the capital furrowed by long files of priests, chanting psalms and litanies, dragging devout in their suite the King, the two Chambers, the judiciary, the administration, and the army. Yet was it not just that Charles X. should cause an expiatory ceremony to be celebrated at the place where his unfortunate brother had been guillotined? Was not that for a pious sovereign the accomplishment of a sacred duty? It matters not;

there were those who reproached him with this homage to the most memorable of misfortunes. They would have forbidden to Charles X. the memory of Louis XVI. Yet a king could hardly be asked to have the sentiments of a *conventionnel*, of a regicide. In their systematic and bitter opposition, the adversaries of the Restoration imputed to the royal family as a crime its very virtues and its piety.

Charles X. was not unaware of this half-expressed hostility. That evening he wrote to M. Villèle, President of the Council of Ministers: —

"In general I have been content with the ceremony and the appearance of the people; but I wish to know the whole truth, and I charge you to see M. Delavau, and to know from him if the reality corresponds to appearances, if there was any talk against the government and the clergy. I wish to know all, and I trust to you to leave me in ignorance of nothing."

M. de Villèle was not a flatterer. He responded discreetly, but without concealing the truth: —

"The aspect of the people," he wrote, "permitted the thoughts agitating its spirit to be recognized. We were following the King at a slight distance and could judge very well of it. It was easy to read in all eyes that the people were hurt at seeing the King humbly following the priests. There was in that not so much irreligion as jealousy and animosity toward the rôle played by the clergy."

It might have been asked, in these circumstances, whether the criticisms of the opposition were just.

If a ceremony was to be observed, such as the laying and blessing the corner-stone of an expiatory monument, it must be religious. If it were religious, was not the presence of the clergy in large numbers natural?

At heart, there was something noble and touching in the thought of Charles X., and the true royalists sincerely respected it. From the monarchical point of view, a monument to Louis XVI. had much more *raison d'être* than the obelisk since erected in its place, which represents nothing, and has, moreover, the inconvenience of obstructing the fine perspective of the Champs Élysées and the Tuileries. But there were two camps in France, and these processions, expiations, prayers, which, according to the royalist journals, opened a new era of sanctity, glory, and virtue, exasperated the Voltairians. The opposition determined to make of the King's piety a weapon against royalty.

And yet, we repeat, this piety had nothing about it not worthy of respect. As the Abbé Védrenne remarks in his *Vie de Charles X.*, this Prince "had a perfect understanding of the duties and *convenances* of his rank, never refused his presence at fêtes where it was desirable, never seemed to blame or fear what a sensible indulgence did not condemn; he loved the charm of society, and increased it by his kindliness, but he was not dazzled by it. He remained to the end the most amiable prince in Europe, but he was also the severest. A surprising thing in a convert, his religion was always full of true charity for others. He excused those who neglected their Christian duties, remembering his delay in practising his own, without ever compromising his own beliefs. He sincerely respected the good faith of those who did not share them. This faith, this piety — a legacy from love — which he guarded so faithfully, was the consolation of his long misfortunes and the principle of his unchanging serenity. It banished even the idea of hatred from his heart. Never did any one forgive as he did."

It must not be forgotten that the pamphleteers and song-writers of the Restoration, violent, unjust, and even cruel as they were toward Charles X., never breathed an insinuation against the purity of his morals. His life was not less exemplary than that of his son, the Dauphin, or of his niece and daughter-in-law, the Orphan of the Temple. Despite the great piety of the sovereign, the court was not melancholy or morose. Charles X. had a foundation of benevolence and gaiety to his character. He was not surprised to see committed about him the gentle trespasses of love, of which he had been himself guilty in youth, and he had become — the very ideal of wisdom — severe for himself, indulgent for others.

XVIII

THE DUCHESS OF GONTAUT

THE Governess of the Children of France was the Viscountess of Gontaut, who, as a recompense for the manner in which she had accomplished her task, was made Duchess by Charles X. in 1826. Here is the opening of her unpublished Memoirs: —

"January, 1853. To Madame the Countess and Monsieur the Count Georges Esterhazy. My dear children, you have shown a desire to know the events of my long life. Wishing to teach them to your children, I yield to this amiable and tender purpose, promising myself, meanwhile, to resist the too common charm of talking pitilessly about myself. I shall search my memory for souvenirs of the revolutions I have often witnessed to give interest to my tales. One writes but ill at eighty, but one may claim indulgence from hearts to which one is devoted."

The amiable and intelligent octogenarian had no need of indulgence. Her Memoirs possess irresistible attraction, grace, exquisite naturalness, and we are convinced that when they are published — as they must be sooner or later — they will excite universal interest.

Born at Paris in 1773, the Duchess of Gontaut was the daughter of Count Montault-Navailles and of the Countess, *née* Coulommiers. All her memories of childhood and early youth were connected with the old court. She had seen Marie Antoinette in all her splendor, Versailles when it was most dazzling, and she was formed in the elegant manners of that charming world whose social prestige was so great. At seven she was held at the baptismal font by the Count of Provence (the future Louis XVIII.) and by the wife of this Prince.

"I had for this ceremony," she says, "a *grand habit* and a *grand panier*. I was so proud of them that I caused much amusement at the Queen's, whither my mother took me after the baptism. Being connected with the Duchess of Polignac, she often took me to Versailles; there I saw Madame Royale, younger than I, and the poor, little, handsome, delightful Dauphin. The Queen, wishing to give them a little fête, organized a children's spectacle, in which I was entrusted with a part. The piece chosen was *Iphigénie en Aulide*. Mademoiselle de Sabran and her brother, as well as a young Strogonoff, were, it is said, perfect actors. Armand de Polignac had a little part. Tragedy was not my *forte*. But in the second piece I achieved a little success, which the Chevalier de Boufflers was kind enough to celebrate in a very bright couplet, sung at the close. He gave me the name of the Little White Mouse. After that the Queen called me her little white mouse, and showed me a thousand kindnesses. After the play there was a children's supper; the princes waited on us and were much diverted by our enjoyment; Louis XVI. stood behind my chair for a moment, and even gave me a plate. The Queen sent me home in her sedan chair; footmen carried great torches; the body-guard presented arms to us. So much honor would, perhaps, have turned my head, but for my prudent mother who knew how to calm it."

The sorrows of exile followed rapidly on the first enchantments of life. It was in England, during the Emigration, that the future Governess of the Children of France married M. de Saint-Blanchard, Viscount de Gontaut-Biron. She was then residing at Epsom, where she lived on the proceeds of little pictures which she painted. She gave birth to twin daughters October 9th, 1796. "I nursed them both," she says, "our means not permitting us to have two nurses in one little household, and I felt strong enough for this double task. Brought into the world at seven and one-half months, their frail existence required my care night and day." In 1797, Madame de Gontaut visited Paris under a false name, and after this journey, on which she ran many risks, she returned to England, where she was the companion in exile of the princes. Monsieur, the Count d'Artois, the future Charles X., was then pursued by his creditors. The Castle of Holyrood, privileged by law, sheltered its occupants from all legal process. That is why the Prince Regent offered its hospitality to the brother of Louis XVIII., seeking in every way to soften the severity of the old palace.

"But the saying is true," adds Madame de Gontaut, "that there are no pleasant prisons. The Castle of Holyrood, as well as the park, was spacious. The governor visited there, and also several Scotch families, very agreeable socially. Monsieur could not 'leave the limits' except on Sunday, when the law allows no arrest. He had a carriage that he loaned to us, reserving it only for Sunday, when he was out from morning to night. To these excellent Scotch people a visit from him was an honor, a festival. Our little society comedies amused Monsieur as much as us; I always had, unluckily, a part that I never knew; I could never in my life learn anything by heart; I listened, filled my mind with the subject, and went ahead, to the great amusement of the audience and the despair of my fellow-players." After a while the suits against the Prince came to an end, and he could quit Holyrood, his debtor's prison.

Madame de Gontaut made a very good figure at Louis XVIII.'s little court at Hartwell. By her wit and her tact, she won the friendship of all the royal family, and much sympathy in high English society. She returned to France with Louis XVIII., and no lady of the court was regarded with greater respect. At the time of the marriage of the Duke of

Berry, she became lady companion to the new Duchess, whom she went to meet at Marseilles.

The King, Monsieur, the Duke and Duchess of Berry, all showed equal confidence in Madame de Gontaut, and her nomination as Governess of the Children of France was received with general approval and sympathy. A woman of mind and heart, she performed her task with as much zeal as intelligence, and though strict with her two pupils, she made herself beloved by them. She especially applied herself to guard them against the snares of flattery. On this subject she relates a characteristic anecdote. One day a family that had been recommended to her asked the favor of seeing, if only for a moment, the Duke of Bordeaux and his sister. The two children, vexed at having to leave their play, were not communicative, and nevertheless received an avalanche of compliments. The visitors were in ecstasy over their gentleness, their beauty. They admired even their hair. These exaggerations embarrassed the children, who were full of frankness and directness, and displeased Madame de Gontaut. She quickly closed the interview. As the visitors were going out, a half-open door allowed the little Prince and Princess to overhear their observations. "It was not worth while to come so far to see so little," said an old lady, in an irritated tone. "Oh, as to that, no," said a big boy, "they hardly had two words of response for all the compliments that papa and mamma strained themselves to give them. You made me laugh, papa, when you said, 'What fine color, what pretty hair!' She's as pale as an egg and cropped like a boy." — "That's true," said the old lady, "she needs your medicines, doctor; and then they are very small for their age." — "Did you see the governess?" resumed the big boy. "She did not seem pleased when you complimented her on the docility of her pupils, and I could see that they were teasing each other." The Duke of Bordeaux and his sister, who heard all this, were petrified. "They are very wicked!" they cried. "They are simply flatterers," replied Madame de Gontaut. Little Mademoiselle resumed: "After having praised us without end, and telling us a hundred times that we were pretty, — for I heard it all perfectly, — to want to give me medicine because I was so homely and ill-looking! Oh, this is too much! I know now what flattery is, — to say just the contrary of the truth. But it's a sin. I shall always remember it!"

Madame de Gontaut succeeded beyond her hopes in the task confided to her. Morally and physically the little Prince and Princess were accomplished children.

The moment was approaching when the Duke of Bordeaux, born September 20, 1820, was about to begin his seventh year. That was the period fixed by the ancient code of the House of France for the young Prince to pass from the hands of women to those of men, who were thereafter to direct his education. On the 15th of October, 1826, the transfer

THE DUKE OF BORDEAUX AND HIS SISTER.

was made of the Duke of Bordeaux to his governor, the Duke de Rivière, at the Chateau of Saint Cloud, in the Hall of the Throne, in the presence of all the members of the family, the first officers of the crown, etc. The child, brought by his governess before the King, was stripped of his clothing and examined by the physicians, who attested his perfect health. When he was clad again, the King called the new governor and said to him: "Duke de Rivière, I give you a great proof of my esteem and confidence in remitting to you the care of the child given us by Providence — the Child of France also. You will bring to these important functions, I am sure, a zeal and a prudence that will give you the right to my gratitude, to that of the family, and to that of France."

Charles X. then turned to Madame de Gontaut, whom he had just named Duchess in witness of his gratitude and satisfaction. "Duchess of Gontaut," he said, "I thank you for the care you have given to the education of this dear child." Then, pointing to Mademoiselle, "Continue and complete that of this child, who is just as dear to me, and you will acquire new claims on my gratitude." The little Princess then seized the hands of her governess with such effusion that the latter could hardly restrain her tears.

That evening the Duchess of Gontaut addressed to the Duke de Rivière a letter in which she depicted the character of the child she had brought up with such care: —

"I have always followed the impulses of my heart," she wrote, "in easily performing a task for which that was all that was needed. Monseigneur and Mademoiselle believe me blindly, for I have never deceived them, even in jest. A pleasantry that a child's mind cannot understand embarrasses him, destroys his ease and confidence, humiliates and even angers him, if he believes that he has been deceived. Monseigneur has more need than most children of this discretion. The directness and generosity of his character incline him to take everything seriously. When he thinks he sees that any one is being annoyed, the one oppressed straightway becomes the object of his lively interest; he will take up his defence warmly and will not spare his rebukes; he shows on these occasions an energy quite in contrast with the natural timidity of his character. With such a child, I have had to avoid even the shadow of injustice. He loves Mademoiselle, is gentle, kind, attentive to her. I have always carefully shunned for Their Royal Highnesses the little contests of childhood; however unimportant they may seem at first, they end by embittering the disposition."

We commend to mothers and teachers the letter of the Duchess of Gontaut. It is a veritable programme of education, conceived with high intelligence and great practical sense. What more just than this reflection: "The method of teaching by amusement is fashionable, and appears to me to lead to a very superficial education. That is not what I have sought.

Let the teacher explain readily, but let him allow the pupil to take some pains, for he must learn early the difficulties of life and how to overcome them. A child prince, exposed to flattery, runs the risk of thinking himself a prodigy. To obviate this Monseigneur and Mademoiselle have often been subjected to little competitions with children of their age. I have sought by this means to give them the habit of witnessing success without envy, and to gain it without vanity." And what a fine and noble thing is this. "I have tried on all occasions to lead the mind of Monseigneur to the moral teaching of religion; I have used it as a restraint; I have presented it as a hope."

The Duchess of Gontaut was proud of her pupil: —

"It will require time," she says, in this same letter, "kindness, and tenderness to gain the confidence of Monseigneur. His features show his soul; he talks little of what he undergoes; he has much sensibility, but a power over himself remarkable at his age; I have seen him suffer without complaint. The efforts that he has made to overcome a timidity that I have tried hard to conquer, have been noteworthy. I have been able to make him understand the necessity, for a prince, of addressing strangers in a noble, gracious, and intelligible fashion. I have always sought to remove all means and all pretext for concealing his faults; bashfulness leads imperceptibly to dissimulation and falsehood. I am happy in affirming that Monseigneur is scrupulously truthful.

I have believed it requisite, by reason of the vivacity of his disposition, and the high destiny awaiting him, to constrain him to reflect before acting. The word *justice* has a real charm for him; I have never seen a heart more loyal."

The woman who wrote these lines so firm and honest, so sensible and forcible, was no ordinary woman. In contrast with so many *émigrés* who had learned nothing and forgotten nothing, she had learned much and retained it. The difficulties and bitternesses of exile were an excellent school for her. She remained French always, — in ideas, tastes, feelings. Sincerely royalist, but with no exaggeration, she took account perfectly of the requirements of modern society. Very devoted to her princes, she knew how to tell them the truth. She spoke frankly to Charles X., whom she had known from an early day, and had seen in such diverse situations.

It is to be regretted that the King did not consult her oftener. She would have saved him from many errors, notably from the fatal ordinances which she disapproved. She was a woman not merely of heart, but of head. Her Memoirs are the more interesting, that not the least literary pretension mingles with their sincerity. They have a character of intimacy that doubles their charm. This talk of a venerable grandmother with her grandchildren is not only solid and instructive, it is agreeable and gracious, tender and touching.

XIX

THE THREE GOVERNORS

IN the space of three years, from 1826 to 1828, Charles X. named three governors for the Duke of Bordeaux. One, the Duke of Montmorency, never entered on his duties. The others were the Duke de Rivière and the Baron de Damas. The Duke of Montmorency was named in anticipation the 8th of January, 1826, although his task did not begin until the 29th of September. Mathieu de Montmorency, first Viscount and then Duke, was born in 1766. After having been through the war in America, he had adopted the ideas of Lafayette, and had been distinguished by his extreme liberalism. He took the oath of the *Jeu de Paume*, and was the first to give up the privileges derived from his birth on the celebrated night of the 4th of August. The 12th of July, 1791, he was one of the deputation that attended the solemn transfer of the ashes of Voltaire, and, August 27th, he sustained the proposition to decree the honors of the Panthéon to Jean Jacques Rousseau. In his *Petit Almanach des Grands Hommes de la Révolution*, Rivarol wrote, not without irony: —

"The most youthful talent of the Assembly, he is

still stammering his patriotism, but he already manages to make it understood, and the Republic sees in him all it wishes to see. It was necessary that Montmorency should appear popular for the Revolution to be complete, and a child alone could set this great example. The little Montmorency therefore devoted himself to the esteem of the moment, and combated aristocracy under the ferrule of the Abbé Sieyès."

Mathieu de Montmorency did not adhere to his revolutionary ideas. After the 10th of August, 1792, he withdrew to Switzerland, at Coppet, near his friend Madame de Staël. Under the Empire he held himself apart. He had become as conservative as he had been liberal, as religious as he had been Voltairian. Under the Restoration, he was one of the most convinced supporters of the throne and the altar. Minister of Foreign Affairs in 1821, he showed himself a distinguished diplomat, and during the session of 1822 made the *amende honorable* for what he called his former errors.

As he had always been sincere in his successive opinions, the Duke of Montmorency deserved general esteem. His profound piety, his unchanging gentleness, his exhaustless charity, made him a veritable saint. He was the complete type of the Christian nobleman. His name, his character, the very features of his countenance, were all in perfect harmony. The adversaries of the Revolution could not refrain from honoring this good man. On receiving the title of governor to the Duke of Bordeaux, he felt rewarded for the devotion and virtue of his whole life. But he regarded this grave employment as a heavy burden, "an immense and formidable honor, the terror of his feebleness, and the perpetual occupation of his conscience." This was the thought expressed in his reception discourse at the French Academy. The Count Daru replied to him. At the same session M. de Chateaubriand read a historic fragment. It was the first time since leaving the ministry that the celebrated writer had appeared in public, and he chose to do so to adorn the triumph of him whose rival he had been.

The Duke Mathieu de Montmorency died six months before he was to enter upon his functions as governor to the Duke of Bordeaux. It was Good Friday of the year 1826, at three o'clock in the afternoon. Before the tomb in the Church of Saint Thomas Aquinas, his parish, the Duke was praying like a saint, when suddenly he was seen to waver, and then to fall. Those near him ran to him, raised him; he was dead. The news had hardly spread when the church was filled with a crowd of poor people, who wept hot tears over the loss of their benefactor. On the morrow the Duchess of Broglie wrote to Madame Récamier, for whom the deceased had had an almost mystic tenderness: —

"Holy Saturday. Oh, my God! my God! dear friend, what an event! I think of you with anguish. All the past comes up before me. I thought I could see the grief of my poor mother, and I think of yours, my dear friend, which must be terrible. But what a beautiful death! Thus he would have chosen it — the place, the day, the hour! The hand of God, of that saviour God, whose sacrifice he was celebrating, is here!"

Father Macarthy said, in a sermon preached in the Chapel of the Tuileries: —

"Happy he, O God, who comes before Thy altar, on the day of Thy death, at the very hour when Thou didst expire for the salvation of the world, to breathe out his soul at Thy feet, and be laid in Thy tomb!"

Lastly, the Duke de Laval-Montmorency wrote to Madame Récamier: —

"I say it to you, my dear friend, I avow it without false modesty, I never have had any merit or any honor in life, save from action in common with my angelic friend. He alone is happy; he is so beyond doubt; from heaven he sees our tears, our desolation, our homage; he will be our protector on high as he was our friend, our support, upon the earth."

The death of the virtuous Duke caused Charles X. great grief. He said: "There are in me two persons, the king and the man, and I know not which is the most affected."

M. de Chateaubriand desired — and the desire was quite natural — to replace the Duke of Montmorency in the office of governor of the Duke of Bordeaux, but the wish was not gratified. In his *Life of Henry of France*, M. de Pène makes the following reflections on this point: —

"Chateaubriand lacked neither the knowledge nor the virtue to be the Fénelon of a new Duke of Burgundy. The *éclat* of his literary renown, the political sense of which he had given proof in the Spanish war, the popularity that surrounded him, were certainly arguments in his favor. But looking at things coolly, it was clear that an irregular genius was not suited for the part of Mentor, when he still had all the wayward impulses of Télémaque."

The choice of Charles X. fell on one of his oldest and most faithful friends, the Lieutenant-General Duke Charles de Rivière. He was a soldier of great valor, of gentle disposition, full of modesty and kindness, believing devoutly and practising the Christian religion, a descendant of those old knights who joined in one love, God, France, and the King.

Born the 17th of December, 1763, M. de Rivière had been the companion and servitor of the princes in exile and misfortune, and they had confided to him the most difficult and dangerous missions. He was secretly in France in 1794, and was arrested and condemned to death as implicated in the Cadoudal case. At his trial, he was shown, at a distance, the portrait of the Count d'Artois, and asked if he recognized it. He asked to see it nearer, and then having it in his hands, he said, looking at the president: "Do you suppose that even from afar I did not recognize it? But I wished to see it nearer once more before I die." And the martyr of royalty religiously kissed the image of his dear prince.

Josephine intervened, and secured the commutation of the sentence, as well as that of the Duke Armand de Polignac. Napoleon, who admired men of force, caused to be offered to M. de Rivière his complete pardon, and a regiment or a diplomatic post, at choice. The inflexible royalist preferred to be sent to the fort of Joux, where Toussaint Louverture had died, and remained a prisoner up to the time of the marriage of the Empress Marie Louise.

Under the Restoration, M. de Rivière, who was Marquis and was made Duke only in 1825, became lieutenant-general, Peer of France, ambassador at Constantinople, captain of the body-guards of Monsieur. At the time of his accession, Charles X. did for his faithful servitor what had never before been done; he created for him a fifth company of the King's body-guards. "My dear Rivière," he said, "I have done my best for you, but we shall both lose by it; you used to guard me all the time, now you can guard me but three months in the year." The 30th of May, 1825, the morrow of the coronation and the day of the reception of the Knights of the Holy Spirit, Charles X. conferred the title of duke on his devoted friend. "By the way, Rivière, I have made you a duke." It recalled the words of Henry IV. to Sully in like circumstances.

When he chose the Duke de Rivière as governor of the Duke of Bordeaux, the King said to Madame de Gontaut: "In naming Rivière, I have followed, I confess, the inclinations of my heart; I am under obligations to him; he has incessantly exposed himself for our cause; he has borne captivity, poverty; I love him, and I am used to him."

The new governor, who was very modest, was frightened at the task confided to him.

"You congratulate me," he wrote to a friend; "console me, rather, pity me. An employment so grave must be a heavy burden. I am easy about the instruction my royal pupil will receive; the wise prelate named by the King as his preceptor will be a powerful auxiliary for me. But my share is still too great. It requires something more than fidelity for such a place, — firmness without roughness, unlimited patience, address, intelligence. I am frightened at the mission I have to fill. I begged the King to release me. He insisted. I asked him to make it a command; he replied: 'I will not command you, but you will give me great pleasure.' I did not conceal from the King that I should have preferred to remain captain of his guards; he answered: 'Well, you made that place for yourself; make this for me.' How could one resist such language from the lips of such a prince? There was but one choice to make, — to do all that he wished."

Charles X. named as sub-governors two distinguished military men, the Colonel Marquis de Barbançois and the Lieutenant-Colonel Count de Maupas. He named as preceptor Mgr. Tharin, Bishop of Strasbourg, and as sub-preceptor the Abbé Martin de Noirlieu and M. de Barande. The Bishop of Strasbourg was a pious and learned priest, of great benevolence and extreme affability. But his appointment exasperated the Opposition, because he had formerly taken up the defence of the Order of the Jesuits against the attacks of M. de Montlosier. All the liberal sheets cried aloud. *Le Journal des Débats*, furious that its candidate to the succession of the Duke de Montmorency, M. de Chateaubriand, had not been named, wrote, regarding the appointment of Mgr. Tharin:—

"Such imprudence amazes, such blindness is pitiable. It awakens profound grief to see this chariot rush toward the abyss with no power to restrain it."

The Duke de Rivière gave himself up entirely to the task confided to him. He never quitted the young prince. He slept in his room and watched over him night and day. In the month of February, 1828, he fell ill. The princes and princesses visited him frequently. The sovereign himself, putting aside for this faithful friend the etiquette which forbade him to visit any one out of his own family, went constantly to see him and remained long with him. The Duke had no greater consolation, after that of his religion, than the visit of his King. He said to his family as the hour of the expected visit approached, "Do not let me sleep," and if he felt himself getting drowsy, "For pity's sake," he said, "awaken me if the King comes; it is the best remedy for my pains." Charles X. could hardly restrain his tears; on leaving the room he gave way to his grief. The little Duke of Bordeaux, also, was much saddened.

One day, when he was told that the sick man had passed a bad night, he said to his sister: "Let's play plays that don't amuse us to-day."

Another day, when it was reported that his governor was a little better: "In that case," he cried, "general illumination," and he went in broad day, and lighted all the candles in the salon. The Duke de Rivière died the 21st of April, 1828; by order of the King, his son lived from that time with the Duke of Bordeaux, and received lessons from the preceptors of the young Prince.

The Liberals wished the successor of the Duke to be one of their choice. They maintained that the son of France belonged to the nation, and that it had too much interest in his education to permit the parents alone to dispose of it, as in ordinary families. The ministry wished to be consulted. Charles X. replied that he took counsel with his ministers in all that concerned the public administration, but that he should maintain his liberty as father of a family in the choice of masters for his grandson.

The King named the Lieutenant-General Baron de Damas (born in 1785, died in 1858). He was a brave soldier and a good Christian. M. de Lamartine said that he had "integrity, obstinate industry, virtue incorruptible by the air of courts, patriotic purpose, cool impartiality, but no presence and no brilliancy," and that "his piety was as loyal and disinterested as his heart." He had been Minister of War, and of Foreign Affairs, and distinguished himself under the Duke of Angoulême, during the Spanish Expedition. But under the Revolution and the Empire, he had served in the Russian army, and this did not render him popular. The Abbé Védrenne, in his *Vie de Charles X.*, wrote: —

"To watch over the person of the son of France, not quitting him night or day; to make sure that the rules of his education are followed in the employment of his time, in the routine of his lessons; to let no one save persons worthy of confidence come near him; to ward off all dangers, and notify the King of the least indisposition, — such is the duty of the governor. It requires more prudence than learning, more probity than genius. M. de Damas was a royalist too tried, too fervent a Christian, for his nomination not to provoke many murmurs. His place, moreover, had been desired by so many people, that there was no lack of those who were displeased and jealous. There was a general outcry over his incapacity and ignorance. One would have thought that he was to perform the task of a Bossuet and a Fénelon, while in reality he filled the place of a Montausier or a Beauvilliers. Had he not their virtues, and especially their devotion?"

The Duchess of Gontaut thus relates the first interview of the young Prince with his new governor: "Monseigneur was a little intimidated, when the Baron, coming up near to him, made a profound bow, and said: 'Monseigneur, I commend myself to you.' To which Monseigneur, not knowing what to say, said nothing, and as no one spake a word, the King dismissed us. When the Duke of Bordeaux learned that M. de Damas had six or seven boys nearly his age and only one girl, and that the girl would not be any trouble, his gaiety returned." The little Prince got used to his new governor, who had the most solid qualities, and who performed his task with the same devotion and zeal as his predecessor.

XX

THE REVIEW OF THE NATIONAL GUARD

CHARLES X. was always much beloved by the court, but less so by the city. In vain, in his promenades, he sought the salutations of the crowd, and exerted himself by his affability to provoke acclamations; the public remained cold, and the monarch returned to the Tuileries, saddened by a change in his reception which he charged to the tactics of the liberal party and the calumnies of the journals. The anti-religious opposition went on increasing, and tried to persuade the crowd that the King was aiming at nothing less than placing his kingdom under the direction of the Jesuits.

The person of the sovereign was still respected, but the men who had his confidence were the object of the most violent criticisms. A coalition of the Extremists and the Left fought savagely against the Villèle ministry, which was reproached particularly for its long duration.

From 1827, Orleansism, which Charles X. did not even suspect, existed in a latent state, and sagacious observers could perceive the dangers of the near future. A review of the National Guard of Paris was a forerunner of them.

Each year the 12th of April, the anniversary of the re-entrance of Monsieur to Paris in 1814, the National Guard alone was on duty at the Tuileries. This privilege was looked upon as the reward of the devotion it had then shown to the Prince, whose sole armed force it was for several weeks. In 1827, the 12th of April fell on Holy Thursday, a day given over wholly by the sovereign to his religious duties. In consequence, he decided that the day of exceptional service reserved to the National Guard should be postponed to Monday, the 16th. The morning of that day, detachments from all the legions, including the cavalry, assembled in the court of the Château, and were received by Charles X. He received a warm welcome, such as he had not been used to for a long time, and the crowd joined its shouts to the huzzas of the Guard. Charles X., filled with delight, said to the officers who joined him as the troops filed by: "I regret that the entire National Guard is not assembled for the review." Then the officers replied that their comrades would be only too happy if the King would consent to review the whole Guard. Marshal Oudinot, Duke of Reggio, who was the commandant-in-chief, warmly supported this desire, and the sovereign responded by promising for April 29 the review thus urged.

Charles X. believed he had returned to the pleasant time of his popularity. He wished to confirm it by withdrawing a law as to the press, proposed in the Chambers, and which, though called by the ultras a "law of love and justice," encountered bitter opposition even in the Chamber of Peers. The law was withdrawn April 17, the very day that the *Moniteur* announced the promise given the day before for the review of the 29th. On learning of the withdrawal of the unpopular law, the liberals uttered cries of joy and triumph. Columns of working printers traversed the streets with cries of " Long live the King ! Long live the Chamber of Peers ! Long live the liberty of the press ! " In the evening Paris was illuminated. A victory over a foreign foe would not have been celebrated with greater transports of enthusiasm. The ministry was disquieted by these wild manifestations of delight, which, in reality, were directed against it. It tried in vain to induce the King to countermand the review of the 29th. M. de Chateaubriand wrote to Charles X. a long letter to beg him to change his ministry. It contained the following passage : —

"Sire, it is false that there is, as is said, a republican faction at present, but it is true that there are partisans of an illegitimate monarchy; now these latter are too adroit not to profit by the occasion, and mingle their voices on the 29th with that of France, to impose on the nation. What will the King do? Will he surrender his ministers to the popular demand? That would be to destroy the power of the State. Will he keep his ministers? They will cause all the unpopularity that pursues them to fall on the head of their august master."

Chateaubriand closed as follows: —

"Sire, to dare to write you this letter, I must be strongly persuaded of the necessity of reaching a decision. An imperative duty must urge me. The ministers are my enemies. As a Christian I forgive them, as a man I can never pardon them. In this position I should never have addressed the King, if the safety of the monarchy were not involved."

All this urging was futile. Charles X. did not change his ministry, and the review took place on the Champ-de-Mars on the day appointed.

It is Sunday, April 29th, 1827. The weather is magnificent. The springtime sun gives to the capital a festive air. All the people are out. The twelve legions and the mounted guards — more than twenty thousand men — are under arms awaiting the King on the Champ-de-Mars. An enormous crowd occupies the slope. At one o'clock precisely, Charles X., mounted on a beautiful horse, which he manages like a skilled horseman, leaves the Tuileries with a numerous escort, including the Dauphin, the Duke of Orleans, the young Duke of Chartres, and a number of generals. The princesses follow in an open calèche. Everything appears to be going perfectly. The National Guards have pledged themselves to satisfy the King by their conduct. A note has been read in the ranks in these words: "Caution to the National Guards, to be circulated to the very last file. The rumor is spread that the National Guards intend to cry 'Down with the ministers! Down with the Jesuits!' Only mischief-makers can wish to see the National Guard abandon its noble character."

A general movement of curiosity on the Champ-de-Mars is noticed. Charles X. arrives. He has a serene brow, a smile upon his lips. It hardly seems possible that before the end of the year he will be a septuagenarian; he would be taken for a man of fifty, powdered. An immense cry of "Long live the King," raised by the National Guards, is repeated by the crowd. The monarch, radiant, salutes with glance and hand.

He passes along the front of the battalions. Here and there are heard cries of "Hurrah for the Charter! Hurrah for liberty of the press!" But they are drowned by those of "Long live the King!" Everything seems to go as he wishes, and Charles X. feels that the review, which his timid ministers regarded as dangerous, is an inspiration. So far it is for him only a triumph. But suddenly, as he appears in front of the Seventh Legion, he remarks the persistence with which a group of the Guards is crying, "Hurrah for the Charter!" The monarch perceives a sentiment of unfriendliness. A National Guardsman ventures to speak: —

"Does Your Majesty think that cheers for the Charter are an outrage?"— "Gentlemen," responds the King in a severe tone, "I came here to receive homage, not a lesson." The royal pride of this response had a good effect. The cries of "Long live the King!" are renewed with energy. The face of Charles X. again becomes calm and serene. Seated in his saddle before the Military School, the sovereign sees file by the twelve legions, with unanimous cheers. The review closed, the King says to Marshal Oudinot, commandant-in-chief of the National Guard : " It might have passed off better ; there were some mar-plots, but the mass is good, and on the whole, I am satisfied."

The Marshal asks, if, in the order of the day he may mention the satisfaction of the King. " Yes," replied Charles X., "but I wish to know the terms in which this sentiment is expressed."

The sovereign returns on horseback to the Tuileries, while each legion goes to its own quarter. When he arrives at the Pavillon de l'Horloge, he is received by his two grandchildren. Mademoiselle throws herself upon his neck : " *Bon-papa*, you are content, aren't you ? " — " Yes, almost," he answers. The Count de Bourbon-Busset, who is in the sovereign's suite, says to the Duchess of Gontaut, his mother-in-law, that all has passed off well. The Duchess of Angoulême, who has just alighted from her carriage, as well as the Duchess of Berry, hears this phrase ; she cries : " You are not hard to please." The two princesses are as agitated as the King is calm. At the moment of their return they have been greeted with violent cries of " Down with the ministers ! Down with the Jesuits ! " It is even said that there was a cry of " Down with the Jesuitesses ! "

The clang of arms rendered these violent clamors more sinister. The daughter of Louis XVI. and the widow of the Duke of Berry believed themselves doubly insulted as women and as princesses. The Duchess of Angoulême, with intrepid countenance, but deeply irritated, trembled with indignation. It seemed to her that the Revolution was being revived. The scenes of horror that her uncle Charles X. had not beheld, but of which she had been the witness and the victim, arose before her again, — the 5th and the 6th of October, 1789, the 20th of June, and the 10th of August, 1792.

While the Dauphiness gives herself up to the gloomiest reflections, the Third Legion of the National Guard is passing under the windows of the Minister of Finance in the Rue de Rivoli. The minister, M. de Villèle, has passed the day at the ministry, receiving from hour to hour news of the review. The blinds of his windows are closed. At the moment when the Third Legion files through the street, the band ceases to play, the drums stop beating. Cries of fury break from the ranks: "Down with the ministers! Down with the Jesuits! Down with Villèle!" The guards brandish their arms; the officers themselves make menacing gestures; the tumult is at its height. M. de Villèle, on the inside, follows from window to window the march of the legion, and so traverses the salons to the apartments occupied by his old mother and her family, whom he wishes to reassure by his own calm. Opposite the ministry, a great crowd fills the Terrasse des Feuillants, without taking part in the manifestation. But the clamors of the National Guards increase. They continue their march, enter the Rue Castiglione, reach the Place Vendôme, where the Ministry of Justice is situated, and recommence their cries: "Down with the ministers! Down with the Jesuits! Down with Peyronnet!"

Invited to dine by Count Opponyi, ambassador of Austria, with all the ministers, M. de Villèle waits to the last moment before going to the Embassy, still believing that he will be summoned by the King. As his waiting is in vain, he goes to the house of Count Opponyi and takes part in the dinner. At dessert, a messenger of Charles X. glides behind his chair, and says to him in a low voice: "The King charges me to tell you to come to him immediately." M. de Villèle takes leave of the ambassadress, and sets out for the Tuileries. He finds Charles X. there, very calm, quite reassured, and having called him only to give expression to his confidence and sympathy. The minister exerts himself to make the sovereign see the situation in a very different light. He represents the incident of the Minister of Finance as secondary, but insists on the facts occurring at the Champ-de-Mars, notably the shouts around the carriage of the princesses. "It is a fact," replies the King. "I did hear them complain. Well, what do you advise me to do?" The minister responds: "This very evening, before the bureaux are closed, dissolve the National Guard of Paris; order the marshal on duty near your person, to have the posts held by the National Guard occupied at four o'clock in the morning by the troops of the line; to resort to this measure of force and justice to forestall the consequences of the most audacious attempt at revolution since the commencement of your reign. To-morrow, there are to arrive at Paris fifteen thousand men to replace the fifteen thousand of the actual garrison. It suffices to retain these latter, and thirty thousand men will be enough to hold the factions in check if they have the least intention of rising." — "Very well," resumes Charles X.; "go and consult your colleagues, and return after the soirée that I shall attend with the Duchess of Berry."

This soirée is a concert given by the Duchess at the Tuileries. The music is but little heard. The incidents of the review are the subject of all conversation. The courtiers wonder whether, to please the King, they should take a dark or a rose-colored view of things. The optimists and pessimists exchange impressions. Charles X. seems to lean to the former. "Apparently," he says, with his habitual *bonhomie*, "my bad ear has done me a friendly service, and I am glad of it, for I protest I heard no insults." Plainly it costs the sovereign pain to dismiss the National Guard. It gave him so brilliant a welcome in 1814. He was its generalissimo under the reign of Louis XVIII. He has liked to wear its uniform, the blue coat with broad fringes of silver that becomes him so well. But the ministers, except the

Duke of Doudeauville and M. de Chabrol, pronounce strongly in favor of disbandment. Their idea prevails. After the concert Charles X. signs the decree, which appears in the *Moniteur* on the morrow, and is enforced without resistance. "The King can do anything!" cries the Duke de Rivière, with enthusiasm; and May 6th M. de Villèle addresses to the Prince de Polignac, then ambassador at London, a letter in which he says: "The dissolution of the National Guard has been a complete success; the bad have been confounded by it, the good encouraged. Paris has never been more calm than since this act of severity, justice, and vigor." The monarchy thinks itself saved; it is lost.

XXI

THE FIRST DISQUIETUDE

THERE were still great illusions among those about Charles X., and the Duchess of Berry had not for a single instant an idea that the rights of her son could be compromised. They persuaded themselves that the Opposition would remain dynastic and that the severest crises would end only in a change of ministry. Nevertheless, even at the court, the more thoughtful began to be anxious, and perceived many dark points on the horizon. Certain royalists, enlightened by experience of the Emigration and Exile, had a presentiment that the Restoration would be for them only a halt in the long way of catastrophes and sorrow. They mourned the optimist tranquillity in which some of the courtiers succeeded in lulling the King. There were courageous and faithful servitors who, at the risk of displeasing their master and losing his good graces, did not recoil from the sad obligation of telling him the whole truth. From the beginning of his reign, Charles X. heard useful warnings, and later he blamed himself for not having listened better to them. This justice, however, must be done him, that if he had not the wisdom to profit by such counsels, he never was offended at the men of heart who dared to give them to him.

In this number was the Viscount Sosthènes de La Rochefoucauld, son of the Duke of Doudeauville, son-in-law of Mathieu de Montmorency, charged with the department of the fine arts, at the ministry of the King's household. In publishing the reports addressed by him to Charles X. from his accession to the Revolution of 1830, he writes: —

"These are respectful and tender warnings of which too little account was taken, and which might have saved the King and France. I put them down here with the gloomy predictions contained in them, which have been only too completely realized. They are not prophecies after the event. We saw in advance the misfortunes of the King, the fall of the monarchy, the ruin of legitimacy. Each page, then each line, and soon every word of this part of my Memoirs will be a cry of alarm: 'God save the King!' Alas! He has not saved him. One is always wrong if one cannot get a hearing and make one's self believed. It is then, with no pride in my previsions, but with bitter regret, that I could not get them accepted, that I recall this long monologue addressed to Charles X."

From the beginning of the reign, as he foresaw that one day the Chamber would sign the Address of the 221, and that M. Laffitte would be the banker of the revolution of July, the Viscount wrote to the sovereign in December, 1824: —

"The King has two things to combat for the glory and strength of his rule, the encroachments of the Chamber of Deputies, and the power of money in Europe. Four bankers could to-day decide war, if such was their pleasure. Sovereigns cannot seek too earnestly to free themselves from the sceptre which is rising above their own. The triumph of moneyed men will blight the character and the morals of France."

M. de La Rochefoucauld added (report of January 31, 1825) this prediction, which shows to what length his frankness went in his loyal explanations with his King: —

"We are between two rocks, equally dangerous: revolution with the Duke of Orleans, and ultraism with the good Polignac. The by-word now is: 'These princes will end like the Stuarts.' Madame de ——, who is agitating against the laws now under discussion, has said: 'Yes, it's the second throne of the Stuarts.' The Left compare the Archbishop of Rheims to Father Peters, the restless and ambitious confessor of King James. It is not easy for me to write thus to the King, and I have assumed a hard task in promising myself to conceal nothing from him. Sometimes my heart is oppressed and my hand stops; but I question my conscience, which seems troubled, and the indispensable necessity of telling all to the King, that he may judge in his wisdom, decides me to go on."

How many sagacious warnings given by the brave

courtier, or, better, by the faithful friend, during the year 1825, the year of the coronation: "The good Madame de M—— of the Sacred Heart was saying the other day: 'We had a King with no limbs, and with a head; now we have limbs and no head.' It is unheard of, the trouble taken in certain circles to make out that the King has no will. The future must give to all a complete refutation; the future must teach them that the King knows how to distinguish those that betray from those that serve him." (Report of March 1, 1825). "Does the King wish to run the chances of a complete overturning by throwing himself into the hands of the ultras? That would be to fall again under the blows of the Revolution, which counts on these to push the monarchy into the abyss always held open at its side."

From 1825, criticism of the King began. He was accused of giving himself up too much to the pleasures of the chase. The time was approaching when his enemies would say of him — a cruel play on words: "He's good for nothing but to hunt," and would translate the four letters over the doors of houses M. A. C. L. (*maison assurée contre l'incendie*) by this phrase: *Mes amis, chassons-le.*

The 17th of June, 1825, M. de La Rochefoucauld wrote: —

"I must tell all to the King. I have prevented the giving of a play at the Odéon called *Robin des Bois* (Robin Hood), because it is a nickname criminally given by the people to him whom they accuse of hunting too often, an accusation very unjust in the eyes of those who know that never did a prince work more than he to whom allusion is made. When the King takes this distraction so necessary to him, why hasten to make it known to the public? All news comes from the Château, and the *Constitutionnel* and the *Quotidienne* are always the best informed."

He returned to the same subject October 6 : —

"I am in despair at seeing the journals recounting hunt after hunt. I know the effect that produces. I wanted to get at the source of these mischievous reports, and M—— communicated to me confidentially that these reports came to him from the court, and at such length that he always cut them down three-fourths. In this case, it is for the King to give orders."

Let us put beside this report the following passage from the Memoirs of the Duke of Doudeauville : —

"I must justify Charles X. in this passion for the chase, so bitterly laid up against him in that time when malice and bad faith seized on everything that could injure him. Five whole days every week he remained in his apartment, busy with affairs of state, working with the ministers, examining by himself their different reports with a sensitive heart, much soul, and more intellect than had been believed; he had much reason and a very sound judgment. We were often astonished at it in the Council, over which he presided, and which he prolonged two, three, four, and five hours, without permitting himself the least distraction or showing any sign of weariness. Often, in the most difficult discussions, he would open up an opinion that no one had conceived, and which, full of sagacity, smoothed every difficulty.

"Twice a week, and often only once, when the weather permitted, he went hunting, perhaps gunning, perhaps coursing. It will be conceded that it was a necessary exercise after such assiduous toil and occupations so sedentary.

"I certify that this was the extent of the hunting of which calumny, to ruin him, made a crime. Every time he went hunting, the Opposition journals did not fail to announce it, which persuaded nearly all France that he passed all his time in the distractions of this amusement."

The tide of detraction of the sovereign steadily rose. The Viscount de La Rochefoucauld perceived it clearly. He wrote to the King, 13th October, 1825:—

"The interior of France, as regards commerce, agriculture, industry, wealth, offers a most striking spectacle. Let Charles X., as King and father, rejoice in his work; but let him reflect that the lightest sleep would be followed by a terrible awakening."

The 12th of January, 1826, when his father-in-law, the Duke Mathieu de Montmorency, had just been named governor to the Duke of Bordeaux, M. de La Rochefoucauld again wrote to the King:—

"Shall I thank the King for the nomination of

M. de Montmorency? Six months ago, it would have been useful. To-day, it is merely good. But alas, how far is that interesting Prince from the crown! and what shocks and revolutions he must traverse first. If ever — God watch over France; the Orleans are making frightful progress."

The signs of the coming storm accumulated in the most alarming manner. Read this other report of the Viscount de La Rochefoucauld (August 8, 1826): —

"Indifference to religion, hatred of the priests, were the symptoms of the Revolution. God grant that the same things do not bring the same results. The unfortunate priests no longer dare to go through the streets; they are everywhere insulted. Three days since, a well-dressed man, passing by the sentinel of the Luxembourg said to him, pointing to a priest: 'Never mind; in a year you'll see no more of all these wretches.' The poor Curé of Clichy was in real danger, surrounded by two or three hundred madmen, who cried; 'Down with the black-hats!' Every day there is a scene of the same sort."

The popularity of Charles X., so great at the beginning of his reign, was dwindling every day at Paris. M. de La Rochefoucauld did not fear to declare it to him.

"By what inconceivable fatality is it," he wrote, February 6, 1827, "that the king amid all the care he takes to ensure the happiness of his people, is losing from day to day in their love and affection?

At the play — and it is there, to use an expression of Napoleon, that the pulse of public opinion is to be felt — the most seditious and hostile allusions are eagerly caught up. Saturday last, verses, of which the sense was that kings who have lost the love of their people encounter only silence and coldness, were greeted with triple applause and furiously encored."

The report of May 12, 1827, was like an alarm bell:

"Circumstances are so grave that the calmest minds betray fear regarding them; there are now but one opinion and one feeling, — doubt and fear. It is said openly, as eight years since: This branch cannot keep the crown; it is impossible; who will succeed it? How many things, great Heavens, done in eight years; how many things forgotten!"

Exposed to an outpouring of enmities and of incessant intrigues, taken between two fires, — the extreme Right and the Left, — M. de Villèle no longer had the strength to govern. His ministry was about to come to an end. Later, in retracing in his journal this phase of his career, he wrote: —

"All that took place was of a feebleness destructive of all government, and disheartening for him who bears all the responsibility for it, with the weight of affairs besides. But he was not, and did not pretend to be, the Cardinal Richelieu. He had not his character, nor his ambition, nor his superior gifts. He did not even envy them. Had he been quite different in this regard, to repress and annul his king, to oppress the daughter of Louis XVI. and the widow of the Duke of Berry, to exile from France the new Gaston d'Orléans, and his numerous family, to bring down the heads of the court pygmies,—more dangerous, perhaps, with their influence over the King and his family and their vexatious intrigues in the Court of Peers than the Montmorencys and the Cinq-Mars,— this was a rôle to which he never aspired and would not have accepted."

Charles X. sacrificed M. de Villèle, who, however, had his sympathy, and replaced him with a liberal minister, perhaps with a mental reservation as to a ministry, before long, from the extreme Right. The retiring minister wished to remain in the Chamber of Deputies, to defend his acts. For their part, his successors, fearing his influence in that body, wished his transfer to the Chamber of Peers, where, in their judgment, he would be less dangerous. At the last Council of Ministers attended by M. de Villèle, the King passed to him a note in pencil, announcing that he had called him to the peerage. The statesman declined, in a note also in pencil. "You wish then to impose yourself upon me as minister?" wrote the King once more. M. de Villèle appeared moved, and passed to the sovereign this response: "The King well knows the contrary; but since he can write it, let him do with me what he will." The next day the Martignac ministry entered on its duties, and the Duchess of Angoulême said to Charles X.: "It is true, then, that you are letting Villèle go? My father, you descend to-day the first step of the throne."

XXII

THE MARTIGNAC MINISTRY

M. DE MARTIGNAC, who succeeded M. de Villèle in the Ministry of the Interior, was a man of merit, honest, liberal, and sincerely devoted to the King. Born in 1776, at Bordeaux, he was at first an advocate at the bar of that city, and at the same time made himself known by some witty vaudevilles. On the return of the Bourbons, he entered the magistracy, became procureur-general at Limoges, was elected a deputy in 1821, and distinguished himself in the tribune. He was Minister of the Interior from January, 1828, to August, 1829, and his name was given to the ministry of which he was a member. He had for colleagues enlightened and moderate men, such as Count Auguste de La Ferronnays, M. Roy, Count Portalis. He tried to reconcile the different parties, and to preserve the throne from the double danger of reaction and revolution. Taken between two fires, the extreme Right and the extreme Left, he was destined to fail in his generous effort.

The royalist sentiment was becoming constantly more feeble. The 24th of January, 1828, some days after the formation of the Martignac ministry, the

Viscount Sosthènes de La Rochefoucauld wrote, in a report to the King: —

"In going to Saint-Denis, the 21st of January (the anniversary of the death of Louis XVI.), and seeing the lightness with which the court itself conducted itself there, it was impossible for me not to make many reflections on the futility of an age in which no memory is sacred. And by what right can the people be asked to have a better memory when such an example is given to them? No cortège, no coaches draped, none of the pomp that strikes the imagination and the eye. Some isolated carriages, passing rapidly over the route, as if every one longed to be more promptly rid of whatever is grave and mournful in this day of cruel memory."

The ultras were thinking much less of the real interests of the monarchy than of their own spites and their personal ambitions.

These pretended supports of the throne were digging the abyss in which the throne was to be swallowed up. Charles X., blinded, was already thinking of calling the Prince de Polignac to power, and regarded the Martignac ministry as a provisional expedient. To the despair of the members of this ministry, he maintained relations with M. de Villèle, whose fall he regretted. After the opening of the session, he wrote to his former minister, February 6, 1828: —

"What do you think of my discourse? I did my best; but as it was a success with some persons of doubtful opinions, I am afraid that it is not worth much. Everything appears to me so confused, that I know not what to count upon. The eulogies of the *Débats* and the *Constitutionnel* make me fear I have said stupid things. Yet I hope not, and I shall continue to arrest with firmness what may lead to dangerous concessions."

On the other hand, if there were among the liberals some sincere and well-intentioned men, who meant to remain faithful alike to the throne and the Charter, there were others who already masked treachery under the appearance of devotion to the King. Those who two years later were to boast of having labored during the entire restoration for the ruin of the elder branch,—actors in the comedy of fifteen years, as they called themselves,—gave themselves out, in 1828, as partisans and enthusiastic admirers of Charles X. At the commencement of the session a deputy of the Left, having affected to say in the tribune that the King had not a single enemy, the Right permitted itself some exclamations of doubt. One of its members, M. de Marinhac, cried: "As a good prince I believe that His Majesty has no enemies, but as King, he has many, and I know them," added he, looking at his opponents. The entire Left was indignant, and caused the orator to be called to order. M. Dupin thanked the president, and said in an agitated voice: "It is a calumny, an insult, that we cannot endure. Nothing wounds us more than to hear ourselves accused of being the enemies of him whom we adore, cherish, bless."

The tactics of the Opposition were to flatter the King, but to disarm him and to make him look on those who were really revolutionists as ministerialists. M. de Martignac was a man of good faith, but many who boasted of supporting him were not so, and perhaps M. de Villèle was right when he wrote to Charles X. in June, 1828: —

"I could serve Your Majesty only with the light and the character God has given me. It would have been, it would be, impossible for me to believe that authority can be maintained by concessions and by leaning on those who wish to overthrow it."

Meanwhile there were still some fine days for the old King. His journey in the departments of the east, in 1828, was a continual ovation that recalled to him the enthusiasm of the beginning of his reign. Setting out from Saint Cloud the 31st of August, he arrived at Metz the 3d of September. All the houses of this great military city were hung with the white flag adorned with fleurs-de-lis. After having visited some of the fortifications, Charles X., following the ramparts, came to an elegant pavilion erected on the site of the ancient citadel. Long covered seats were arranged for the ladies of the city; a prodigious number of spectators occupied the ramparts. In the presence of the sovereign a regiment made a simulated attack on a "demi-lune" and a bastion.

On September 6, Saverne arranged a very picturesque reception for the King. All the cantons and all the communes sent thither, together with their mayors and their richest farmers, their prettiest village girls in Alsatian costume. Five hundred peasants, clad in red vest and long black coat, the head covered with a great hat turned up on one side, a white ribbon tied about the left arm, were on horseback at the place of meeting. The young girls, bearing flags and garlands, were brought in wagons, each containing a dozen or sixteen. In other wagons were the musicians. The pretty Alsaciennes presented the monarch with a basket of flowers; then he breakfasted with the authorities, and, at a signal, fires were lighted at the same time on the plain and on the surrounding mountains.

The 7th of September, Charles X. entered Strasbourg in triumph. At a league from the city, on a height from which it was to be seen, and whence the wooded hills of the Black Forest were visible, he was awaited by a crowd of young girls in Alsatian costume, in three hundred wagons, with four or six horses to each. There were also twelve hundred horsemen, divided into squadrons, the mayors with their scarfs at their head and carrying the fleur-de-lis standards. The royal cortège passed, under arbors of verdure and flowers, amid this long file of vehicles and horsemen, who escorted it to the walls of Strasbourg. Delighted with the enthusiasm of which he was the object, the sovereign proceeded to the Cathedral, where a *Te Deum* was sung. In the evening the spire of this marvellous church was illuminated: it was like a pyramid of stars.

The King of Würtemberg, the Grand Duke of Baden, and his three brothers came to greet the King of France in the capital of Alsace. He showed them at the arsenal sixteen hundred pieces of ordnance on their carriages, and arms sufficient for a hundred thousand men.

"Sire, and gentlemen," he said with a smile, in which kingly pride mingled with perfect urbanity, "I have nothing to conceal from you. This is something I can show to my friends as to my enemies."

Yes, France was great then, and no one could have predicted for Alsace the fate reserved for her forty-two years later. The army was the admiration of Europe. The navy had just recaptured at Navarino the prestige and power of the time of Louis XVI. Charles X. said to Mr. Hyde de Neuville: —

"France, when a noble design is involved, takes counsel only with herself. Thus whether England wishes or not, we shall free Greece. Continue the armaments with the same activity. I shall not pause in the path of humanity and honor."

And at the moment when the very Christian King was greeted by the German Princes in the Alsatian capital, his victorious troops were completing in the Morea the enfranchisement of Greece.

Charles X. returned by Colmar, Lunéville, Nancy, and Champagne. At Troyes he found himself surrounded by all the liberal deputies, and he decorated Casimir Périer. Everywhere he had an enthusiastic welcome. On his return to Saint Cloud he was warmly congratulated by all his court. Nevertheless, as the Duchess of Gontaut said to him: —

"Sire, you must be happy." — "What do cheers signify?" he answered, not without sadness. "These demonstrations, all superficial, should not dazzle — a friendly gesture of the hand, a prince's, a king's, expression of satisfaction will obtain them."

Despite this philosophic reflection, Charles X. was triumphant. If his ministers wished to credit their liberal policy with the ovations he had received in the east, he called their attention to the fact that he had been not less well received the year before under the Villèle ministry at the time of his visit to the camp of Saint Omer. In the enthusiasm manifested by the people, he saw an homage to the monarchical principle, not to the policy of one or another ministry.

"You hear these people. Do they shout hurrah for the Charter? No, they cry long live the King!" Still confident of the future, he wished to persuade himself that the obstacles piled up before his dynasty were but clouds that a favorable wind would scatter soon. "Ah, Monsieur de Martignac," he cried, with deep joy, "what a nation! what should we not do for it!"

At the moment that Charles X. traversed the provinces of the east in triumph, the Duchess of Berry was making in the west a journey not less brilliant than that of the sovereign.

XXIII

THE JOURNEY IN THE WEST

NEVER was a princely journey more triumphal than that of the Duchess of Berry in the provinces of the west in 1828. Madame, who left Paris June 16, returned there October 1, and there was not a day in these three months that she was not the object of enthusiastic ovations. In a book of nearly six hundred pages, Viscount Walsh has described, with the fidelity of a Dangeau, this journey in which the mother of the Duke of Bordeaux was treated like a queen of a fairy tale.

The 16th of June, the Princess slept at Rambouillet, where two years later such cruel trials were to come to her. The 18th, she visited Chambord, where she was received by Count Adrien de Calonne, the author of the project of the subscription, thanks to which this historic château became the property of the Duke of Bordeaux.

In the face of the wind, which was blowing with force, Madame ascended to the highest point of the château, the platform of the lantern called Fleur-de-Lis at the end of the famous double balustered staircase. From there her glance wandered over the vast extent of the park, with a circumference of eight leagues, and enclosing, besides six or seven thousand acres of woodland, twenty-three farms, whose buildings, cultivated fields, and scattered flocks, animated the view in all directions. On descending, she said: "I should like to mark my name here; I shall love to see it again when I come to visit the Duke of Bordeaux." And with a stiletto she cut these words: "18th June — Marie Caroline." Some young girls presented her with lambs white as snow, decorated with green and white ribbons, and with a tame roe, on whose collar was engraved: "Homage of the people of Chambord." The same day she paid visits at their châteaux to Marshal Victor, Duke of Bellune, and to the Duke d'Avaray. In the evening she returned to Blois. Madame left there the 19th of June, after examining the Salle des États, the room in which the Duke of Guise was assassinated, and the tower where Catharine de' Medici used to consult the astrologers. The 20th, she attended at Saumur a brilliant tournament given in her honor by the Cavalry School. The 21st, she entered Angers amid shouts and cheers. The 22d, she visited the château of Count Walsh de Serrant. Her carriage passed under vaults of verdure adorned with flowers and banners.

The Princess arrived the same day at Saint Florent, which, in 1793, had given the signal for the war of the Vendée, and where the Vendéan army had effected the famous passage of the Loire, comparable to that of the Berezina. There the aged witnesses of the struggles described by Napoleon as "a war of giants," had assembled near the tomb of Bonchamp to await the Duchess of Berry. All the neighboring heights were bristling with white flags. From afar they were seen fluttering on the church-towers, on the châteaux, over cottages, on isolated trees. They were to be seen even above the graves in the cemeteries. A son had said: "My father died for the white flag; let us plant it on his grave; the dead should rejoice, for Madame comes to honor their fidelity." The example was followed, and the tombs bore the rallying sign of those who rested there. When on the borders of the Loire, the Princess paused a moment, struck with the majesty of the scene. The cannon mingled their noble voices with the acclamations of fifteen thousand Vendéans. The stream was covered with a swarm of boats, dressed with flags. A magnificent sun lighted up this fête.

It was ten o'clock when Madame arrived at Milleraye, opposite Saint Florent. It was there that General de Bonchamp, one of the heroes of the Vendée, had given up his soul to God. The cottage where the soldiers had laid him to die was shown. His widow awaited the Duchess of Berry. What contrast between the festivity of Saint Florent and the consternation of the days of grief and misfortune, when, in October, 1793, its people fled to the right bank of the Loire, leaving their houses a prey to the flames! The cries of distress and despair which sounded along the banks of the stream in that fatal year, were now replaced by shouts of joy. Madame embarked amid cheers. Her boat was escorted by a great number of others, six of which contained Vendéans bearing flags torn by bullets in the battles of Fontenay and of Torfou, of Laval, and of Dol. Grouped on the hill-slopes of Saint Florent, more than fifteen thousand spectators followed with their gaze the flotilla, in the midst of which they saw the Duchess of Berry, standing, visibly agitated. She landed upon the plateau of Saint Florent, and ascended on foot the hill that led to it. When she reached the summit, she found herself in the midst of a camp of five thousand Vendéan soldiers who had taken part in the war of 1793 or in the arming of 1815. There it was that Cathelineau, as in the time of the crusades, cried: "It is God's will. Let us march!"—"Oh, what a people!" said the Princess. "What fine and honest faces! What an accent in their cries of 'Long live the King!' Yes, plainly they love us." She proceeded to the church of Saint Florent, where, kneeling beneath a canopy, she heard Mass. She regarded with attention the tomb of Bonchamp, and said, as she beheld his statue: "He looks as if he were still commanding."

On leaving the church, she went to see the place where Bonchamp is buried, and, under a tent, partook of a repast offered her by the Countess d'Autichamp. She had recounted to her in detail the celebrated passage of the Loire, the disastrous period when all the city of Saint Florent was burned by order of the Convention, and the only house left standing was the one occupied by the republican General Léchelle as his headquarters.

At three o'clock in the afternoon, Madame embarked anew on the steamboat awaiting her at the point of Varades, and proceeded in this way to Nantes. The inhabitants from the two banks of the stream greeted her upon her passage. The red aprons and white caps of the women contrasted, in the landscape, with the sombre costume of the men. That she might be better recognized by the crowd, the Princess, clad in a simple robe of brown silk, with a long chain of gold at the neck, separated herself from her suite, mounted to the highest point on the boat, and greeted with voice and gesture all these faithful people. The men waved banners and standards. The women raised their little children in their arms and said: "Look at her well; it's the mother of the Duke of Bordeaux."

The people seemed to walk upon the water to get a nearer view of Madame. Not a rock pushing out into the stream that was not occupied. Where the Loire was too wide for the features of the Princess to be seen from the shore, the dwellers on the banks had, so to speak, brought them together, by forming in the middle of the stream streets of boats, with their flags and their triumphal arches. At a league from Saint Florent a rock juts into the water of the Loire. Here was an aged Vendéan, all alone, his white hair fluttering in the wind. Erect upon the rock, he was holding a white flag, and at his feet was a dog. It was, according to the *Moniteur*, a symbol of faithful Vendée.

The same day, June 22, at seven in the evening, the Princess reached Nantes. She passed on foot from the Port Maillard to the Prefecture, and had difficulty in getting through the innumerable multitude. The next day she was at Savenay, where, on leaving the church, she paused to contemplate the monument raised to the memory of the victims of the battle of the 23d of September, 1793. The 24th, she went to Saint Anne d'Auray, a pilgrimage venerated throughout all Brittany, and visited the *Champ des Martyrs*, the little plain where thirty-three years before, the *émigrés* taken at Quiberon had been shot, despite their capitulation. When Madame appeared on the consecrated field, the crowd cheered her, then became still, and amid solemn silence, sang the *De Profundis*.

The 25th, the Princess was at Lorient, and there laid the corner-stone of the monument erected to Bisson, the lieutenant of the navy who, in the Greek expedition, October, 1827, being charged with the command of a brig taken from the Turks by Admiral de Rigny's fleet, blew up the vessel, with the crew, rather than surrender. After visiting Rennes, she returned to Nantes, the 28th of June. A triumphal arch had been constructed on the Place des Changes, with this inscription : " Lilies for our Bourbons. Laurels for Henry. Roses for Louise." The flower and fruit girls had written on their arch of verdure: "Our flowers, our fruits, our hearts, are Madame's." The 29th, the Duchess attended a magnificent ball given by the city. The next day she visited the Trappist Convent at Melleray. It was difficult to persuade her to go away. "Where shall I find more happiness than here?" she said. "Elsewhere there are pleasures and distractions, but none here. Since I make them happy, I would remain; and I am very well pleased."

The 30th, at evening, Madame arrived at Trémicinière, at the house of the Countess de Charette, the sister-in-law of the famous Vendéan chief. July 1, she entered Bocage. From there no more wide roads, no more cities of easy approach; bad ways, long distances without relays, obstacles of all sorts. Clad in a green riding-habit, with a gray felt hat and a gauze veil, Madame galloped between Madame de la Rochejaquelein and Madame de Charette. At her arrival at Saint Hilaire, the Marquis de Foresta, Prefect of La Vendée, said to her: "Madame does not like phrases; La Vendée does not make them; it has but one sentiment and one cry to express it: Long live the King! Long live Madame! Forever live the Bourbons!"

The peasants never wearied of admiring her intrepidity. When her horse, excited by the cries and the beating of the drums, pranced and reared, they were heard to say: "Oh! the brave little woman; she is not frightened." A villager exclaimed: "I have never regretted my old father so much as today; one day like this would have repaid him for all the hardships he suffered."

Madame passed the night at the Château of Lagrange, the property of the Marquis de Goulaine. On entering her chamber she found by her bed a night-lamp, with this motto: "Rest tranquilly; La Vendée is watching."

On the 3d of July, she visited the Champ des Mattes, where in 1815 the Marquis Louis de La Rochejaquelein was killed at the head of the Vendéans in insurrection against Napoleon. The same day she was at Bourbon-Vendée. The 5th of July, at the crossing of the Quatre Chemins, in sight of the roads from Nantes, from Bourbon, from Saumur, and from La Rochelle, she laid the first stone of a monument to perpetuate the memory of the Vendéan victories. She returned afterward to the Château de Mesnard, the property of her first equerry, the one who traced so well the itinerary of her journey. All the inhabitants of the bourg of Mesnard had taken part in the great Vendéan war, and, their curé at their head, marched as far as Granville. The mother of the first equerry, then a widow, and whose two sons were in the army of Condé, had followed her former peasants, with her daughter, and died at Lagrande at the time of the disastrous retreat. Madame de la Rochejaquelein, in her Memoirs, speaks of the sad state in which she saw her. In memory of so much devotion, Madame wished to open a *bal champêtre* with a veteran of the bourg of Mesnard.

That night the Princess slept at the Château of Landebaudière, belonging to Count Auguste de La Rochejaquelein. Everywhere the villagers came to the gates of the châteaux to enlist in their joys as formerly they had enlisted in their combats,—Lescure, La Rochejaquelein, d'Elbée, Charette. The 6th, Madame visited the field of the battle of Torfou. A former officer of the army of La Vendée, noting that she wore a green riding-habit, said to her: "We were always attached to our uniform, but we cherish it more than ever to-day, when we see that we wear the colors of Madame."—"Gentlemen," replied the Princess, "I have adopted your uniform." She breakfasted in the open air, amid the Vendéans under arms.

Madame continued her journey on horseback. Nothing could stop her, neither oppressive heat nor rain-storms. When she was spoken to of her fatigues, "It is only fair," she responded, "that I should give myself a little trouble to make the acquaintance of those who have shed their blood for us." Most of the time she took her repast in the open air. The peasants strolled around the table and fired salutes with their old muskets; for in Vendée there is no fête without powder. Then to the sound of the *biniou* and of the *vèze* they moved in joyous dances in which the daughter of kings did not disdain to take part. On entering every village she was greeted by the curés of the parish and the neighboring parishes. Nearly all were old soldiers whose hands had borne the sword before carrying the cross.

Near the boundaries of the department of La Loire-Inférieure Madame alighted. "Here is a farm," she said; "let us knock and ask for some milk." The doors were not closed. On entering the room of the farm-wife, — who was absent, — the Princess found only a very little infant asleep and swaddled in a cradle. Then she seated herself on a stool, and after the fashion of the country, set herself to rocking, with her foot, the babe of the poor peasant-woman. The 6th of July, at nine in the evening, she reached Beaupréau. The city, built in the form of an amphitheatre, was illuminated; an immense bonfire had been lighted. The next day Madame laid the corner-stone of a monument in honor of d'Elbée, and saluted at Pin-en-Mauges, the statue of Cathelineau. The 8th of July, she was at the Château of Maulévrier, whose owner, M. de Colbert, had erected a monument to the memory of Stofflet, the heroic huntsman. The same day, at Saint Aubin, she laid the first stone of another monument raised to the four heroes of La Vendée, — Dornissan, Lescure, Henry and Louis de La Rochejaquelein.

The 10th of July, the Princess was at Luçon, the 11th at La Rochelle, the 12th at Rochefort, the 13th at Blaye, the 14th at Bordeaux. The "faithful city," as the capital of the Gironde was then named, distinguished itself by its enthusiasm. A little girl of eight years, Mademoiselle du Hamel, surrounded by her young companions, daughters of members of the municipal government read a welcome to the mother of the Duke of Bordeaux as follows: —

"Madame, while our fathers have the honor to offer you their hearts and their arms, permit us, children, to offer to you the flowers and the prayers of innocence. In choosing me as their interpreter, my young companions have doubtless wished to recall to you an angel who is dear to you; but if alone of them all I have the fortune to count the same number of years as Mademoiselle, we all rival each other in cherishing you, we all repeat with an enthusiasm rendered purer and more simple by our age, Long live the King! Long live Madame!"

In the evening the "Mother of the Little Duke," as the Bordelais called the Princess, went to the chief theatre, where she was received with frenzied applause. The statue of the Duke of Bordeaux, supported by soldiers under a canopy of flags, and crowned with laurels, was brought to the front of the stage, while a cortège formed by a detachment of troops of the line, and by all the company of the theatre, filed by, military music resounded. Then a cantata was sung.

On the morrow, at a grand ball offered to her by

the city, Madame was seated upon a platform that was surmounted by a fine portrait of her son. Eight hundred women, crowned with white plumes, flowers, and diamonds, cheered her. The 18th, she slept at Pau, the native place of Henry IV. The mountaineers, descending from their heights, banner in hand, with their Basque costumes, came to meet her. The next day she visited the castle where was born the Béarnais, whose cradle, formed of a great tortoise-shell, she saw: it was shaded by draperies and white plumes. The following day she visited the environs. To descend into the valley of Ossun, she donned the felt hat and the red sash worn by the peasants of Béarn. As she was looking at the spring of Nays, a mountaineer offered her some water in a rustic dish, and said naïvely: "Are you pleased with the Béarnais, Madame?"—"Am I not pleased!" replied the Princess, eagerly. "See, I wear the hat and sash of the country!"

The 24th, she was at the Ile des Faisans, famous in the souvenirs of Louis XIV.; the 25th, at Bayonne, where she assisted at a military fête. In all her excursions, Madame carried her pencils with her, and almost every day sketched some picturesque site. Eight Béarnais, with an amaranth belt and hats of white and green, served her as a guard of honor. She passed all the month of August and a part of the month of September in the Pyrenees. The mountaineers never wearied of admiring the hardihood, the gaiety, the spirit, shown by her in making the most difficult ascensions. The 9th of September, she quitted Bagnères-de Luchon to return to Paris, passing through Toulouse, Montauban, Cahors, Limoges, and Orleans. It was one long series of ovations. The 1st of October, Madame returned to the Tuileries. She had been accompanied all through her journey by the Maréchale Duchess of Reggio, lady of honor; by the Marchioness of Podenas, lady companion; and by Count de Mesnard, first equerry.

The Duchess of Berry returned enchanted. Could she suspect the reception that awaited her, four years later, in the places where she had just been the object of veritable worship? When she was received at Nantes as a triumphant sovereign, could she believe that the time was approaching when, in that same city, she would have hardly a stone on which to lay her head and where she would seek a futile refuge in the chimney-piece — mysterious hiding-place — of the house of the Demoiselles Duguigny? At Blaye could she imagine that the citadel, hung with white flags, whose cannon were fired in her honor, would so soon become her prison? Poor Princess! She had taken seriously the protestations of devotion and fidelity addressed to her everywhere. They asked her to promise that if ever the rights of her son were denied, she would defend them on the soil of La Vendée, and she had said to herself: "I swear it." The journey of 1828 held the germ of the expedition of 1832.

XXIV

THE MARY STUART BALL

NO society in Europe was more agreeable and brilliant than that of the Duchess of Berry. The fêtes given by the Princess in the salons of the Pavillon de Marsan at the Tuileries were marked by exceptional elegance and good taste; the *petit château*, as her vivacious social staff was called at that time, had an extraordinary brightness and animation. At the carnival of 1829 Madame organized a costume ball, which, for its brilliancy, was the talk of the court and the city. All the costumes were those of one period,— that at which the dowager queen of Scotland, Marie of Lorraine, widow of James V., came to France to visit her daughter, Mary Stuart, wife of the King, Francis II. It was decided that Mary Stuart should be represented by the Duchess of Berry, and the King, Francis II., by the oldest of the sons of the Duke of Orleans, the Duke of Chartres, who was then eighteen and one-half years old, and who was, the next year, to take the title of Duke of Orleans, on the accession of his father to the throne. The apartments of the Children of France in the Pavillon de Marsan were chosen for the ball, and the date was fixed at Monday, March 2, 1829.

The King, the Dauphin and Dauphiness, the Duke and Duchess of Orleans, appeared at the fête, but not in costume. Charles X. came after the hour of giving out the general orders. The Dauphin, the Dauphiness, and the Duke of Orleans arrived at 8 P.M. The entry of the four queens, Mary Stuart, Marie of Lorraine, Catharine de' Medici, Jeanne d'Albret, was announced by the band of the body-guards which preceded them. The cortège was magnificent, the costumes of the princes and their ladies resplendent. To increase its richness, the Dauphiness had lent not only her own jewels, but a part of those of the crown. The invited guests not taking part in the cortège occupied places already assigned them. They wore a uniform costume of silver gauze and white satin. This coolness of tone produced a charming effect when at the arrival of the cortège all rose. In the ball-room a platform had been prepared with a throne for Mary Stuart. The Duchess of Berry, as the famous queen, wore with great grace a dazzling toilet — crown of diamonds, high collar, blue velvet robe with wide sleeves, front of white satin bordered with ermine. The Duke of Chartres, a handsome boy and brilliant cavalier, as King Francis II., wore a cap with white plumes, and a dark blue velvet doublet with ornaments of gold. His brother, the Duke of Nemours, fourteen years old, was in the character of a page to the King, with a white satin doublet, and recalled in his features the youth of Henry IV. The Duchess of Berry, playing to perfection her rôle of queen, advanced to the throne. The Duke of Chartres gave her his hand to ascend the steps. Then she made a sign to be seated; but the young Prince remained standing. Placing himself behind the throne, and removing his cap with white plumes, he bowed low and said: "Madame, I know my place." The Duchess of Gontaut spoke to the Duchess of Orleans, and asked her if she had remarked the tact of her son the Prince. "I remarked it," replied the Princess, "and I approve of it."

The ball commenced. There was present a great Scotch lord, the Marquis of Huntley, who belonged to a very illustrious Jacobite house. In his youth he had been what was then called a *beau danseur*, and had had the honor of opening a fancy dress ball at the Château of Versailles with the Queen Marie Antoinette. Charles X. remembered it and wished that the Marquis, then nearly eighty, should open the ball with little Mademoiselle, who was but nine. Still a *beau danseur*, the old Englishman had not forgotten the pirouettes of Versailles; all the court admired, and the young princes were greatly amused.

The ball was a marvellous success. It was a revival of the beautiful fêtes of the Renaissance. The sixteenth century, so elegant, so picturesque, lived anew. A painter, who was then but twenty-nine, and who had already a great vogue, M. Eugène Lamy, perpetuated its memory in a series of twenty-six water-colors, which have been lithographed, and form a curious album. (A copy of this album is in the National Library, in the Cabinet of Engravings.) It contains, besides, four water-colors, representing one, the ascent of the stairway of the Pavillon de Marsan by the guests; another, Mary Stuart seated on the throne; a third, one of the dances of the ball; a fourth, the entrance of the Dowager Queen of Scotland — twenty-two reproductions of the principal personages at the fête. At the left are the arms of the historic personages represented, and at the right those of the representative. Then above the portrait of the Duchess of Berry there are at the left the arms of Scotland and France, and at the right those of France and the Two Sicilies, and above the portrait of the Duke of Chartres at the left the arms of France, at the right the ducal blazon of Orleans.

Here are the names of the twenty-two persons who figure in the album of M. Eugène Lamy, with the personages represented: —

1. The Duchess of Berry (Mary Stuart).
2. The Duke of Chartres (Francis II.).
3. The Duke de Nemours (a king's page).
4. Lady Stuart de Rothsay (Marie de Lorraine). Daughter of Lord Hardwicke, she was the wife of Lord Stuart de Rothsay, ambassador of England at Paris.
5. The Marquis of Douglas, since Duke of Hamilton (the Duke de Châtellerault), a finished type of the great Scotch lord; he married in 1843 the Princess Mary of Baden, and under the reign of Napoleon III.

added to his titles of Hamilton and of Brandon in Scotland and England, the title of Duke de Châtellerault, in France, which had formerly belonged to the Hamilton family.

6. The Marchioness of Podenas, *née* Nadaillac (Catharine de' Medici). Lady companion of the Duchess of Berry, she was one of the brightest women of the court.

7. The Count de Pastoret, married to a de Neufermeil (Duke of Ferrara).

8. The Marquis de Vogué (the Vidame de Chartres). Married to a Mademoiselle de Machault d'Arnouville; his son was the diplomat who was ambassador under the presidency of Thiers and of Marshal Macmahon.

9. Count Ludovic de Rosanbo (Duke de Guise). He was one of the handsomest men of his time. He had married the daughter of the Count de Mesnard, lady companion to the Duchess of Berry.

10. The Countess de La Rochejaquelein, daughter of the Duke de Duras (a lady of honor to the Queen). She was honorary lady companion to the Duchess of Berry.

11. Miss Louise Stuart (a page to the Queen-Mother of Scotland).

12. Miss Pole Carew (Mary Seaton, maid of honor to the same queen).

13. The Count de Mailly (René de Mailly, officer of the guard to Mary Stuart). The Count was the son of the Marshal de Mailly, defender of the Tuile-

ries on August 10, who paid for his devotion on the scaffold of the Revolution. Aide-de-camp of the Duke of Bordeaux, and lieutenant-colonel; he was a brilliant officer who had received glorious wounds in the Russian campaign. He was married to a Mademoiselle de Lonlay de Villepail.

14. The Countess d'Orglandes, *née* Montblin, one of the prettiest women of the court (Louise de Clermont-Tonnerre, Countess of Crussol).

15. The Duchess de Caylus, *née* La Grange, a great beauty, remarried afterwards to the Count de Rochemure (Diane de Poitiers).

16. Mademoiselle de Béarn, a charming young girl, married afterwards to the Duke of Vallombrosa, and dying so young and so regretted (a maid of honor to Mary Stuart).

17. Count de Mesnard, peer of France, field marshal, first equerry of the Duchess of Berry, aide-de-camp of the Duke of Bordeaux (Admiral de Coligny).

18. Marquis de Louvois, peer of France, married to Mademoiselle de Monaco (Count Gondi de Ritz).

19. The Duke of Richelieu, nephew of the President of the Council of Ministers of Louis XVIII. (Jacques d'Albon, Marshal of Saint André).

20. The Baron de Charette (François de Lorraine). He had married a daughter of the Duke of Berry and of Miss Brown. His son was the general of the Papal Zouaves.

21. Countess de Pastoret, *née* Neufermeil (the Duchess of Montpensier).

22. The Countess Auguste de Juigné, *née* Durfort de Civrac (Jeanne d'Albret).

Among the pages were the Duke de Maillé, who carried the banner of France, and Count Maxence de Damas.

Eugène Lamy, at the age of eighty-seven, exhibited in 1887 a charming water-color, of which the subject was "A Ball under Henry III." He has the same talent, the same brightness, the same freshness of coloring as when, fifty-eight years before, he painted the water colors of the Mary Stuart ball. The Duke de Nemours, one of the last survivors of the guests of this ball, could recount its splendors. Even in the time of the old régime no more elegant ball was ever seen. If such a fête had been given in our time, the detailed accounts of it would fill the papers; but under the Restoration the press was very sober in the matter of "society news," and the dazzling ball of 1829 was hardly mentioned. On the morrow, the *Journal des Débats* said: —

"PARIS, 2d of March.

"The ball given at the Pavillon Marsan, in the apartments of the Children of France, was honored by the presence of the King, M. the Dauphin and Madame the Dauphiness. Mgr. the Duke of Orleans and his family arrived at eight o'clock.

"To-morrow there will be a play at the Court Theatre; the actors of the opera will play *La Muette de Portici*."

Beside the persons who figure in the album of M. Eugène Lamy many others were to be noted. Let us mention the Countess Henri de Biron, the Marchioness Oudinot, the Countess de Noailles, who represented Margaret of Savoy, Claude Duchess of Lorraine, the Princess de Condé, the Princess of Ferrara; the Count A. de Damas, as Lanoue Bras-de-Fer; Monsieur de San Giacomo, as François de' Medici; the Countess de Montault, as Countess de Coligny; the Marchioness de Montcalm, as the Duchess de Bouillon; the flower of the English aristocracy, — Lady Aldborough, Lady Rendlesham, Lady Cambermere, Lady Vernon, Lord Ramlagh, Captain Drummond, Lord Forwich, Lord Abayne, Miss Caulfuld, Miss Thelusson, Miss Baring, Miss Acton, and, lastly, the Counts de Cossé de Biron, and de Brissac, representing the three marshals of France whose names they bore.

In donning the costume of the unfortunate queen whose sorrows could only be compared to those of Marie Antoinette, the Duchess of Berry proved how free her mind was from all gloomy presentiments, forgetting that the family of the Bourbons had already had its Charles I., and not foreseeing that it was soon to have its James II., the amiable Princess hardly suspected that in the course of next year, she would be an exile in Scotland in the castle of Mary Stuart.

XXV

THE FINE ARTS

FROM 1824 to the end of the Restoration, the department of the Fine Arts, connected with the ministry of the King's household, was confided to the Viscount Sosthènes de la Rochefoucauld, son of the Duke de Doudeauville. He was then at the head of the museums, the royal manufactures, the Conservatory and the five royal theatres, — the Opéra, the Français, the Odéon, the Opéra-Comique, and the Italiens.

From the point of view of arts and letters the reign of Charles X. was illustrious. The King encouraged, protected, pensioned the greater number of the great writers and artists who honored France. What is sometimes called in literature the generation of 1830 would be more exactly described as the generation of the Restoration. This régime can claim the glory of Lamartine, as poet. A body-guard of Louis XVIII., he was the singer of royalty. He published, in 1820, the first volume of his *Méditations poétiques*, in 1823 the second, and in 1829 the *Harmonies*. His literary success opened to him the doors of diplomacy. He was successively attaché of the

Legation at Florence, Secretary of Embassy at Naples and at London, Chargé d'Affaires in Tuscany. When the Revolution of 1830 broke out, he had just been named Minister Plenipotentiary to Greece.

Victor Hugo published his *Odes et Ballades* from 1822 to 1828. "La Vendée," "Les Vierges de Verdun," "Quiberon," "Louis XVII.," "Le Rétablissement de la Statue de Henri IV.," "La Mort du duc de Berry," "La Naissance du duc de Bordeaux," "Les Funérailles de Louis XVIII.," "Le Sacre de Charles X.," are true royalist songs. Alexandre Dumas, *fils*, in receiving M. Leconte de Lisle at the French Academy, recalled "the light of that little lamp, seen burning every night in the mansard of the Rue Dragon, at the window of the boy poet, poor, solitary, indefatigable, enamoured of the ideal, hungry for glory, of that little lamp, the silent and friendly confidant of his first works and his first hopes so miraculously realized." Who knows? without the support of the government of the Restoration the light of that little lamp might less easily have developed into the resplendent star that the author of *La Dame aux Camélias* indicated in the firmament.

The author of *Méditations poétiques* and the author of the *Odes et Ballades* were sincere in the expression of their political and religious enthusiasm. These two lyric apostles of the throne and the altar, these two bards of the coronation, obeyed the double inspiration of their imagination and their conscience. Party spirit should not be too severe for a régime that suggested such admirable verses to the two greatest French poets of the nineteenth century — to Lamartine and to Victor Hugo.

Let us recall also that in Victor Hugo it was not only the royalist poet that Charles X. protected, it was also the chief of the romantic school; for the government, despite all the efforts of the classicists, caused *Hernani* to be represented at the Français, a subsidized theatre. When the Academy pressed its complaint to the very throne to prevent the acceptance of the play, the King replied wittily that he claimed no right in the matter beyond his place in the parterre. The first representation of *Hernani* took place the 25th of February, 1830, and the author, decorated, pensioned, encouraged by Charles X., did not lose the royal favor, when, on the 9th of March following, he wrote in the preface of his work: "Romanticism, so often ill-defined, is nothing, taking it all in all — and this is its true definition, if only its militant side be regarded — but liberalism in literature. The principle of literary liberty, already understood by the thinking and reading world, is not less completely adopted by that immense crowd, eager for the pure emotions of art, that throngs the theatres of Paris every night. That lofty and puissant voice of the people, which is like that of God, writes that poetry henceforth shall have the same matter as politics! Toleration and liberty!"

The first representation of a work that was a

great step forward for the romantic school, *Henri III. et Sa Cour*, by Alexandre Dumas, had already taken place at the Français, February 11, 1829. The 30th of March, 1830, the Odéon gave *Christine de Suède*, by the same author.

In 1829, Alfred de Vigny had represented at the Français his translation in verse of *Othello*. It was from 1824 to 1826 that the poet published his principal poems. It was in 1826 that his romance of Cinq-Mars appeared. Victor Hugo published *Les Orientales* in 1829; Alfred de Musset, *Les Contes d'Espagne et d'Italie* in 1830. It may be said then that before the Revolution of 1830, romanticism had reached its complete expansion.

Note, also, that the government of Charles X. always respected the independence of writers and artists, and never asked for eulogies in exchange for the pensions and encouragement it accorded them with generous delicacy. It named Michelet Maître de Conferences at the École Normale in 1826. It pensioned Casimir Delavigne, so well known for his liberal opinions, and Augustin Thierry, a writer of the Opposition, when that great historian, having lost his eyesight, was without resources. It ordered of Horace Vernet the portraits of the King, the Duke of Berry, and the Duke of Angoulême, as well as a picture representing a "Review by Charles X. at the Champ-de-Mars," and named the painter of the battles of the Revolution and the Empire director of the School of Rome.

From the point of view of painting as well as of letters, the Restoration was a grand epoch. Official encouragement was not wanting to the painters. Gros and Gérard received the title of Baron. There may be seen to-day in one of the new halls of the French School at the Louvre, the pretty picture by Heim, which represents Charles X. distributing the prizes for the Exposition of 1824, where *Le Vœu de Louis XIII.* by Ingres had figured, and where the talent of Paul Delaroche had been disclosed. In the *Salon Carré* of the Louvre, the King, in the uniform of general-in-chief of the National Guards, blue coat with plaits of silver, with the cordon of the Saint Esprit, and in high boots, himself hands the cross of the Legion of Honor to the decorated artists, among whom is seen Heim, the author of the picture.

Ingres, chief of the Classic School, and Delacroix, chief of the Romantic School, shone at the same time. In 1827, the first submitted to general admiration *L'Apothéose d'Homère* and *Le Martyre de Saint Symphorien.* The same year Delacroix, who had already given in 1824 *Le Massacre de Scio,* in 1826 *La Mort du Doge Marino Faliero,* exhibited *Le Christ au jardin des oliviers,* acquired for the Church of Saint Paul; *Justinien,* — for the Council of State; and *La Mort de Sardanapale.*

When the *Musée Charles X.* (the Egyptian Museum) was opened at the Louvre, the government ordered the frescoes and ceilings from Gros, Gérard, Ingres, Schnetz, Abel de Pujol. M. Jules Mareschal says: —

"The right-royal munificence of Charles X. was not marked by niggardliness in the appreciation of works of art any more than in the appreciation of the works of science and letters. But, as is known, it is not by interest alone that the heart of the artist is gained and his zeal stimulated. They are far more sensitive to the esteem shown them, to the respect with which their art is surrounded, and to the taste manifested in the judgment of their productions. Now, who more than Louis XVIII. and Charles X. possessed the secret of awakening lively sympathy in the world of artists and men of letters? Who better than their worthy counsellor seconded them in the impulses of generous courtesy so common with them? Thus from this noble and gracious manner of treating men devoted to art and letters, which marked the royal administration of the Fine Arts under the Restoration, sprang an emulation and a good will which on all sides gave an impetus to genius, and brought forth the new talents."

In theatrical matters, the Viscount Sosthènes de La Rochefoucauld exercised a salutary influence. He loved artists, and wishing to raise their situation, moral and social, he deplored the excommunication that had been laid on the players.

Speaking of the stage, he wrote in a report addressed to Charles X., June 20, 1825: "I perceive that I have forgotten the most essential side, — the moral,

I will even say the religious side. What glory it would be for a king to raise this considerable class of society from the abject situation in which it is compelled to live! Sacrificed to our pleasures, it has been condemned to eternal death, and a king believes his conscience quiet! For a long time I have cherished this thought; we must begin by elevating these people, as regards their art, by reforming, little by little, the swarming abuses that awaken horror, and end by treating with Rome in order to obtain some just concessions that would have important results."

In another report to the King, dated October 21, 1826, M. de La Rochefoucauld wrote, apropos of the obsequies of Talma: —

"A profound regret for me is the manner of the great tragedian's death. Sire, would it not be worthy of the reign, the breast, the conscience of Charles X., to draw this class of artists from the cruel position in which they are left by that excommunication that weighs upon them without distinction? Whether they conduct themselves well or ill, the Church repels them; this reprobation holds them perforce in the sphere of evil and disorder, since they have no interest in rising above it. Honor them, and they will honor themselves. It is time to undertake the reform of what I call a pernicious prejudice. The clergy itself is not far from agreeing on these ideas."

In his relations with authors, artists, directors of theatres, the Viscount was courtesy itself. We read in one of his reports (June 17, 1825) : —

"Rossini is the first composer of Europe; I have succeeded in attracting him to the service of France; he had before been tempted in vain. Jealous of his success, people have cried out that he was an idler, that he would do nothing. I secured him by the methods and in the interest of the King; I can do with him as I will, as with all the artists, though they are most difficult people. They must be taken through the heart. Rossini has just composed a really ravishing piece; and, touched by the manner in which he is treated, he wishes to present it to the King in token of his gratitude, and wishes to receive nothing. He is right, but the King cannot accept gratis so fine a present; I propose that the King grant him the cross of the Legion of Honor and announce it himself to him to-morrow — which would be an act full of grace. All favors must come always from the King."

Great tenacity was needed in the government of Charles X. to get the *chefs-d'œuvre* of Rossini represented at the Opéra. A little school of petty and backward ideas rushed, under pretext of patriotism, but really from jealousy, systematically to drive from the stage everything not French. For this coterie Rossini and Meyerbeer were suspects, intruders, who must be repulsed at any cost. The government had the good sense to take no account of this ridiculous opposition, which refused to recognize that art should be cosmopolitan. Before seeing his name on the bills of our first lyric stage, Rossini required no less than nine years of patience. All Europe applauded him, but at Paris he had to face the fire of pamphleteers rendered furious by his fame. The government finally forced the Opéra to mount *Le Siège de Corinthe.* Its success was so striking that the evening of the first representation (October 9, 1826), the public made almost a riot for half an hour, because Rossini, called loudly by an enthusiastic crowd, refused to appear upon the stage.

The maëstro gave at the Opéra *Moïse*, March 26, 1826; *Le Comte Ory*, August 20, 1828; *Guillaume Tell*, August 20, 1829. (At this time the first representations of the most important works took place in midsummer.) The evening of the first night of *Guillaume Tell*, the orchestra went, after the opera, to give a serenade under the windows of the composer, who occupied the house on the Boulevard Montmartre, through which the Passage Jouffroy has since been cut. The 10th of February, 1868, on the occasion of the hundredth representation of the same work, there was a repetition of the serenade of 1829. The master then lived in the Rue Chaussée d'Antin, No. 2. Under his windows the orchestra and chorus of the opera commenced the concert about half an hour after midnight, by the light of torches, and Faure sang the solos.

The government which secured the representation of *Guillaume Tell* was not afraid of the words "independence" and "liberty." A year and a half before, the 20th of February, 1828, there had been given at the Opéra the *chef-d'œuvre* of Auber, *La Muette de Portici*, and the Duchess of Berry, a Neapolitan princess, had applauded the Naples Revolution put into music.

The government of Charles X. protected Meyerbeer as well as Rossini. *Robert le Diable* was only played under the reign of Louis Philippe, but the work had already been received under the Restoration.

During the reign of Charles X. the fine royal theatres reached the height of their splendor: the Français and the Odéon were installed in their present quarters; the Opéra in the hall of the Rue La Peletier, excellent as to acoustics and proportions; the Italiens in the Salle Favart (where they remained from 1825 to 1838); the Opéra Comique in the Salle Feydeau, until the month of April, 1829, when it inaugurated the Salle Ventadour. Talma, Mademoiselle Duchesnoir, Mademoiselle Mars, triumphed at the Français; Mademoiselle Georges, at the Odéon; Nourrit, Levasseur, Madame Damoreau, Taglioni, at the Opéra; Sontag, Pasta, Malibran, and Rubini at the Italiens.

The Viscount de la Rochefoucauld wished in every way to raise the moral level of the theatre. He forbade subscribers, even the most influential, the *entrée* behind the scenes of the Opéra, because these persons had not always preserved there the desirable decorum. Thence arose rancor and spite, against which he had to contend during his entire administration. He wrote to the King, July 29, 1828: —

"A cabal is formed to deprive me of the direction of the theatres; and by whom and for what? It is a struggle, Sire, between good and evil. It is sought to maintain, at any cost, the abuses I have dared to reform. They throw a thousand unjust obstacles in my way. Gamblers are mixed up in it too; they wish to join this ignoble industry and the theatres. It is a monstrous infamy. The opera must be reached at all hazards, the coulisses must be entered; these are the abuses that must be revived. How can it be done? By removing the theatres from troublesome authority. . . . Sire, Your Majesty shall decide, and must defend me with a firm will in the interest, I venture to declare, of order; you must defend yourself also in the interest of morals and of art, and of a great influence of which it is sought to deprive you."

M. de La Rochefoucauld had the last word, and remained at the head of the direction of the Fine Arts until the close of the Restoration. To the credit of his administration there must still be added the creation of the school of religious music, directed by Choron, and the foundation of the concerts of the conservatory with Habeneck, and a little against the wishes of Cherubini. The *chefs-d'œuvre* of German music were brought out as well as those of Italian music. The Viscount performed his task *con amore*, as they say on the other side of the Alps. He wrote to Charles X. January 12, 1830: —

"How many reflections must have come to the

King on regarding the picture of the Coronation! I divined the thought that he did not complete, and my eyes filled with tears. Oh, how much I feel and imagine all the ennui given to the King by these barren and unfortunate politics! I detest them more even than the King detests them. Ungrateful offspring of the times, they fly away, rarely leaving even a memory. How much I prefer the arts!"

This was also the feeling of the Duchess of Berry, who, during all the Restoration, fled from surly politics to live in the region, radiant and sacred, of art and charity. The taste of this Italian lady for painting and music was a veritable passion. She was forever to be found in the museums, the expositions, the theatres. She caught the melodies by heart and was always interested in new works. An expert, a dilletante, was no better judge of pictures and operas; the great artists who shone in the reign of Charles X. received from the amiable Princess the most precious encouragements. Nor did she forget to encourage the efforts of beginners. "Who, then," she said, "would buy the works of these poor young people, if I did not?"

XXVI

THE THEATRE OF MADAME

ONE of the most agreeable theatres of Paris, the Gymnase, owed its prosperity, not to say its existence, to the high protection of Madame the Duchess of Berry. Our old men recall its vogue, at the time when they used to applaud Ferville, Gontier, Numa, Léontine Fay, Jenny Verspré, and when they used to gaze at the greatest ladies of the court, the most fashionable beauties; and they remember that on its façade, from the month of September, 1824, to the Revolution of 1830, there was this inscription in letters of gold: "Théâtre de Madame." Placed under the patronage of the Princess, this fortunate theatre was a meeting-place of the most elegant society of Paris. It had the same audiences as the Opéra and the Italiens, and they enjoyed themselves as much in the entr'actes as during the acts. The spectacle was in the hall as well as on the stage.

The origin of the Gymnase goes back to 1820. According to the privilege accorded to the new stage under the Decazes ministry, it was to be only a *gymnase* composed of the young pupils of the Conservatoire, and other dramatic and lyric schools, and was authorized only to present fragments from the various repertories. But from the beginning it transgressed the limits set for it. Not content with simple pupils, it engaged actors already well known. In place of borrowing *débris* of the repertories of other theatres, it created one of its own. At first the authorities shut their eyes. But when M. de Corbière became Minister of the Interior, he tried to enforce the regulations and to compel the new theatre to confine itself to the limits of its privilege. The Gymnase asked for time, was very meek, prayed, supplicated. It would have succumbed, however, but for the intervention of the Duchess of Berry. Scribe composed for the apartments of the Tuileries a vaudeville, called *La Rosière*, in which he invoked the Princess as protectress, as a beneficent fairy. She turned aside the fulminations of M. de Corbière. The minister was obstinate; he wished the last word; but the Princess finally carried the day. The day after he had addressed to the director of the Gymnase a warning letter, he was amazed to hear the Duchess of Berry say: "I hope, Monsieur, that you will not torment the Gymnase any longer, for, henceforth, it will bear my name."

The minister yielded. The Gymnase was saved. It kept its company, its repertory; it gained the right to give new pieces. From the first days of September, 1824, it took the name of Madame the Duchess of Berry. After the death of Louis XVIII., the 16th of that month, the Duchess of Angoulême having replaced her title of Madame by that of Dauphiness, and the Duchess of Berry taking the former, the Gymnase was called the Théâtre de Madame.

The programme of the Gymnase was constantly being renewed. Scribe, whose *verve* was inexhaustible, wrote for this theatre alone nearly one hundred and fifty pieces. It is true that he had collaborators, — Germain Delavigne, Dupin, Mélesville, Brazier, Varner, Carmouche, Bayard, etc. It was to them that he wrote, in the dedication of the edition of his works: —

"To my collaborators: My dear friends, I have often been reproached for the number of my collaborators; for myself, who am happy to count among them only friends, I regret, on the contrary, that I have not more of them. I am often asked why I have not worked alone. To this I will reply that I have probably neither the wit nor the talent for that; but if I had had them I should still have preferred our literary fraternity and alliance. The few works I have produced alone have been to me a labor; those I have produced with you have been a pleasure."

Eugène Scribe was born December 25, 1791, at Paris, Rue Saint-Denis, near the Marché des Innocents. His father, whom he lost early, kept a silk store, at the sign of the *Chat Noir*, where he had made a considerable fortune. Eugène commenced his career as a dramatic writer in 1811. From that time to his death (February 20, 1861), he composed alone, or with associates, and had represented on the various stages of Paris, more than four hundred plays. M. Vitel said, at the reception of M. Octave Feuillet, at the French Academy, March 26, 1863: —

"There was in Scribe a powerful and truly superior faculty, that assured to him and explained to me his supremacy in the theatre of his day. It was a gift of dramatic invention that perhaps no one before him has possessed; the gift of discovering at every step, almost apropos of nothing, theatrical combinations of a novel and striking effect; and of discovering them, not in the germ only, or barely sketched, but in relief, in action, and already on the stage. In the time needed by his confrères to prepare a plot, he would finish four, and he never secured this prodigious fecundity at the expense of originality. It is in no commonplace mould that his creations are cast. There is not one of his works that has not at least its grain of novelty."

On his part, M. Octave Feuillet, a master in things theatrical, said in his reception discourse: —

"One of the most difficult arts in the domain of literary invention, is that of charming the imagination without unsettling it, of touching the heart without troubling it, of amusing men without corrupting them; this was the supreme art of Scribe."

They are very pretty, very alert, very French, these plays of the Théâtre de Madame. They have aged less than many pretentious works that have aimed at immortality. There is hardly one of them without its ingenious idea, something truly scenic. We often see amateurs seeking pieces to play in the salons; let them draw from this repertory; they will have but an embarrassment of choice among plays always amusing and always in good form.

Scribe said, in his reception discourse at the French Academy (January 28, 1836):—

"It happens, by a curious fatality, that the stage and society are almost always in direct contradiction. Take the period of the Regency. If comedy were the constant expression of society, the comedy of that time must have offered us strong license or joyous Saturnalia. Nothing of the sort; it is cold, correct, pretentious, but decent. In the Revolution, during its most horrible periods, when tragedy, as was said, ran the streets, what were the theatres offering you? Scenes of humanity, of beneficence, of sentimentality; in January, 1793, during the trial of Louis XVI., *La Belle Fermière*, a rural and sentimental play; under the Empire, the reign of glory and conquest, the drama was neither warlike nor exultant; under the Restoration, a pacific government, the stage was invaded by lancers, warriors, and military costumes; Thalia wore epaulettes. The theatre is rarely the expression of society; it is often the opposite."

Scribe was an exception to the rule thus laid down by him. The Théâtre de Madame is an exact painting of the manners, the ideas, the language of the Parisian *bourgeoisie* in the reign of Charles X. Villemain was right in saying to Scribe, on receiving him at the Academy: —

"The secret of your success with the theatre lies in having happily seized the spirit of your century and in making the sort of comedies to which it is best adapted and which most resemble it."

The world that the amiable and ingenious author excels in representing, is that of finance and the middle classes; it is the society of the Chaussée d'Antin, rather than that of the Faubourg Saint Germain. His Gymnase repertory is of the Left Centre, the *juste milieu*, nearer the National Guard than the royal guard. The protégé of Madame the Duchess of Berry never flattered the ultras. There is not in his plays a single line that is a concession to their arrogance or their rancor; not a single phrase, not one word, that shows the least trace of the prejudices of the old régime; not one idea that could offend the most susceptible liberal. It is animated by the spirit of conciliation and pacification. We insist on this point because we see in it a proof that a Princess who took under her protection a kind of literature so essentially modern and *bourgeois*, never thought of reviving a past destroyed forever.

The 28th of June, 1828, when the struggles of the liberals and the ultras were so heated, Eugène Scribe, in connection with M. de Rougemont, wrote for the Gymnase a piece entitled *Avant, Pendant, Après*, historical sketches in three parts. *Avant* was a critique of the view of the old régime; *Pendant*, a critique of those of the Revolution; *Après* an appeal for harmony under the Charter and liberty. This piece seems to us very curious, as a true programme, a faithful reflection of the ideas of the *haute bourgeoisie* of Paris a little before 1830.

The principal personage is a great liberal noble, the General Count de Surgy, who has served gloriously in the armies of the Republic and of the Empire, and at the close is named as deputy to represent an intelligent and wise royalism. By the side of the General is a certain Viscount, who has lived in a savage island since the wreck of *La Pérouse*, and who, more royalist than the King, finds himself among strangers and is utterly dumfounded on beholding the new France. Let us cite some fragments of this piece in which there is more acuteness, more observation, more truth, than in many of the studies called psychologic or historic : —

"THE GENERAL. Ah, do not confuse Liberty with the excesses committed in her name. Liberty, as we understand her, is the friend of order and duty; she protects all rights. She wishes laws, institutions, not scaffolds.

THE MARQUIS. Alas! of what service to you are your courage and your wise opinions? You are denounced, reduced as I am, to hiding, after shedding your blood for them.

THE GENERAL. Not for them but for France. The honor of our country took refuge in the armies, and I followed it there. I have done a little good;

I have hindered much evil, and if the choice were still mine, I should follow the same route.

A Voice (*in the street*). A great conspiracy discovered by the Committee of Public Safety.

The General. Still new victims.

The Marquis. They who did not respect the virtues of Malesherbes, the talents of Lavoisier, the youth of Barnave, will they recoil from one crime more?

The General. Decent people will get weary of having courage only to die. France will reawaken, stronger and more united, for misfortune draws to each other all ranks, all parties; and already you see that we, formerly so divided, are understanding each other better at last, and love each other more than ever.

The Marquis (*throwing himself into the General's arms*). Ah, you speak truly."

This scene passes in the midst of the Terror. The conclusion, the moral of the piece, is as follows:—

"The General. My friends, my fellow-citizens, we who, after so many storms have finally reached port, and who, under the shelter of the throne and the laws, taste that wise and moderate liberty which has been the object of our desires for forty years; let us guard it well, it has cost us dear. Always united, let us no longer think of the evil done, let us see only the good that is, let us put away sad memories, and let us all say, in the new France, 'Union and forgiveness.'"

Among the spectators more than one could recognize himself in the personages of the piece. But the allusions were so nicely made that no one could be offended. Liberals and ultras could, on the contrary, profit by the excellent counsels given them in the little play of the Théâtre de Madame.

Let us add, moreover, that Scribe never wished to be anything but a man of letters. There could be applied to him the words said by him of his confrère, friend, and nephew, Bayard: —

"A stranger to all parties, he speculated on no revolution; he flattered no one in power, not even those he loved. He solicited no honors, no places, no pension. He asked nothing of any one but himself. He owed to his talent and his labor his honor and his independence."

The device chosen by Scribe is a pen, above which is the motto: *Inde fortuna et libertas*. The Duchess of Berry knew how to understand and appreciate this man of wit and good sense. For his part, Scribe avowed for the Princess a sentiment of gratitude that he never falsified. When the days of ill fortune came for her, he journeyed to bear his homage to her upon a foreign soil.

XXVII

DIEPPE

DIEPPE has not forgotten the benefits received from the Duchess of Berry. It was this amiable Princess that made fashionable the pretty Normandy city and made it the most elegant bathing resort of Europe. She made five visits there, of several weeks each, in 1824, 1825, 1826, 1827, and 1829.

The Duchess came for the first time to Dieppe some time before the death of Louis XVIII. She arrived the 29th of July, and left the 23d of August. She conceived immediately a passion for the picturesque town, as famous for its fine beach as for its smiling environs. The enthusiasm manifested for her by the inhabitants touched her. She said to the mayor: "Henri IV. was right when he called the Dieppois his good friends. I shall imitate my ancestor in his love for them."

The next year — the year of the coronation — Madame returned to her favorite city. She arrived there the 2d of August, 1825. More than twenty thousand persons were awaiting her at the boundary of the district, and her entry was triumphal. The

6th of August, the actors of the Gymnase, come from Paris, gave a theatrical representation in her honor.

Madame made many excursions by sea. There was on her boat a tent of crimson silk, above which floated the white flag. The little flotilla of the royal navy had manœuvres in her honor, and saluted her with salvos of artillery. The 10th of September, the Princess made an excursion to Bacqueville, where there awaited her a numerous cortège of Cauchois women, all on horseback, in the costume of the country. The 12th, she breakfasted in the ship *Le Rodeur*, and a recently constructed merchant vessel was launched in her presence. She departed the 14th, promising to return the following year.

Accordingly, Madame left Paris for Dieppe the 7th of August, 1826. The morrow of her arrival, she assisted at the inauguration of a new playhouse that had been built within six months. The mayor presented the Princess with some keys, artistically worked—the keys to her loge and to her salon. The prologue of the opening piece, entitled *La Poste Royale*, was filled with delicate allusions and compliments. The 17th of August, there was a performance offered by Madame to the sailors and soldiers of the garrison. From his place in the parterre a subordinate of the 64th regiment of the line sang, in honor of the Princess, some couplets expressing the sentiments of his comrades.

The 19th, there was a visit to the ruins of the Château of Arques, immortalized by the victory of

Henry IV. An agreeable surprise for Madame was a comedy for the occasion improvised by the actors of the Vaudeville. When the Princess presents herself before the Château, a little peasant girl at first refuses her admittance. She has received orders, she says, from her father and mother to open to no one, no matter whom. But the air *Vive Henri IV.* is heard, and straightway both doors are opened wide to the Princess. An old concierge and his wife sing piquant verses about their first refusal to open to her. From here Madame is guided by the little peasant girl to the entrance of an ancient garden, where she perceives the whole troupe in the costume of gardeners and garden girls. She is offered bouquets and escorted to a dairy at the extremity of the ruins. The band of the guard plays for her her favorite air, *Charmante Gabrielle*. A young milk-maid—the pretty actress Jenny Colon—offers her a cup of milk and sings couplets that please her greatly. Then comes the husband of the dairy-maid and recounts to the grand-daughter of Henry IV. the victory won by her ancestor over the Duke of Mayenne. A little later, Madame is conducted to the foot of an ancient tower, whence there is a view of immense extent. Here she is arrested by the songs of an ancient minstrel, whose voice is accompanied by mysterious music hidden in the hollows of the ruins.

Going from surprise to surprise, the Princess traverses a long arch of verdure where she reads on escutcheons the dates dear to her heart. At the end of this long avenue, she again finds the entire troupe of the Vaudeville, who re-escort her to the gates of Château, singing a general chorus of farewell, amid cries of "Long live the King! Long live Madame!" the effect of which is doubled by repeated salutes of artillery.

Some days later, the 7th of September, the Duchess of Berry learned, during the day, that a frightful tempest threatened to engulf a great number of fishing-boats which were coming toward port. Instantly she countermanded a ball that she was to give that evening. She proceeded in all haste to the point whence aid could be given to these unfortunates. Clinging to a little post on the jetty, which the waves covered from all sides, she directed and encouraged the rescue. The Dieppe correspondence of the *Moniteur* said:—

"What has been seen at Dieppe alone, is a young Princess, braving all the dangers of a wild sea, remaining on the end of the jetty to direct the succor of the fishing-boats that were seeking refuge in the harbor. She seemed placed there by the Deity as a protecting angel, and the sailors who saw her took courage again."

She withdrew from the dangerous place, which she called her post, only when all the barks had entered port. One man only had perished. Before even changing her clothing the Princess sent relief to his widow.

By her kindness, her charity, her grace, Madame won all hearts. Her protection revived at Dieppe the commerce in ivory and laces. She gave two brevets, one in her own name, the other in that of Mademoiselle, to the best two manufacturers in the city, and made considerable purchases. She founded at her expense, under the direction of the Sisters of Providence, a manufactory of laces where a large number of young girls obtained at the same time the means of living and the benefits of a Christian education. Between the Princess and her good city of Dieppe there was a constant exchange of delicate attentions and proofs of sympathy. When she was spoken to of preparations for departure, "Already?" she said sadly. She left the 19th of September, 1826, and returned the following year.

The 6th of August, 1827, Madame made an entry to Dieppe by the hamlet of Janval. A great crowd went to visit her, and greeted her with enthusiastic cheers. The 13th of August, the city offered her a great ball, at which more than twelve hundred persons attended. On the 16th, the portrait of the Princess was unveiled at the Hôtel de Ville. At the moment that the veil was raised, the band of the fifth regiment of the royal guard played the air of *Vive Henri IV.* amid long applause. The mayor of Dieppe, M. Cavalier, pronounced a discourse in which he expressed the gratitude of the inhabitants, and promised that the cherished image should be surrounded, age after age, by the veneration of a city whose history was one of constant devotion to its Kings. In the evening Madame gave a soirée at which the hereditary Princess of Hesse-Darmstadt was present. Rossini was at the piano and sang with his wife and with Balfe; Nadermann played the harp.

The Duchess of Berry made numerous excursions by sea, even in the worst weather. One day, at least, she was in some danger. The sailors admired her good spirits and her courage. "Oh," they said, "she is indeed a worthy descendant of Henry IV."

The 4th of September, 1827, Mademoiselle, with her governess, the Duchess of Gontaut, came to join her mother at Dieppe. The little Princess was to be eight years old the 21st of the month. A formal reception was given her. Her arrival was announced by the noise of cannon and the sound of bells. The Baron de Viel-Castel, sub-prefect of the city, made a complimentary address to her. She responded in the most gracious manner, "I know how much you love my mother, and I loved you in advance."

Madame, who had gone to meet her daughter at Osmonville, three leagues from Dieppe, took her in her carriage. The horses proceeded at a walk, and the people never wearied of admiring the gentle little Princess. On the morrow, Madame received the homage of the functionaries. The mayor said to her: "Your Royal Highness is in a country filled with your ancestors, in a city honored by Henry IV. with special benevolence, which Louis XIV. rewarded for its fidelity by calling it 'his good city,' which your august aunt, Madame the Dauphiness, deigned to choose for her return to France, and which received her, triumphant and adored."

An elegant breakfast service in ivory, with her arms, was presented to Mademoiselle by a group of very young people. She next received a deputation of the fisherwomen of Du Polet, the faubourg of Dieppe. They came in their picturesque costumes, — a skirt falling a little below the knee, men's buckled shoes, a striped apron of white and red, an enormous head-dress, with broad tabs, and great ear-rings. They sang couplets expressing a lively attachment to the family of the Bourbons. In their enthusiasm they asked and obtained leave to kiss the little Princess.

On the 6th of September, there was a fête at the ruins of the Castle of Arques. From seven in the morning the crowd gathered on the hillside of Saint Etienne, at the edge of the coast between Martin-Eglise and the village of Arques. It is a magnificent site, which, towering above the valley, is surrounded on all sides by grim hill-slopes, while in the distance is the sea, along the edge of which extends the city of Dieppe, like a majestic dike. A mimic battle took place in the presence of Madame and her daughter, on the ground where Henry IV. had delivered the famous battle of September 21, 1589. Numerous strokes on the flags of different colors indicated the lines of the Béarnais, and circumscribed the enceinte occupied by his troops. An obelisk had been placed at the highest point of this sort of entrenched camp; in the centre was a post tent, under which a rich breakfast had been prepared for the two princesses. During the repast, both put their names to a subscription to erect a monument commemorating the victory of their ancestor.

The 14th of September, the city offered a ball to Madame and Mademoiselle. The little Princess danced two quadrilles. The 15th, she offered lunch to a great number of children of her own age, and afterward went with them to the theatre. The 18th, at the close of the play, some scenes were represented before Madame, mingled with verses, expressing the regret of the city at the near departure of Madame. The next day, the Princess and her daughter left Dieppe, between double lines of troops and National Guards.

The journey of the Duchess of Berry in the West, in 1828, prevented her from going that year to Dieppe. She came in 1829, but it was for the last time. She arrived the 6th of August, with her daughter. The next day she danced at a subscription ball given by the city and by the visitors to the baths; the 8th she received a visit from the Dauphiness, who passed three days with her.

For every fête there was a corresponding good work. The Princess said: "I wish that while I am enjoying myself the poor may also have their share." The 18th of August, she visited the bazaar opened for the benefit of the indigent. Mademoiselle had conceived the idea of writing her name on little objects of painted wood, which were bid for at their weight in gold. The 24th, Madame gave a concert, at which the Sontag sisters were heard and some stanzas of the Viscount of Castel-bajac were recited. The 25th, the city offered a ball to Mademoiselle, at which the grace of the little Princess, her tact, and her precocious amiability, excited surprise. The 9th of September, the inauguration of the monument commemorative of the victory of Henry IV. took place in the presence of Madame and her daughter. It was a column indicating the point where the army of Mayenne debouched to surround the King's troops, when, the fog rising, the artillery of the castle could be brought into play, and threw into disorder the ranks of the Leaguers. The inauguration interested the Duchess much. The troops of the line and the National Guard had established bivouacs where the princesses read with joy such inscriptions as these: "The young Henry will find again the arquebusiers of Henry IV.—The flag of the 12th will always rally to the white plume!—Two Henrys—one love, one devotion."

A table of forty covers had been arranged under a pavilion draped with flags. After the repast Madame and Mademoiselle danced several quadrilles on the grass. The fête was charming. An expression of joy was depicted on every face.

At the time of her various sojourns at Dieppe, the Duchess of Berry went to visit the Orleans family at the Château d'Eu. She manifested toward her aunt, Marie-Amélie, the liveliest affection, and had no courtier more amiable and assiduous than the young Duke of Chartres, whom, it is said, she wished to have as husband for Mademoiselle. The 9th of September, she had been at the baptismal font, with the Duke of Angoulême, the Duke of Montpensier, the latest son of the Duke of Orleans. She was very fond of her god-son, and nothing was more agreeable to her than a reunion at the Château d'Eu, where Mademoiselle was always happy, playing with her young cousins.

The Duchess of Berry and her daughter returned to Saint Cloud the 16th of September, 1829. On leaving, Mademoiselle said to the Dieppois: "My friends, I will come back next year, and I will bring you my brother." Neither she nor her mother was to return.

XXVIII

THE PRINCE DE POLIGNAC

AT the very moment that the Duchess of Berry, happy and smiling, was tranquilly taking the sea-baths at Dieppe, an event occurred at Paris that was the signal for catastrophes. The 9th of August, 1829, the *Moniteur* published the decree constituting the cabinet, in which were included the Prince de Polignac as Minister of Foreign Affairs; Count de La Bourdonnaye as Minister of the Interior; and as Minister of War, the General Count de Bourmont. The next day the *Débats* said: —

"So here is once more broken the bond of love and confidence that was uniting the people to the Monarch. Here once again are the court with its old rancors, the Emigration with its prejudices, the priesthood with its hatred of liberty, coming to throw themselves between France and her King. What she has conquered by forty years of travail and misfortune is taken from her; what she repels with all the force of her will, all the energy of her deepest desires, is violently imposed upon her. Ill-fated France! Ill-fated King!"

The 15th of August the *Débats* reached a paroxysm of fury: —

"If from all the battle-fields of Europe where our Grand Army has left its members, if from Belgium, where it left the last fragments of its body, and from the place where Marshal Ney fell shot, there arise cries of anger that resound in our hearts, if the column of the Grand Army seems to tremble through all its bronze battalions, whose is the fault? No, no; nothing is lacking in this ministry of the counter-Revolution. Waterloo is represented. . . . M. de Polignac represents in it the ideas of the first Emigration, the ideas of Coblenz; M. de La Bourdonnaye the faction of 1815 with its murderous friendships, its law of proscription, and its *clientèle* of southern massacres. Coblenz, Waterloo, 1815, these are the three personages of the ministry. Turn it how you will, every side dismays. Every side angers. It has no aspect that is not sinister, no face that is not menacing. Take our hatreds of thirty years ago, our sorrows and our fears of fifteen years ago, all are there, all have joined to insult and irritate France. Squeeze, wring this ministry, it drips only humiliations, misfortunes, dangers."

The Abbé Védrenne, historian of Charles X., wrote:—

"How is the language of the writers of the *Débats*, who called themselves royalists, to be understood? Was not Charles X. at Coblenz? Did not Chateaubriand emigrate with the King and the princes? Did he not follow Louis XVIII. to Ghent? Was he not in his council at the very hour of the battle of

Waterloo? They might as well have stigmatized the white flag and demanded the proscription of the King's dynasty. But such was their blindness that they feared nothing for it. 'The throne runs no risk,' said Chateaubriand, 'let us tremble for liberty only.' Yet the nomination of the Polignac ministry was an error. It appeared to be a provocation, a sort of defiance. Charles X. doubtless only wished to defend himself, but in choosing such ministers at such an hour, he appeared to be willing to attack."

From the début of the new cabinet, the Opposition, to use a recent expression, showed itself irreconcilable. It raised a long cry of anger, and declared war to the death on Prince Polignac.

"It is in vain," said the *Débats*, "that the ministers demand of Time to efface with a sweep of his wing their days, their actions, their thoughts, of yesterday; these live for them, as for us. The shadow of their past goes before them and traces their route. They cannot turn aside; they must march; they must advance. — But I wish to turn back. — You cannot. — But I shall support liberty, the Charter, the Opposition. — You cannot. March, then, march, under the spur of necessity, to the abyss of *Coups d'État!* March! Your life has judged and condemned you. Your destiny is accomplished."

The man who excited hatreds so violent was Jules de Polignac. He was born at Versailles, May 14, 1780. As the German historian, Gervinus, has said: "His past weighed upon him like a lash of political interdict. He was the son of the Duchess of Polignac, who had been the object of so many calumnies, and who had never been pardoned for the intimate friendship with which she was honored by the unfortunate queen, Marie Antoinette, a friendship that had evoked against her, first all the jealousies of the envious courtiers, and then all the aversion of the people. It was believed that a like favoritism could be recognized in the relations of the son of the Duchess with Charles X. To this unpopularity, inherited from his mother, was joined another that was directed against the person of the *émigré*."

After having been one of the courtiers of the little court at Coblenz, he had taken service for some time in Russia, and then passed into England, where he had been one of the most intimate confidants, and one of the most active agents of the Count d'Artois. Sent secretly into France, with his elder brother, the Duke Armand de Polignac, he was, like the latter, compromised in the Cadoudal conspiracy. Their trial is remarkable for the noble strife of devotion, in which each of the brothers pleaded the cause of the other at the expense of his own. Armand was condemned to death. His wife threw herself at the feet of the First Consul, who, thanks to the intercession of Josephine, commuted the penalty of death to perpetual confinement. Jules was condemned to prison, and shared the captivity of his brother. Confined at first in the castle of Ham, then in the Temple, then at Vincennes, they obtained, at the time of the marriage of

Napoleon with Marie Louise, their transfer to a hospital. There they knew the General Mallet, but the part they were suspected of taking in his conspiracy was never proven. When the allied armies entered France, they succeeded in escaping, and rejoined the Count d'Artois at Vesoul. They penetrated to Paris some days before the capitulation, and displayed the white flag there the 3d of March, 1814.

Peer of France, field-marshal, ambassador, the Prince Jules de Polignac was one of the favorites of the Restoration. On the proposition of M. de Chateaubriand, then Minister of Foreign Affairs, he had him named, in 1823, ambassador to London, where he had shown a genuine talent for diplomacy. The example of England made him think that in France the liberties of the constitutional régime could be combined with the directing influence of an aristocracy. That was his error and the cause of his fall. Some weeks before his accession to the ministry, he had solemnly affirmed in the Chamber of Peers, that he considered the Charter as a solemn pact, on which rested the monarchical institutions of France, and as the heavenly sign of a serene future. But the liberals did not believe his word, and accused him of striving to re-establish the old régime.

Even at court the accession of the Prince de Polignac did not fail to cause apprehension. Charles X., having announced to the Duchess of Gontaut that he was going to appoint him minister, added: "This news must give you pleasure; you know him well, I

THE PRINCE DE POLIGNAC.

believe." The Duchess replied: "He has been absent a long time. I only knew him when very young." The King resumed: "Do not speak of it; it is my secret as yet." Madame de Gontaut could not keep from smiling, for she held several letters from London in her hand, among others one from the sister-in-law of the Duke of Wellington, announcing the news. Charles X. wished to see the letters. "He is good, loyal," they said, "loving the King as one loves a friend, but feeble, and with bad surroundings. It is doubted whether he can ever rise to the height of the post in which the King wishes to place him."

Charles X., wounded by the indiscretion of the Prince, and also by that of the Duke of Wellington, who divulged what he himself was keeping secret, returned the letter to Madame de Gontaut, and remarked: —

"It is very thoughtless in Jules to have spoken of it so soon, and in the Duke to have published it." The Duchess of Gontaut, who was used to frank talk with the King, said: "In the circumstances existing, I long for, I confess it frankly, and at the risk of displeasing Your Majesty, yes, I long for the Martignac ministry."

Then, adds the Duchess in her unpublished Memoirs, the King, more impatient than ever, turned his back on me, and took his way to his apartment. I had had the courage to tell him my thought and the truth. I did not repent it. When we saw each other again the same day he did not speak to me again of it.

One of those most devoted to the elder branch, the Duke Ambroise de la Rochefoucauld-Doudeauville, also says in his Memoirs: —

"The King sincerely wished for the Charter, whatever may be said, but he wished for the monarchy; he, therefore, decided to change ministers who had made promises that seemed to him fatal, and to replace them by others whose principles suited him better. He was not happy in this choice, it must be agreed. He took as Minister of Foreign Affairs and President of the Council the Prince de Polignac. For a long time public opinion had foreseen this choice, and dreaded it. At the commencement of the Restoration M. de Polignac for more than a year had refused to recognize the Charter and to swear fidelity to it, which made him regarded as the pronounced enemy of our institutions. Was this antipathy real? I do not think so. He had for a long time lived in England, as ambassador, and was thoroughly imbued with principles at once very constitutional and very aristocratic, after the English fashion. His devotion was great, as well as his personal merit, but his resources as a statesman were not so much so; he took his desire to do well for the capacity to do well, and he mistook."

When he assumed the direction of affairs the Prince de Polignac was wholly surprised at the systematic and obstinate opposition that he encountered. As M. Guizot said, "he was sincerely astonished that he was not willingly accepted as a minister devoted to the constitutional régime. But the public, without troubling itself to know if he were sincere or not, persisted in seeing in him the champion of the old régime and the standard-bearer of the counter-Revolution."

Although he had passed a part of his life in England, first as *émigré*, then as ambassador, and had married as his first wife an English lady, Miss Campbell, and as his second another, the daughter of Lord Radcliffe, the Prince de Polignac was French at heart.

No Minister of Foreign Affairs in France had in higher degree the sentiment of the national dignity. Yet this is the way the *Débats* expressed itself, the 16th of August, 1829, about a man who, the next year, at the time of the glorious Algiers Expedition, was to hold toward England language so proud and firm: —

"The manifesto of M. de Polignac comes to us from England. That is very simple. We have a minister who scarcely knows how to speak anything but English. It takes time to relearn one's native tongue when one has forgotten it for many years. It appears even that one never regains the accent in all its freedom and purity. In fact, the English have not given us M. de Polignac; they have sold him to us. That people understand commerce so well."

Despite all the violent criticisms, all the implacable hatreds by which he was incessantly assailed, the Prince de Polignac was a noble character, and no one should forget the justness of soul with which, from the commencement to the end of his career, he supported misfortune and captivity. The Viscount Sosthènes de La Rochefoucauld, afterwards the Duke of Doudeauville, says, in his Memoirs:—

"The purest honor, the loftiest disinterestedness, the sincerest devotion, are not everything, there is needed a capacity for affairs, a knowledge of men, which experience alone procures and which even the strongest will cannot give. M. de Polignac had all the qualities of the most devoted subject, but his talent did not rise to the height of his position. If it had been necessary only to suffer and to march to death, no one, surely, could have equalled him; but more was requisite, and he remained beneath the level of the circumstances he thought he was overcoming; the fall of the throne was the consequence. How he developed, though, and grew great when in duress, and who should flatter himself that he could bear up with a firmness more unshaken against the severest trials? If M. de Polignac is not a type of the statesman, he will at least remain the complete model of the virtues of the Christian and the private citizen."

The Prince de Polignac was mistaken, but he acted in good faith. No one can dispute his faults, but none can suspect the purity of his intentions. Unfortunately his royalism had in it something of mysticism and ecstasy that made of this gallant man a sort of *illuminé*. He sincerely believed that he had received from God the mission to save the throne and the altar, and foreseeing neither difficulties nor obstacles, regarding all uncertainty and all fear as unworthy of a gentleman and a Christian, he had in himself and in his ideas, that blind, imperturbable confidence that is the characteristic of fanatics. In a period less troubled, this great noble would perhaps have been a remarkable minister of foreign affairs, but in the stormy time when he took the helm in hand, he had neither sufficient prudence nor sufficient experience to resist the tempest and save the ship from the wreck in which the dynasty was to go down.

XXIX

GENERAL DE BOURMONT

THE new Secretary of War awoke no less lively anger than the Prince de Polignac. He was a general of great merit, bold to temerity, brave to heroism, and a tactician of the first order. But his career had felt the vicissitudes of politics, and like so many of his contemporaries,— more, perhaps, than any of them, — he had played the most contradictory parts. Equally intrepid in the army of Condé, in the Vendéan army, and in the Grand Army of Napoleon, he had won as much distinction under the white flag as under the tricolor. The Emperor, who was an expert in military talent, having recognized in him a superior military man, had rewarded his services brilliantly. But it is difficult to escape from the memories of one's childhood and first youth.

General Count de Bourmont, born September 2, 1773, at the Château of Bourmont (Maine-et-Loire), amid the "Chouans," had shared their religious and monarchical passions. Officer of the French Guards at sixteen, and dismissed by the Revolution, he followed his father at the beginning of the Emigration, lost him at Turin, then went to join the Count d'Artois at Coblenz. He took part in the campaign of 1792, until the disbandment of the Prince's army, served as a simple cavalryman in the army of Condé, then threw himself into La Vendée in the month of October, 1794. He was second in command of the troops of Scépeaux. The Vendéan insurrection of 1799 recognized him as one of its chiefs. Victor at Louverné, he seized Mans the 15th of October, and was the last to lay down his arms.

Bourmont had a passion for the life of the camp. When the royal troops had laid down their arms, he was ready to fight in the ranks of the imperial troops rather than not to fight at all. He distinguished himself in the Russian campaign, contributed to the victory of Lutzen, made a heroic defence at Nugent during the campaign in France, and was named general of division by the Emperor.

During the Hundred Days, General de Bourmont, guilty as was Marshal Ney, abandoned the cause of Napoleon as the Marshal had that of Louis XVIII. But there were attenuating circumstances for their conduct. One could not resist the prestige of the Emperor, nor the other that of the King. What aggravated the situation of General de Bourmont was that, after having sought a command from Napoleon, as Marshal Ney had from Louis XVIII., he deserted three days before the battle of Waterloo. The royalist, the soldier of the army of Condé, the "Chouan" had suddenly reappeared under the General of the Empire. His King had summoned him, and impelled by a false sentiment of conscience, he had responded to the appeal of his King. But he was wrongly suspected of having delivered to the English and Prussians the plans of Napoleon.

One may read in the Memoirs of the Duke Ambroise de Doudeauville: —

"The Count de Bourmont was appointed Minister of War. He had to meet grave prejudices. It was claimed that, having accepted service under Bonaparte in the Hundred Days, he had deserted a few hours before the battle of Waterloo, taking with him a great part of the troops, and carrying to the enemy the plans and projects of the campaign. I owe it to the truth to say that this story is greatly exaggerated. I have it from Marshal Gérard himself — and his testimony cannot be suspected — that some days before this battle M. de Bourmont had written him that, summoned by Louis XVIII., he believed it his duty to go to him, but promised to guard the most religious silence. He kept his word, went alone, carried away no plan, and faithfully kept the secret."

The Duke adds: —

"I knew, from Charles X. himself, that he was very greatly surprised at the accusation of desertion brought against M. de Bourmont when he appointed him minister. He had not the least idea that that reproach could be addressed to him, for he knew that the General had but obeyed the orders of Louis XVIII., his legitimate sovereign."

Does not this phrase show the illusions of which

Charles X. was the victim? He never even suspected that his choice was a challenge to the old soldiers of the Empire. Yet the violence of the liberal press certainly extended the range of insult. "As for the other," said the *Journal des Débats* disdainfully, "on what field of battle did he win his epaulets? There are services by which one may profit, which may even be liberally paid for, but which no people ever dreamed of honoring." And, as if the allusion was not sufficiently transparent, "I see," added the same writer, "but one kind of discussion in which the minister can engage with credit — that of the military code, and the chapter relating to desertion to the enemy. There are among our new ministers those who understand the question to perfection." As for the *Figaro*, it confined itself to quoting this line from a proclamation of the General during the Hundred Days: "The cause of the Bourbons is forever lost! April, 1815. — BOURMONT."

Despite the virulent attacks of the journals, General de Bourmont, who had distinguished himself on so many battle-fields, had authority with the troops, and the Expedition of Algiers the next year was to show him to be a military man of the first order. If Charles X. committed an error in naming him as minister, he committed a greater one in sending him away from Paris before the "ordinances," for no one was more capable of securing the success of a *coup d'état*. M. de Chateaubriand remarks: —

"If the General had been in Paris at the time of the

catastrophe, the vacant portfolio of war would not have fallen into the hands of M. de Polignac. Before striking the blow, had he consented to it, M. de Bourmont would beyond doubt have massed at Paris the entire royal guard; he would have provided money and supplies so that the soldiers would have lacked for nothing."

We are inclined to think, however, that when he took the portfolio of war General de Bourmont was not dreaming of a *coup d'état*, and that the Prince de Polignac had as yet no thought of it. This minister, who was so decried, showed at the outset such an inoffensive disposition that the Opposition was surprised and disturbed by it.

"The minister," said the *Débats*, "boasts of his moderation, because in the ten days of his existence, he has not put France to fire and sword, because the prisons are not gorged, because we still walk the streets in freedom. From all this, nevertheless, flows a striking lesson. There are men who were going to make an end of the spirit of the century. Well, they do nothing!"

The journals of the Right lamented this inaction.

"If the ministerial revolution," said the *Quotidienne*, "reduces itself to this, we shall retire to some profound solitude where the sound of the falling monarchy cannot reach us."

Then, more royalist than the King, M. de Lamennais wrote on the subject of the new ministers: "It is stupidity to which fear counsels silence." M. Guizot says in his *Mémoires pour servir à l'histoire de mon temps:* —

"This ministry, formed to overcome the Revolution and save the monarchy, remained inert and sterile. The Opposition insultingly charged it with impotence; it called it the hectoring ministry, the dullest of ministries, and, for answer, it prepared the expedition of Algiers and prorogued the Chambers, protesting always its fidelity to the Charter, promising itself to get out of its embarrassments by a majority and a conquest."

The Duchess of Berry had seen without apprehension, and perhaps even with pleasure, the nomination of the new ministers. Tranquillity reigned in France. There was no symptom of agitation, no sign of disquiet in the circle surrounding the Princess, and after an agreeable stay of some weeks at Dieppe, she proceeded to the south, where her journey was a triumph.

XXX

THE JOURNEY IN THE SOUTH

THE journey of the Duchess of Berry in the south of France, in 1829, was scarcely less triumphant than that she had made in the Vendée the year before. The object of the Princess was to meet her family of the Two Sicilies, which was traversing the kingdom on the way from Italy to Spain, to escort to Madrid the young Marie-Christine, who was about to espouse King Ferdinand VII. — his fourth wife.

Born October 13, 1784, King since March 19, 1808, Ferdinand VII. had married, first, Marie Antoinette, Princess of the Two Sicilies; second, Isabelle-Marie Françoise, Princess of Portugal; third, Marie-Josèphe-Amélie, Princess of Saxony. He had chosen for his fourth wife, Marie-Christine, Princess of the Two Sicilies, born April 27, 1806. Sister of the father of the Duchess of Berry, Marie-Christine was the daughter of François I., King of the Two Sicilies, and his second wife, the Infanta of Spain, Marie-Isabelle, born October 13, 1784, and sister of Ferdinand II. The King of the Two Sicilies was escorting his daughter, Marie-Christine, to the King of Spain, where she was to marry at Madrid the 11th of December, 1829.

Ferdinand VII. had a brother, the Infante François de Paule, born March 10, 1784, who had espoused a princess of the Two Sicilies, Louise-Caroline-Marie Isabelle, born October 24, 1804, sister of the Duchess of Berry. From this marriage was born the Infante Don Francisco of d'Assisi, husband of Queen Isabelle. The Infante and Infanta François de Paule traversed the south of France, to meet the Bourbons of Naples. We may add that the Duchess of Orleans, sister of King François I., aunt of Marie-Christine and of the Duchess of Berry, went with her husband to the eastern frontier of France to meet her relatives.

The Duchess of Berry, authorized by Charles X. to go to the south to meet her father, her step-mother, and her sisters, left Saint Cloud, October 10, 1829. The 17th, she was at Lyons, whither she promised to return. At Valence, she found her step-brother and her sister, the Infante and Infanta François de Paule, and returned with them to Lyons, where, October 20, she was greeted by a great crowd, eager to look upon her face. At the Grand Théâtre Their Highnesses assisted at a performance, in which the actor Bernard-León, Jr., played the part of Poudret in *Le Coiffeur et le Perruquier*.

Their Highnesses quitted Lyons, October 23, visited the Grande-Chartreuse the 24th, and were at Grenoble the 25th, where they met the Bourbons of Naples, who arrived in that city the 31st, coming from Chambéry. The Duchess of Berry, the Infante and Infanta François de Paule, the Duke and Duchess of Orleans, received them at their entry into France. Everywhere, from the frontier to Grenoble, the Sicilian Majesties were met by the authorities, the mayors, the clergy. Triumphal arches were erected by various communes. The one constructed by the Marquis de Marcieu, in the wood of the avenue of his Château of Trouvet, was especially remarked. This arch formed three porticoes, surmounted by the arms of France, Naples, and Spain. Above were these words, "Love to all the Bourbons." The grand avenue of the château was draped from one end to the other. Every tree bore a white flag. Garlands of verdure, mingled with these flags, formed an arbor that stretched as far as the eye could see. Thirty young girls, clad in white, crowned with flowers, and holding little flags in their hands, were ranged in two lines near the arch. They offered to the King of Naples, to the Queen and the princesses, bouquets and baskets of fruits. When the cortège arrived before Grenoble, the mayor said: "Sire, the descendants of Louis XIV. have imprescriptible rights to our respect, to our love. We can never forget their origin nor the indissoluble bonds that bind them to our native land, and still less the virtues and goodness that distinguish this illustrious dynasty." He added: "Sire, the city of Grenoble deems itself happy in being the first city of France to present to Your Majesties the homage of our respects, and to thank you for the noble present you have made to our land in the person of your illustrious daughter, Madame, Duchess of Berry. May the future Queen of Spain long embellish the throne on which she is about to take her seat, and reign over the hearts of her new subjects as her heroic sister reigns over ours. Long live the King! Forever live the Bourbons!"

The Duchess of Berry accompanied her relatives to the Pyrenees. The journey was a long series of ovations. Marie-Christine, who was about to ascend the throne of Spain, never ceased to admire the riches and beauty of France. "Ah, my sister," said the Duchess of Berry to her, "do not contemplate it too much. You would not be able to quit it!" During the entire passage — at Valence, Avignon, Montpellier, Nîmes — the people rivalled the authorities in making the welcome as brilliant as possible. Perpignan was reached the 10th of November. The King and Queen of Naples, the Duchess of Berry, and the future Queen of Spain, journeyed together in an uncovered calèche. Madame accompanied her relatives to the frontier at Perthus, where she bade them adieu, the 13th of November. The French troops from the foot of Bellegarde flanked the right of the road. At the first salute fired from the fort, an immense crowd of French and Spanish, who occupied the heights, greeted with harmonious shouts the appearance of the royal carriage. On an arch of triumph, erected on the Spanish side of the frontier, floated the flags of the three peoples placed under the sceptre of the Bourbons. That of France was in the middle and seemed to protect those of Spain and Naples on either side. Thus was indicated the mother branch of the three reigning families. The adieux were made with effusion. The Duchess of Berry fell at the feet of her father, who hastened to raise her and embrace her tenderly. The two sisters threw themselves into each other's arms. Then they parted.

While the Bourbons of Naples were entering on the soil of Spain, the Duchess of Berry returned to Perpignan. She left there the 14th, and the ovations were renewed along the route. The 16th, she passed through Montpellier, where she admired the promenade of the Peyrou, whence are perceived the sea, the Pyrenees, and the Alps, and saw the foundations prepared for an equestrian statue of Louis XIV. The 17th, at Tarascon, she breakfasted with the Marquis de Gras-Préville, and was present at the games instituted by good King René, — tambourine dances and the races of the Tarasque. The 18th, at Arles, she visited the Cloister of Saint Trophime, and the Roman circus. About eighteen thousand persons were crowded on the ancient benches. The galleries resounded with military music which, borne from echo to echo, spread beneath all the arches. In the evening the entire city was illuminated. From a balcony, the Princess assisted at a *pégoulade*, a sort of torchlight promenade of five or six hundred young people, who bore pieces of tarred rope lighted at one end. She desired to see again these bizarre and picturesque effects of light, this joyous procession, this clamorous animation, and she had the enthusiastic cortège file a second time under her windows. The 21st, she visited the Roman theatre at Orange, one of the most curious ruins of the world. The 23d, she passed again through Lyons. The 28th, she was at the Tuileries for dinner.

The Duchess of Berry returned enchanted with her journey. Never had the throne of the Bourbons seemed to her more solid, never were the advantages of the family pact revealed in a more brilliant manner. The *Moniteur* wrote: "The Princess Marie-Christine has heard her name mingling in the air with that of her whose son is one day to be King of France. Happy the new Queen, if her presence shall deliver Spain from the factions that still divide it, and if, finding beyond the mountains the same order, devotion, prosperity, as in our provinces, she can cry, 'There are no longer any Pyrenees.'"

The Duchess of Berry had not found the inclinations of the south less royalist than that of La Vendée. Everywhere protestations were made to her, verging on lyrism, on idolatry; the idea of suspecting such demonstrations never crossed her mind. She persuaded herself that France loved her as much as she loved France.

INDEX

Adélaïde, Madame, remains of, re-interred in Saint-Denis, 27.

Almoner, Grand, the, 90.

Ampulla, the holy, containing the coronation oil, 127.

Angoulême, Duke of, his character and qualities, 48 *et seq.;* deserves credit for his part in the Spanish expedition, 49; marriage of, to the daughter of Louis XVI., 50.

Angoulême, Duchess of, 51 *et seq.;* her character and habits, 51; her apartments, 52; her charity, 52, 53; brusqueness of, 55; not deceived, 55, 56; affection of Charles X. for, 57; absent from the expiatory solemnity at Paris, 173; insulted at the review of the National Guard, 203.

Arques, Château of, reception of the Duchess of Berry at, 267.

Aumale, Duke d', 73.

Avant, Pendant, Après, Scribe's drama, 262.

Barrère, advocates the destruction of the royal tombs at Saint-Denis, 22.

Barthélemy, celebrates the coronation in verse, 159.

Berry, the Duke of, remains interred in Saint-Denis, 38.

Berry, Duchess of, present at the death of Louis XVIII., 3; her optimism, 9; her friendship for the Duchess of Angoulême, 58; her character and manner, 58, 59; her love of freedom, 59; her gaiety, 60; the queen of elegance, 61; never meddled in politics, 62; led an active life, 63; very charitable, 64, 65, 67; her pleasure house Rosny, 65; instances of her charity and kindness of heart, 67 *et seq.;* her devotion to France and to her son, 70; her affection for her aunt, the Duchess of Orleans, 74; refuses to make an arrangement with Madame Feuchères, 88; her household, 114 *et seq.;* order in her household, 121; triumphant journey of, in the west of France, 224 *et seq.;* at Chambord, 224; in the Vendée, 225 *et seq.;* at Nantes, 229; lays the corner-stone of a monument in honor of the Vendéan victories, 231; at Bordeaux, 233 *et seq.;* in the Pyrenees, 235; returns to Paris, 236; brilliancy of her society, 237; the Mary Stuart ball given by her, 237; takes the Gymnase theatre under her protection, 258; her relations with Scribe, 265; her affection for Dieppe, 266; the incidents of her visits there, 267 *et seq.;* her kindness of heart shown at Dieppe, 270; her journey in the south of France, 292 *et seq.;* at Grenoble, 293.

Bonapartism believed to be dead, 10.

Bordeaux, enthusiasm over the Duchess of Berry in, 234.

Bordeaux, the Duke of, 4, 6; and his sister, warned by their governess against flattery, 181, 182;

at his seventh year passes to the hands of the Duke of Rivière, 183; his character described in a letter of the Duchess of Gontaut, 184; his three governors, 187; his sub-governors and preceptor, 193, 195.

Bossuet, funeral oration of Madame Henriette preached by, in Saint-Denis, 37.

Bourbon, Duke of, see Prince of Condé.

Bourbons, remains of, recovered and reinterred in Saint-Denis, 26.

Bourmont, General, Count de, Secretary of War, his life and character, 286 *et seq.*; his military ability, 289.

Cadoudal Conspiracy, the, the Polignacs' part in, 279.

Chabrol, Count of, address of, 46.

Chantilly, the society at, 82; the life at, 86.

Charlemagne, the crown of, 148, 150.

Charles X., accession of, 1 *et seq.*; goes to Saint Cloud, 4; receives the felicitations of the Corps de l'État, 5; makes a solemn entry into Paris, 11; an excellent horseman, 13; attends a review on the Champ-de-Mars, 14 *et seq.*; his popularity, 17; not to be allowed to rest in Saint-Denis, 39; birth of, 41; attraction of his personality, 42; his imposing manner, 43; the dignity of his private life, 44; Lamartine's estimate of his character, 45; his family, 48; had a kindly feeling for the Orleans family, 75, 76; restores the Duke of Orleans to his former privileges and domain, 77 *et seq.*; his affection for the Duke of Bourbon, 86; his civil household, 90 *et seq.*; his military household, 96; routine of his court at Compiègne, 98; deeply religious, 100; set a good example, 101; his generosity, 102; his character summed up, 102; decides to be crowned at Rheims, 125; at Compiègne, 131; received at Rheims by the clergy, 135; summoned to the coronation, 141; takes the oath, 146; anointed, 147; crowned, 148; subsequent ceremonies in which he officiated, 152 *et seq.*; his vestments, 153; confers orders, 155 *et seq.*; visits the hospital and touches scrofulous patients, 157; at the abbey of Saint Remi, 157; reviews the troops, 158; re-enters Paris, 160; fête to, by the city of Paris, 163; his piety a cause of offence, 166; his pledge to Madame de Polastron, 167; his exemplary life, 168; assists at the ceremony of the Jubilee, 170; hostility shown to, at the expiatory ceremony, 173; his amiable yet severe character, 175; his life exemplary, 176; at Holyrood, as the Count d'Artois, 179; beloved by the court, 198; the National Guard received by, at the Tuileries, 199; withdraws the law as to the press, 200; refuses to countermand the review of the National Guards, 200; reviews the National Guards, 201 *et seq.*; unfriendliness to, apparent, 202; dissolves the National Guard, 207; disregards the warnings of his friends, 208, 209; accused of giving too much time to the chase, 211; his popularity dwindling, 214; dismisses M. de Villèle, 216; maintains relations with him, 218; his journey in the departments, 220; reception of, in Alsace, 221; visited by the King of Würtemberg in Alsace, 222; confident of the future, 223; his reign illustrious from the point of view of arts and letters,

245; his generous treatment of writers and artists, 248; maintains a high standard in music and the drama, 255; appoints the Polignac ministry, 276 *et seq.*; frankness of Madame de Gontaut to, 281.

Chartres, Duke of, 72; at the ball of Mary Stuart, 339.

Chateaubriand, pamphlet of, on the accession of Charles X., 7; quoted, 25; urges Charles X. to be consecrated by a public coronation, 123, 131, 137; knighted by the King, 155; *Mémoires d'outre-tombe* quoted, 159; desired to replace the Duke of Montmorency as governor of the Duke of Bordeaux, 190; tries to persuade the King to change his ministry, 200; on General de Bourmont, 289.

Cinq Mars, the, of Alfred de Vigny, 248.

Compiègne, life of the court at, 98.

Condé, Prince of, his career, 81; his household at Chantilly, 83; under the influence of Madame Feuchères, 84; fond of hunting, 85; description of the life at his court, 86.

Corbière, M. de, 258.

Coronation, the, of Charles X., 123 *et seq.*, 139; the persons present, 140; ceremonies of, 141 *et seq.*

Courier, Paul Louis, 78.

Damas, Baron de, appointed governor of the Duke of Bordeaux, 195, 196.

Dawes, Sophie, 83. See Madame de Feuchères.

Débats, the, on the Polignac ministry, 276; on Prince de Polignac, 283.

Delacroix, 249.

Delaroche, Paul, 249.

Delavigne, Casimir, 248.

Dieppe, indebtedness of, to the Duchess of Berry, 266; inauguration of a playhouse in, 267.

Doudeauville, Duke Ambroise, on the King's religion, 101, 104; his early years, 105; his marriage, 106; his career, 108 *et seq.*; minister of the King's household, 111; his death, 112; his conception of a good woman, 112, 113; on the King's passion for the chase, 212, 285; on the King's change of ministers, 282; on the Prince de Polignac, 284; on the Count de Bourmont, 288.

Drapeau Blanc, the, quoted, 46.

Dumas, Alexandre, his *Henri III. et la Cour*, 248.

Dumas, Alexandre, *fils*, 246.

Entrées, the classes of the, 92.

Equerry, the First, 94.

Fare, Cardinal de la, sermon of, before Charles X., 135.

Feuchères, Baron of, his marriage to Sophie Dawes, 83.

Feuchères, Madame de, her influence over the Prince of Condé, 84; her schemes with regard to his will, 87.

Foy, General, subscriptions to the fund for his children, 79.

Funeral ceremonies of Louis XVIII., 30 *et seq.*

Gérard, the painter, 249.

Gervinus, the German historian, quoted, 278.

Gontaut, Madame de, receives the announcement of the death of Louis XVIII., 3; relates an incident of the royal entry into Paris, 12; incident of the King's hat related by, 80; her Memoirs, 177; her birth, 178; exile, 179; at Holyrood with the Count d'Artois, 180; with Louis XVIII. at Hartwell, 180; made governess of the Children of France, 181;

created Duchess, 183; letter of, to the Duke de Rivière concerning the young Duke of Bordeaux, 183; her frankness to Charles X., 186; hears of Polignac's appointment from London, 281.
Grand Chamberlain of France, 91.
Grand Huntsman, the, 95.
Grand Master of Ceremonies, the, 95.
Grand Master of France, the, 90.
Grenoble, the Duchess of Berry at, 293.
Gros, the painter, 249.
Guizot, on Prince de Polignac, 282, 290.
Gymnase, the, called the Théâtre de Madame, 48; under the protection of the Duchess of Berry, 257; origin of, 257 et seq.

Haussonville, Count d', on Charles X., 42; on the coronation, 139, 144; on the ceremony of the Order of the Holy Ghost, 154; on the unsatisfactory reception of the King on re-entering Paris, 161; on the nobility, 164.
Heim, picture of Charles X. distributing the prizes for the Exposition of 1824, 249.
Hernani, first representation of, 247.
Holy Ghost, ceremony of the Order of, at Rheims, 152; persons presented, 152.
Household, civil, of the King, 90.
Households of the Dauphin, Dauphiness, and the Duchess of Berry, 96.
Hugo, Victor, 159; works of, published under Charles X., 246, 247, 248.
Huntley, Marquis of, opens the Mary Stuart ball with Mademoiselle, 239.

Ingres, 249.

Joinville, Prince de, 73.
Jubilee celebrated in Paris in 1826, 169.

La Belle Fermière, 261.
La Rosière, 258.
Lamartine, his estimate of the character of Charles X., 44, 159; the poet of the Restoration, 245, 246.
Lamennais, M. de, on the new ministers, 290.
Lamy, Eugène, painted a picture of the Mary Stuart ball, 243.
Lenoir, Alexander, supervisor of the destruction of the royal tombs at Saint-Denis, 23; his Histoire des Arts en France pour les Monuments, 25.
Lisle, Leconte de, M., 246.
Louis XVI., remains of, transferred to Saint-Denis, 25; remains of, reinterred in Saint-Denis, 27; relics of, preserved by the Duchess of Angoulême, 52; coronation of, 123; expiatory ceremony in honor of, 172.
Louis XVII., relics of his imprisonment, 52.
Louis XVIII., gathering of courtiers in the Tuileries at his death, 1; funeral solemnities of, 20 et seq.; funeral of, 29 et seq.; suspicions of the Duke of Orleans, 75.
Louis Philippe, see Duke of Orleans.

Mademoiselle, her reply when told of the King's death, 4, 6; at Dieppe, 271.
Mallet, General, 280.
Mareschal, M. Jules, as to his royal appreciation of artists and writers, 250.
Marie Amélie, see Duchess of Orleans.
Marie Antoinette, remains of, transferred to Saint-Denis, 25;

INDEX

remains of, reinterred in Saint-Denis, 27; relics of, preserved by the Duchess of Angoulême, 52.
Marie Christine, about to wed Ferdinand VII., 292; her journey with the Duchess of Berry in the south of France, 295.
Marie Thérèse of Savoy, 44.
Marmont, Marshal, on the accession of Charles X., 2.
Martignac, M. de, succeeds M. de Villèle in the Ministry of the Interior, 217.
Mary Stuart ball given by the Duchess of Berry, 237 et seq.; the personages and the costumes, 238 et seq., 242.
Mesnard, Count Charles de, on the reputation for frivolity of the Duchess of Berry, 66; relates instances of her kindness of heart, 67, 68, 119.
Meyerbeer, 254.
Michelet, 248.
Moniteur, the, quoted, 20, 35, 163, 172; on the procession during the expiatory ceremony at Paris, 172.
Montmirail, Mademoiselle de, married to the Duke of Doudeauville, 106; a sister of the Countess of Montesquiou, 110.
Montmorency, Duke Mathieu, his career, 187 et seq.
Montpensier, Duke of, 73.
Musset, Alfred de, 248.

Napoleon intends to provide sepulture for himself at Saint-Denis, 24; coronation of, at Notre Dame, 125.
Napoleon III. not buried in Saint-Denis, 39; magnificent vault built by, in Saint-Denis, 40.
National Guard, the review of, 199 et seq.; goes on guard at the Tuileries, 199.
Nemours, Duke of, 73.
Nettement, M. de, as to the generosity of the Duchess of Berry, 121.
Noailles, Countess of, the, 116.

Orleans, Duke of, his marriage, 72; his children, 73; suspected by Louis XVIII., 75; receives the title of Royal Highness from Charles X., 76; and is restored by him to his former privileges and domain, 77; his share of the indemnity, 78; finesses, 79.
Orleans, Duchess of, on the announcement of the accession of Charles X., 2, 72, 74; intrigues with Madame Feuchères, 88, 89.
Orleans, Mademoiselle d', 72.
Orleanism, as yet a myth, 10; existence of, unsuspected by Charles X., 198.
Orleanist party, the, begins to take form, 78.
Oudinot, Maréchale, lady of honor to the Duchess of Berry, 114; eulogy of, by the Abbé Tripied, 115.

Paris, royal entry into, 12; review of troops by Charles X. at the Champ-de-Mars, 15; celebration of the Jubilee in, 170.
Pène, M. de, on Chateaubriand, 191.
Penthièvre, Duke of, 73.
Polastron, Countess of, 44; her death-bed request of Charles X., 167.
Polignac, Duke Armand de, 279.
Polignac, Prince Jules de, made minister, 276; his history, 278 et seq.; indiscretion of, 281; refused to recognize the Charter, 282; opposition encountered by, 282, 284.
Polignac, Duchess of, 279.
Pontmartin, Count Armand de, his portrait of the Duchess of Berry, 69.
Press, withdrawal of the law as to, 200.

Pujol, Abel de, 250.
Puymaigre, Count de, quoted, 16; on the imposing manner of Charles X., 43; on the Duke of Angoulême, 50; on the Duchess of Angoulême, 54; his account of the Prince of Condé and his household, 82 *et seq.*; his account of the life at court, 98; on the freedom of manners at Charles X. court, 100.

Récamier, Madame de, letters to, on the death of the Duke of Montmorency, 189.
Reggio, Duchess of, 114.
Review of the National Guard, the ministry try to dissuade the King from, 200.
Rheims, cathedral of, repaired for the coronation of Charles X., 126, 130; the rich display in, 141; subsequent ceremonies in, 152; preparations in, for the coronation of Charles X., 129; crowds of tourists in, 131.
Rivière, Duke of, becomes governor of the Duke of Bordeaux, 183; career of, 191 *et seq.*; his devotion to the Duke of Bordeaux, 194; his death, 195.
Robespierre, 52.
Rochefoucauld, de La, Viscount Sosthènes, warns the King of his danger, 209 *et seq.*, 213, 214, 218; on the King's generosity, 102, 104; at the head of the department of the Fine Arts, 245; his report upon the stage, 250; of Talma, 251; of Rossini, 252; aim to raise the moral level of the theatre, 254; letters of, to the King, 255.
Rohan-Soubise, Charlotte-Elisabeth de, 87.
Rosny, the pleasure house of the Duchess of Berry, 65.
Royal Family, members and titles of, 48.

Rossini, 271; first representation of his works in Paris, 252.

Saint-Denis, royal tombs of, 21 *et seq.*; the destruction of, by the revolutionists, 22; the monuments saved of, by Lenoir, 23; Napoleon's intention to provide a sepulture for himself at, 24; remains of the Bourbon's recovered and reinterred in, 26; impressiveness of the church today, 36.
Saverne, reception of the king in, 220.
Schmetz, 250.
Scribe, Eugène, invokes the protection of the Duchess of Berry in a vaudeville, 258; writes for the Gymnase, 259; account of his life and career, 259 *et seq.*; his curious piece *Avant, Pendant, Après*, 263; a man of letters solely, 265.
Scrofulous patients touched by the King at Rheims, 157.
Seraine, Abbé, declaration of, concerning the holy ampulla, 127.
Sévis, Duke de, 118.
Strasbourg, the reception of the King in, 221; munitions of war in, 222.

Talma, 251.
Talleyrand, Prince de, part taken by, at the obsequies of Louis XVIII., 33, 173, 191.
Thierry, Augustin, 248.

Vaudemont, Louise de, 28.
Vaulabelle, M. de, quoted, 18, 173.
Védreune, Abbé, on the character of Charles X., 175; on the duty of the governor of the young prince, 196; quoted, 277.
Vendée, the, the Duchess of Berry's visit to, 225 *et seq.*; enthusiasm of the inhabitants of, for her, 228.
Vernet, Horace, 248.

Victorine, Madame, remains of, re-interred in Saint-Denis, 27.
Vigny, Alfred de, his *Cinq Mars*, 248.
Viel-Castel, M. de, as to the policy of Charles X., 44.
Villèle, M. de, favorite minister of Charles X., 43; knighted by the King, 155; admits to the King that animosity to the clergy was displayed during the expiatory ceremony, 174; assailed by the Guard, 204; advises the King to dissolve National Guard of Paris, 205; dismissed by the King, 216; in relations with, 218; letter of the King, 220.
Villemain, M., quoted, 18; on the secret of Scribe's success, 262.
Villeneuve-l'Étang, the pleasure house of the Duchess of Angoulême, 65.

Wellington, Duke of, 281.
Würtemberg, King of, visits Charles X. at Strasbourg, 222.

www.ingramcontent.com/pod-product-compliance
Lightning Source LLC
Chambersburg PA
CBHW030805230426
43667CB00008B/1073